GERALDENE HOLT'S
CAKES

Also by Geraldene Holt

Cake Stall
Travelling Food
Budget Gourmet
Tuck Box Treats
French Country Kitchen
Recipes from a French Herb Garden
The Gourmet Garden
A Cup of Tea
Complete Book of Herbs
Country House Cooking
Diary of a French Herb Garden

GERALDENE HOLT'S
CAKES

with illustrations
by
Kitty Cox

PROSPECT BOOKS

2011

First published in 2011 by Prospect Books,
Allaleigh House, Blackawton, Totnes, Devon TQ9 7DL.

Geraldene Holt's Cakes is a revised, amended, rewritten and enlarged edition of the same author's *Cake Stall*, first published by Hodder & Stoughton, London, in 1980.

BRITISH LIBRARY CATALOGUING IN PUBLICATION DATA:
A catalogue entry of this book is available from the British Library.

Typeset and designed by Lemuel Dix and Tom Jaine.
The cover illustration is *Still Life* by Samuel John Peploe, *c.* 1913 in the Scottish National Gallery of Modern Art (reproduction courtesy of National Galleries of Scotland).

ISBN 978-1-903018-75-0

Printed and bound by the Gutenberg Press, Malta.

Contents

For Rémy, Raphaël, Sadie, Hannah and Matthew, with love,
and in fond memory of my mother.

Acknowledgements

I shall always be grateful to my customers at Tiverton Pannier Market; little did any of us realize that my making cakes and their buying them would launch me into food writing. In addition to those people named in the text, my thanks go to the late Stanley Foster at Hodder & Stoughton, who had faith in an unpublished author; and to Eleo Gordon of Penguin, who brought *Cake Stall* to an even wider public. For their invaluable advice over the years I thank Philippa Davenport, Alan and Jane Davidson, Josceline Dimbleby, Pamela Todd, Marie-Pierre Moine, Amanda Evans, Celia Rufey, Cortina Butler, Alison Cathie, Rosemary Barron, Vicky Hayward, Ann Bagnall, Anne Collieu, Suzanne and Jeanette Doize, Sri and Roger Owen, Sally and Tom Jaine, Helge and Hilary Rubinstein, Gordon Scott-Wise, Stephen Hayward, Orlando Murrin, and the late Michael Bateman. I am also indebted to all the readers who have encouraged me to re-issue the book which has prompted me to revise and develop the scope of the original.

Warm appreciation goes to my family for their unfailing encouragement: Alexander and Sarah with their children, Hannah and Matthew; and Madeleine and Philip with their children, Rémy, Raphaël, and Sadie. Abundant thanks also to my husband, Maurice, who has never knowingly declined to eat cake.

Geraldene Holt, Oxford 2011
(www.geraldeneholt.com)

Introduction

I sat at the kitchen table and began to write. Page after page, recipe after recipe, I knew them all by heart. When I ran my cake stall I baked thousands of scones, hundreds of sponge cakes, countless biscuits and cookies: so I was certain the recipes worked. I wrote everyday until I'd recorded as accurately as I could all the details of how I baked. My husband typed the pages for me, then I caught the train to London to deliver my book. It was not until, months later, when the first early copy of *Cake Stall* arrived, that I could really believe I'd become an author.

Reviewers were generous in their praise. I shall always be grateful to Philippa Davenport, Josceline Dimbleby, and the late Margaret Costa for their warm encouragement. Letters began to arrive from readers who said they had at last learnt how to make cakes. Others had launched their own cake stalls. 'You saved my marriage,' said one; another was relieved to discover how to keep the family finances afloat by baking cakes when her small children were asleep; and the wife of an English bishop wrote to thank me for helping to launch an employment scheme for disadvantaged young people in her city. And the friend who took over my Devon market stall, using a copy of *Cake Stall* as her guide, was so successful she later opened an old-fashioned tea-shop nearby.

Now that we are seeing a justified enthusiasm for localism, purity of ingredients and the provenance of our food, farmers' markets have sprung up all over Britain. This has brought many more opportunities to sell home baking. Oxford, for example, used to run just one outdoor market a week but now the city holds fifteen markets every month. And I detect a return to cake stalls – there is always a demand for high quality home-made cakes.

Market customers like to meet and talk to the person who produces the food they are buying. Home bakers can offer not just superb oven-fresh fare using the best ingredients but also, if they wish, draw upon a vast repertoire of individual recipes, old and new. Every week, in addition to my usual selection, I introduced one unusual or little-known cake and biscuit on my stall. Supermarkets and commercial bakeries can only offer a restricted range.

When *Cake Stall* was published, Jane Grigson asked me about my next work. 'But I don't know enough to write another book,' I replied. 'That's not the right approach, Geraldene,' she laughed. 'You write about what you care about and find out about your subject on the way.' Now, after writing a dozen books about growing and cooking food in England and France, I have returned to the subject of my first volume.

Cakes still emerge from my kitchen every week because I continue to enjoy the exhilaration and satisfaction of baking – the magic of the oven has never waned. Sometimes my cakes are sold on cake stalls, but these days the proceeds go to charities and other good causes. And grandchildren have come into my life, so I create cakes for them and we work in the kitchen together.

Over the years many readers have written to ask for a new edition of the book – even my own copy is now falling apart – so, at last, I have revised and enlarged the original version. My gratitude goes to the journalists Jane Shilling and Helen Peacocke for urging me to do so. I have included many of my newly created cakes along with improved interpretations of old favourites, though the most popular recipes from the first edition are still here. I hope you enjoy this bigger, better *Cake Stall* and that your talent for baking develops and flourishes, enabling you and your family and friends to appreciate the delectable results.

Abbreviations

teaspoon – tsp
dessertspoon – dsp
tablespoon – tbs
gram – g
kilogram – kg
millilitre – ml
litre – l
millimetre – mm
centimetre – cm
metre – m
ounce – oz
pound – lb
fluid ounce – fl oz
pint – pt
inch – in.
foot – ft

Unless stated otherwise: all cake tins are round; spoonfuls are level; butter is unsalted; sugar is caster; and eggs are large.

Weights and Measures

Metric and Imperial Equivalence Tables

Weight		Volume	
Grams	*Ounces*	*Millilitres*	*Fluid Ounces*
7	¼	7	¼
15	½	15	½
22	¾	30	1
30	1	60	2
45	1 ½	100	3 ½
60	2	125	4
75	2 ½	150	5 = ¼ pt
90	3	175	6
100	3 ½	200	7
120	4	250	9
135	4 ½	300	10 = ½ pt
150	5	350	12
160	5 ½	400	14
175	6	425	15 = ¾ pt
200	7	450	16
230	8	500	18
265	9	600	20 = 1 pt
300	10	700	1 ¼ pt
325	11	850	1 ½ pt
350	12	1 l	1 ¾ pt
375	13	1.2 l	2 pt
400	14	1.5 l	2 ¾ pt
425	15	2 l	3 ½ pt
450	1 lb	2.5 l	4 ½ pt
500	1 lb 2 oz	3 l	5 ¼ pt
680	1 ½ lb		
900	2 lb		
1 kg	2 lb 3 oz		
1350	3 lb		

Level Spoonfuls

1 teaspoon holds 5 ml or 5 g
1 dessertspoon holds 10 ml or 10 g
1 tablespoon holds 15 ml or 15 g

Length

mm and cm	inches	mm and cm	inches
3 mm	1/8	7.5	3
5 mm	1/4	10	4
1	1/2	13	5
2	3/4	15	6
2.5	1	18	7
3	1 1/4	20	8
4	1 1/2	23	9
4.5	1 3/4	25.5	10
5	2	28	11
6.5	2 1/2	30	12 = 1 foot
		100 = 1 m	39 1/2 in.

Temperature

Electricity & Solid Fuel	Gas Mark	Degrees Fahrenheit	Degrees Celsius
Cool	1/4	200	100
Cool	1/4	225	110
Cool	1/4 – 1/2	250	120
Very slow	1	275	140
Slow	2	300	150
Slow	3	325	160
Moderate	4	350	180
Moderate	5	375	190
Moderately hot	6	400	200
Hot	7	425	220
Very hot	8	450	230
Very hot	9	475	250

Steps to Success

THE CONTENTS OF THIS CHAPTER

BAKING INGREDIENTS

I am often asked about ingredients in home baking. So here are a few notes about the principal ones I use in this book.

Butter

Unsalted butter is my preferred fat for baking cakes, though slightly salted butter is fine for pastry. English, French and Dutch unsalted butter softens quickly, making mixing easier, and it imparts a delicate yet rich flavour to baking. Use butter at room temperature in cakes; for pastry, use chilled butter straight from the fridge.

Clarified butter

Clarified butter is invaluable for greasing baking tins and moulds. I usually line baking sheets and the the flat base of a cake tin with non-stick baking parchment, but the sides of the tin are often best brushed with clarified butter. And patterned baking tins such as the scallop-shaped Madeleine cake moulds that cannot be lined with paper require greasing with clarified butter for the best result. The advantage of clarified butter is that the milk solids – which cause a cake to stick to the tin – have been removed.

> *To make clarified butter:* melt some unsalted butter in a pan over low heat. When liquid, gently pour the clear yellow part into a cup or jar leaving the milky solids in the pan – these can be added to cakes and biscuit mixtures. Leave the pot of clarified butter in a cool place to set and use as needed.

Dairy cream

Fresh double cream is the type I use most often, for filling or decorating a cake. Double cream is easily whisked to a thick, glossy mixture. But take care in a hot kitchen with cream at room temperature – it's easy to overdo the whisking so that the cream separates, producing a grainy, butter-like result. The high proportion of butterfat in double cream not only makes it the richest liquid cream but also gives it versatility: it can be thinned with milk to produce a lighter whipping cream; and it can absorb up to a quarter of its weight in extra liquid, so a few spoonfuls of black coffee or fruit juice stirred into the whipped cream can transform its flavour and lighten the consistency. If you wish to sweeten double cream, fold in a teaspoon or so of caster or icing sugar.

Single cream contains 20 % butterfat
Whipping cream contains 30–36 % butterfat
Crème fraîche contains a range of butterfat from 5–30% as stated on the label
Soured cream contains 18–20 % butterfat
Double cream contains 48% butterfat

Yoghurt

Dairy milk cultured with lactic-acid-producing bacteria results in the healthy and delicious product known by its Turkish name of yoghurt. Plain, natural yoghurt is the kind used in baking. It may be organic, full-fat, or low-fat, and made from the milk of cows, goats or sheep. A few spoonfuls of plain yoghurt folded into whipped double cream lightens the mixture and gives an attractive flavour that resembles crème fraîche and soured cream.

Sugar

Sugar is one of the quartet of ingredients common to most cake-making. While you can make a cake without butter or eggs or flour, sugar is almost always present. Sugar used in baking comes either from sugar cane grown in a tropical or sub-tropical climate (although in the Middle Ages it was grown as far north as Sicily) or from the turnip-like sugar beet of northern latitudes. Refined beet sugar is white in colour and is inexpensive, while unrefined cane sugar retains its natural golden-brown colour and varies in flavour from fudge to dark toffee. All types of sugar should be stored in an air-tight container or bag to prevent lumps forming – and even then sugar may need to be sieved before adding to a mixture. For most sugars 1 rounded tablespoon is approximately 30 g / 1 oz.

Beet sugar: there are three grades of white beet sugar.

Granulated, the cheapest type, with fairly coarse grains, can be used for cooking fruit or in rubbed-in cake mixtures.

Caster, finer grains than granulated, widely used in cake-making since it dissolves easily and produces a light mixture when blended with butter.

Icing sugar, a powdered sugar used for making meringues, icings and for dusting over cakes and biscuits. It must be stored in a sealed container to prevent lumps forming, and it is advisable to sieve before use.

Cane sugar: I list the types in ascending order of depth of colour and flavour.

Golden granulated, coarse grain can be used in place of white granulated.

Golden caster, fine grain with delicately caramel flavour, use in place of white caster sugar in many recipes.

Demerara, large amber grains that take longer to dissolve, but are good for sprinkling over the top of a cake before baking, and have a light caramel flavour.

Light brown soft, fine-grained, can be used in place of caster sugar where a fudge flavour is welcome, recommended for biscuits and cookies.

Light muscovado, fine-grained, use where a more pronounced flavour is called for, in light fruit cakes and in fudge frosting.

Dark brown soft, fine-grained, moderately strong caramel flavour, excellent in dark fruit, chocolate and spice cakes.

Dark muscovado, moist and fine-grained, with a strong toffee flavour, good for dark fruit cakes and gingerbread.

Molasses, dark brown, moist, superb rich toffee flavour, use in celebration fruit cakes and mincemeat.

Flavoured sugars

Sugar scented with spices, herbs and flowers brings a charming and individual character to your baking. Traditionally, the aromatic element is layered with sugar in an air-tight jar – pour some white or golden caster sugar into the container, add sprigs of fresh rosemary leaves or lavender blossom, broken bark of cinnamon, a split vanilla pod, or loveliest of all, fresh scented rose petals. Then add more sugar and repeat the layers until the jar is full. Seal the jar securely and place on a warm windowsill, turning it every few days to distribute the flavour. After a few days, taste the sugar and, if already strongly scented, use as soon as possible, sieving it first to remove the herbs or spices. A speedy alternative for a herb- or flower-scented sugar is to chop the fresh leaves or petals in a processor with a few spoonfuls of sugar. Chop until you have a fairly fine aromatic mixture – though fragile rose petals should be chopped only briefly to produce a fragrant pink-speckled sugar – which can be used straight away, without sieving, in a raw mixture or for scattering over a baked cake, icing or a cream filling.

Golden syrup

Intensely sweet liquid sugar produced from white sugar. It has a slightly caramel flavour and it helps to keep cakes moist. One level tablespoon weighs about 30 g / 1 oz.

Black treacle and molasses

A dark, almost black syrup made from raw cane sugar with a strong toffee flavour. Use in rich fruit cakes and gingerbread. One level tablespoon weighs roughly 30 g / 1 oz.

Honey

Honey is a naturally produced form of sugar, mainly fructose and sucrose, and is a wonder food with more than 150 constituents and many health-promoting properties. Honey helps to keep a cake moist and gives an attractive sheen when brushed over the top. Set honey can be converted into clear honey by standing the jar in warm water or a hot cupboard for a day or longer. The colour and flavour of honey depends on the flowers and nectar foraged by the bees. This is is usually stated on the label. Specialist honeys with a pronounced flavour include lavender and chestnut honey from France and the dark amber honey from Greece with its pine-rich taste. As a one-time bee-keeper, I try to support my local honey producers – they and their insects are an endangered species. A level tablespoon of honey weighs close to 30 g / 1 oz.

Eggs

Eggs are the principal raising agent in cake-making. If you are able to use fresh, organic eggs you'll notice the difference in the colour and size of a baked cake. Keep eggs cool, then allow them to reach room temperature before use. Always break an egg into a cup or saucer before adding it to the mixing bowl – this way you can check the soundness of the egg and, if necessary, remove any specks of shell. Left-over yolks and whites can be stored, covered, in the fridge for a few days until used in a recipe that requires only yolks, for instance, the Gold Cake on p. 260, or just egg whites as do meringues (p. 196). It's also worth remembering that in mixtures that are not expected to rise a great deal, such as a heavy fruit cake or crisp biscuits, 2 egg yolks can often replace 1 egg white. The recipes in this book use large eggs, each weighing approximately 60 g / 2 oz.

Flour

Wheat flour is the most common form of ground cereal used in British baking. Wholegrain wheat is milled and sifted to produce a fine powder and several types are available to the home baker.

Bread flour, usually described as 'strong' flour, is ground from a 'hard' wheat with a high gluten content which contributes elasticity to the dough.

Cake flour, is made from a 'soft' low-gluten wheat which combines well with fat and other ingredients, making it suitable for a wide range of home baking.

Wholemeal or wheatmeal flour, is a brown speckled mixture which includes all of the nutritious wheat-germ and bran. The proportion of the whole grain retained in the flour is stated on the packet – this varies from 100% (wholemeal) downwards (various extractions, usually 85%, called wheatmeal). Both plain and self-raising wholemeal and wheatmeal flour are available.

Plain white flour, is produced by removing the bran and brown particles in wholemeal flour by 'bolting' through a series of fine-mesh sieves – for sponge-cakes use the finest grade flour you can find, I particularly recommend French and Italian cake flours; plain flour does not contain a rising agent such as baking powder and is therefore suitable for a wide range of cakes, biscuits and pastry. Plain flour can replace self-raising flour in a recipe if you add 10 g / 2 teaspoons of baking powder to 230 g / 8 oz plain flour, sifting them together before adding to a mixture.

Self-raising white flour, is made by combining plain white flour with a raising agent; some recipes such as scones and quick-mix cakes call for self-raising flour plus baking powder. For a recipe to work properly it is important to use the type of flour specified.

Cornflour

Also described as cornstarch, cornflour is a fine white powder produced from refining maize or cornmeal. It contributes a soft texture to cakes and is sometimes added to wheat flour in sponge cake, biscuit and pastry recipes.

Rice flour

Also known as ground rice, this is a cream-coloured granular powder made from white rice, occasionally used as a partial replacement for wheat flour or ground almonds.

Potato flour

This cream-coloured fine grain mixture is made from dried potatoes. It appears in some Continental cake recipes in place of wheat flour.

Baking powder

Before factory-made baking powder was available, cooks prepared their own – as Alison Uttley describes in *Recipes from an Old Farmhouse.* Today's baking powder is a blend of bicarbonate of soda and cream of tartar, with a dried starch added to prolong its active life. When mixed with liquid, it effervesces and releases carbon dioxide. So if you have prepared a mixture that contains baking powder, it should be baked as soon as possible or the raising effect will be reduced.

Bicarbonate of soda

Also known as baking soda, bicarbonate is an alkali used as a raising agent with a more gentle action than baking powder. It has a stronger effect when mixed with cream of tartar or lemon juice or buttermilk, but care must be taken not to use too much in a recipe or its bitter flavour will predominate.

Cream of tartar

This mildly acidic raising agent begins to react, as does bicarbonate of soda, at room temperature as soon as it is in contact with a liquid. A pinch of cream of tartar is often added to liquid egg whites when making meringues.

Spices

Whole spices such as cloves and coriander will store quite well in a cool place for some months, but finely ground spices tend to lose their intense flavour and aroma after a few weeks. Ideally, spices should be freshly ground just before use. An electric coffee mill (reserved for this purpose) will grind most spices quickly and easily, though a reasonable result can be obtained with a pestle and mortar – if necessary, sieve the pounded spice, discarding the coarser grains. Some spices, such as cinnamon and dried ginger root, are so hard that it is difficult to grind them satisfactorily at home – both these spices are best bought ready-ground. Store ground spices in small refillable, lidded glass jars in a dark, cool place. From time to time – and because I'm very fond of allspice or Jamaican pepper – I mix my own spice blends for cakes, either by combining the whole spices before grinding or by stirring the ground spices together until I have the flavour I like. Most spice companies produce good spice blends, it's a matter of taste which you prefer. I also recommend bringing back small packets of blended spices from abroad – the countries that specialize in gingerbread, such as Holland, Sweden and Germany, produce particularly attractive blends.

Dried fruit

I remember my mother opening the grocer's mid-blue paper bag to spread out the dried fruit on the kitchen table so that the stalks and small stones could be discarded. But these days dried fruit is normally edible straight from the bag – washed, dried and gleaming with a thin layer of vegetable oil. The occasional stalk still gets through, and some whole fruit such as dried figs will need the stalks removed before chopping and adding to the mixing bowl.

The bulk of dried fruit used in home baking is grown on the vine: seeded and seedless raisins, sultanas, and currants.

To save time, look for the pitted form of stone fruits such as prunes, dates, apricots and cherries, and the ready-to-eat kind do not need soaking to soften the flesh. Chopped or sliced, these fruits can go straight into the mix.

Tree fruits such as dried apples and pears can be used as you buy them, provided they are chopped quite small. To use the fruit in bigger pieces, first soften it in a little apple juice or warm water.

Dried berries such as cranberries and blueberries are excellent in baking – they can be used straight from the bag.

Candied fruit, such as pineapple, ginger, angelica and citrus peel, has a reasonably long shelf-life. If still soft and pliable, candied fruit can be used straight away. If encrusted with sugar, soften it in warm water before chopping or slicing.

Fresh fruit

Fresh fruit baked in or on a cake develops a delicious flavour, subtly different from that when cold and raw. Akin to the scent of freshly made jam, the aroma of ripe summer fruit straight from the oven is one of the great pleasures of home baking. When fruit is plentiful, I invariably incorporate some in a cake. Use ripe fruit that is dry and firm because it retains its shape in the heat of the oven and will not leak too much juice into the mixture.

Raspberries, small strawberries, black and red currants, gooseberries, blueberries, cranberries, blackberries, cherries, apricots, peaches, nectarines, figs, pineapple, dessert apples and pears all work well in a cake, either folded into the mixture or baked on top so that the fruit is encrusted with caramelized sugar. For the best flavour, serve fresh-fruit cakes straight from the oven or while still warm.

Nuts

A wide variety of nuts is now available from grocers and supermarkets, though health-food shops usually have the biggest choice. Nuts are good value, delicious and an important ingredient in many cakes, biscuits and cookies imparting both flavour and texture. A further virtue is their fat content, which keeps cakes fresh. But this also means that nuts should stored in the freezer and not at room temperature, to prevent deterioration. Whole nuts are usually cheaper and retain their taste, but if time is short, buy them already prepared for a recipe.

Almonds

Almonds are the most versatile nuts in baking, either whole, halved, chopped, slivered or ground.

To blanch almonds: tip the shelled nuts, still in their brown skins, into a saucepan and cover with cold water. Bring to the boil, pour off the brown liquid and cover again with cold water. When cool enough to handle, slip the brown skins from each almond and discard. Dry the nuts on kitchen paper.

To halve almonds: cut whole freshly blanched almonds in half by sliding a small knife into the side of each nut to separate it.

To sliver almonds: cut each freshly blanched almond half into three or four long slim shreds.

To chop almonds: allow the blanched and halved nuts to dry, either on kitchen paper in the sun or in a warm oven. Then chop them with a knife on a wooden board, or use a Zyliss hand-held chopper. The quickest method is to chop the almonds to the grade you require in a food processor.

To toast almonds: spread either whole or halved blanched almonds in a single layer on a baking sheet and place under a hot grill. Watch them like a hawk – as soon as they are beginning to change to an appetizing brown, remove from the heat and set aside to cool. Toasted almonds are used whole or chopped in recipes and for cake decoration.

Flaked almonds are blanched, then cut into very thin slices. This is tricky to do at home, and it's usually easier and quicker to buy them already prepared.

Ground almonds are made at home by grinding dry blanched almonds – adding a spoonful of cornflour helps – in a processor until the mixture resembles fine breadcrumbs. Ready-prepared ground almonds are also widely available in supermarkets.

Hazelnuts

Hazelnuts are the next most popular nuts in baking. Again, I buy these whole but still in their shiny brown skins.

> *To blanch and toast hazelnuts:* this intensifies the flavour of the nuts and also removes their papery skin. Spread the hazelnuts in a single layer on a baking sheet and toast under a hot grill until they turn a caramel brown. Remove from the heat and tip the nuts into a clean teacloth, wrap the cloth over the nuts and rub off the outer covering with your fingers. Ideally, do this out-of-doors where the papery skin can blow away in a breeze. Sort out the whole nuts and set aside to cool.

> *Halved hazelnuts* are made by cutting the nuts in half with a sharp knife.
> *Chopped hazelnuts* are produced in the same way as for almonds.
> *Ground hazelnuts* are produced in the same way as ground almonds.

Walnuts

Walnuts can be bought shelled and halved or, more cheaply, in broken pieces. Other nuts that appear in my recipes are pine nuts – these are toasted in the same way as almonds – pecans, pistachios, cashews, peanuts, coconut, Brazil and macadamia nuts.

Chocolate

For the best flavour in baking, use the highest quality chocolate you can afford. I prefer to use dark chocolate with 55–70% cocoa solids – the proportion is stated on the label – which has a more intense flavour than chocolate with a smaller proportion. Store chocolate in a cold, dry place but not the refrigerator. Which brand you use will depend on personal preference and the particular recipe involved. I normally use bars of organic Green & Black's Maya Gold.

Chocolate chips are now available in dark and milk versions, and even in white chocolate which is not a true chocolate. Alternatively, you can grate or chop bar chocolate to make home-made chocolate chips.

Chocolate melts easily when hot: break the chocolate into pieces in a heat-proof bowl and place in a hot oven until liquid. Alternatively, melt the chocolate by placing the bowl over simmering water, or use a microwave oven, making sure that the dish is suitable. As a last resort, and only for a small quantity of chocolate, melt it with a hand-held hair-dryer on the highest setting.

Cocoa powder

In some chocolate cake mixtures, cocoa powder is used instead of melted chocolate. To retain moistness in a baked cake, cocoa powder usually replaces some of the flour in the recipe. Cocoa powder is added to a cake mixture either by sieving it with the flour or other dry ingredients, or by first blending the powder with hot water to make a smooth paste. I prefer dark cocoa powder with an intense flavour of chocolate, such as Green & Black's organic cocoa.

Coffee

Coffee is one of the most seductive flavours in baking. When it is used to flavour a cake mixture, the taste withstands the heat of the oven surprisingly well. But the flavour is at its best when coffee is freshly brewed and incorporated in French butter cream, glacé icing and whipped dairy cream. Either espresso coffee or double-strength filter coffee produces the finest flavour. Alternatively, infuse fresh ground coffee in milk or cream over low heat for 3–4 minutes, set aside until cool then strain through a fine mesh. Occasionally, ground coffee itself can be used to flavour a mixture, but if you are not a coffee drinker it may be that instant coffee powder or liquid coffee essence is more convenient for you to use, though the taste is not quite as rich. In baking, the flavour of coffee combines well with either vanilla or chocolate.

Flavourings, essences and extracts

Whenever possible I prefer to use the actual flavouring: for instance, the zest of an orange or lemon, or a purée of fresh fruit such as raspberries or blackcurrant, rather than a chemical replacement. The only essence or extract I buy is *Bitter Almond* – look for the best quality since just a drop or two are needed each time.

Vanilla pods
Vanilla pods are now widely available. The best quality are lustrous, dark brown and pliable. The pod needs to be cut open lengthways with a sharp knife or scissors then scraped to extract the tiny aromatic seeds. A more delicate flavour is obtained by infusing the whole pod in hot milk or cream – the pod can be wiped dry and reused. It's also worth looking for a jar of finely powdered vanilla pod from Italy for adding to a cake mixture and for sprinkling over icing or frosting.

Vanilla essence
If you are going to use vanilla essence in a recipe, either buy a high-quality vanilla extract or make your own vanilla essence as described on page 292.

Vanilla sugar
To make vanilla sugar, cut open a vanilla pod and use the tip of a teaspoon to scrape out some of the seeds. Snip the pod into pieces and place in a large lidded jar with the vanilla seeds. Fill the jar with caster sugar and seal the top firmly. Store in a warm dark place and shake the jar from time to time to distribute the vanilla scent. Top up the jar with sugar as necessary.

Food colourings
Small bottles of food colours are occasionally useful in baking. The liquid is usually quite strong and is best added to a mixture cautiously, drop by drop from the end of a skewer. Stir in each drop before adding another. To obtain all seven colours of the rainbow you need only red, yellow and blue: red and yellow make orange, blue and yellow make green, red and blue make violet, and blue and violet make indigo.

Gelatine
This is a setting agent produced from animal bones, available as a granulated powder or in clear perforated sheets. Both forms are usually softened in a little warm water before being dissolved in a warm liquid. Due to its lack of flavour, I prefer sheet gelatine. The vegetarian alternative to gelatine is agar-agar made from seaweed. To obtain a satisfactory result with any setting agent, it is advisable to follow the instructions on the packet.

BAKING EQUIPMENT

Given the daunting amount of baking equipment on show in kitchenware shops these days, it's useful to know which items are really essential. And remember that you can start with only a few items and gradually add others as you need them. Even so, when necessary one can improvise – I've mixed a cake in a saucepan and baked it in a roasting pan, and it was fine. However, part of the pleasure in cake-making is using utensils specially designed for the purpose. And if you buy the best quality equipment you can afford, it represents a sound investment that should last for many years.

Mixing bowls
It helps to have at least three bowls of different sizes that stack inside each other. I prefer clear, heat-proof glass because it's scratch-resistant, can be warmed in the oven, and the mixture is visible through the side of the bowl.

Wooden spoons
You can't have too many smooth, birch-wood spoons. Even their handles are useful, for example when making brandy snaps.

Flexible spatulas
Two or three plastic or rubber spatulas are indispensable for scraping cake mixture and icing from bowls.

Palette knife
A stainless steel palette knife with 18 cm / 7 in. blade is invaluable, plus a smaller version with a 13 cm / 5 in. blade.

Whisks
One large and one small stainless steel balloon whisk are excellent not only for whisking mixtures by hand but also for folding one mixture into another

or for adding sieved flour to a mixture. Egg whites are traditionally whisked by hand in a copper bowl, but it takes time and energy, even though the resulting foam is higher and more stable than by any other method. Normally, I use a hand-turned egg beater, or a hand-held electric beater with whisking blades, for this task.

Weighing scales

Faulty scales are a pest and probably cause more spoiled cakes than an unreliable oven. Successful baking depends upon accuracy and if you wish to repeat your triumphs, and also try new recipes, it is essential to measure quantities correctly. I prefer balance scales to spring ones. Dependable and easy to use, balance scales can be used with both metric and imperial measures – extra sets can be bought separately if need be. And the double pans make it simple to measure equal weights. For dry ingredients, I usually place a sheet of kitchen paper in the measuring pan in order to transfer its contents easily and to save on the washing up. Balance scales are not cheap but they last a lifetime.

Measuring jugs and spoons

For measuring liquids, one or two clear, heat-proof glass jugs are needed with both metric and imperial scales marked on the side. If one of the jugs is wide rather than tall, it can double as a mixing bowl. Sets of plastic measuring spoons are cheap and reliable. For all ingredients, a spoonful is measured level unless stated otherwise.

Mixers and processors

When I ran my cake stall I invested in two Kenwood mixers and they are still going strong. Years ago, the mixing bowls were made of white glass. I remember the disastrous day when I broke one. With cake orders piling up, I had to dash into Exeter to buy another. Fortunately, the bowls are now made from plastic or stainless steel. If you bake a great many cakes, a food mixer with stand, and possibly a bowl cover, is indispensable – the machine works away while you're doing something else. On the other hand, for many households a hand-held electric mixer with one or two sets of blades is perfectly adequate.

Although I don't use a food processor to mix cakes, it can be useful for making some kinds of pastry and for chopping ingredients such as nuts, chocolate, and dried fruit. Small quantities of nuts can be chopped in a Zyliss hand-held chopper.

Sieves

A stainless steel sieve with fine mesh is used for adding air to flour, and to remove lumps from icing and muscovado sugars – spoon the sugar into the sieve and stir it with a wooden spoon, pressing down to push the sugar through the mesh. Discard any lumps that refuse to be flattened. For small amounts of fresh fruit such as raspberries I use a sieve rather than a blender or processor to produce a purée, and it's simple to press a few tablespoons of jam through a sieve to make a smooth mixture for brushing over a cake. A fine-mesh sieve is required when dredging caster sugar or dusting a cake with icing sugar: spoon a little sugar into the sieve and tap the side with your hand or the spoon to produce a light layer as you move it across the cake.

Kitchen timer

A timer helps you to bake accurately again and again. And although you may have a timer on your cooker, if you leave the kitchen while a cake is baking you'll probably need a portable 60-minute timer – preferably with a loud ring!

Baking tins

Dedicated cake-makers acquire cake tins, lots of them. A fluted *brioche* tin or a *kugelhopf* mould is both a utensil and a beautiful object, worthy of display in any kitchen. Many of my most handsome tins are antique, but it is my modern ones that are in frequent use. I recommend heavy-grade tins (sometimes described as commercial-quality on the label). This avoids any buckling in the heat of the oven and ensures an even golden crust. Almost all cake tins are now Teflon-coated and non-stick. It is also best to look for those with a removeable base or a spring-clip for the side wall. These features make removing the cake a simple operation while ensuring it stays upright.

The latest cake moulds are pliable and made from silicone. These cake moulds need to rest on a baking tray in the oven: this helps to transmit the heat to the mould and makes handling easier. Before using for the first time, wash and dry the mould and brush a thin coat of sunflower oil over the inside.

What kind of cake tins you need, and how many, depends on your baking preference. If you make only shortbread biscuits and cup cakes, a couple of baking sheets and some patty tins will suffice. Or if sponge cakes are your speciality, sets of shallow sandwich cake tins with sloping sides are indispensable.

Some of my cake tins have been bought abroad – tiny patty tins known as Pixie cake tins from America, *moules à manqué* from France with sloping sides that flatter a cake and make decorating it far easier, and prettily-shaped ring tins from Portugal and Germany – all of them practical holiday mementos.

To prepare the recipes in this book I have used the most popular and easily available shapes and sizes of cake tin. The majority of my recipes are baked in round tins, which are measured by their diameter or the widest distance from rim to rim. So a round cake tin is described, for example, as *20 cm / 8 in. tin – lined.* Other cake tins are specified according to their shape – square, oblong and so on. Square cake tins are measured by the length on one side.

Sponge sandwich tins, 18 cm / 7 in., 20 cm / 8 in., 23 cm / 9 in., 25.5 cm / 10 in.
Round and square cake tins, ideally with spring-clip or detachable base, 18 cm / 7 in., 20 cm / 8 in., 23 cm / 9 in.
Ring tins, 18 cm / 7 in., 20–23 cm / 8–9 in., 25 cm / 10 in.
Baking sheets, 38 x 26 cm / 15 x 10 in.
Swiss roll tin, 32 x 23 cm / 13 x 9 in.
Shallow baking tins, 25–28 cm / 10–11 in x 15–18 cm / 6 x 7 in., 30 cm / 12 in x 20–23 cm / 8–9 in.
Loaf tins, 0.5 kg / 1 lb, 1 kg / 2 lb.
Tart tins , 20 cm / 8 in., 28 cm / 11 in, 30 cm / 12 in.
Patty or bun tin, tray of 12 x 6 cm / 2½ in. cake cups.
Muffin tin, tray of 12 small or large sized muffin cups.
Madeleine tin, tray of 12 shell-shape cups.

For the best result, it is, of course, sensible to use the size of tin specified in a recipe. But bear in mind that modifications can sometimes be made by replacing one size with another. What usually matters is that the capacity of the tin remains the same, though you may have to adjust the baking time to compensate for a different depth of mixture. To check the capacity or volume of a tin, fill with cold water and pour into a measuring jug.

Baking paper and liners

Silicone baking paper or parchment is a brilliant invention that makes life easier for cake-makers. Buy it in rolls and cut as needed for lining cake tins and baking sheets. When making several cakes of the same size, fold the paper into layers and cut once to produce multiple liners. Smear small dabs of butter on the cake tin to hold the paper in place, drop the paper liner in place and smooth it out. It's also worth looking out for packets of baking paper, pre-cut to size for lining the base and sides of cake tins. A useful trick when using a cake tin without a loose base or a spring-clip side is to place two long strips of baking paper, about 5 cm / 2 in. wide, at right angles to each other across the base of the cake tin so that the ends protrude above the sides and act as handles when lifting out the baked cake. This avoids having to turn the cake upside down when removing it from the tin.

For cake-stall bakers, fluted paper cases are also available for round and rectangular cakes. Cup cakes and fairy cakes are neater and quicker to produce with small fluted paper cases, either plain, patterned or in coloured foil.

Baking sheets and cake tins can also be lined with non-stick baking fabric which is great boon for the busy baker. Not as flexible as baking paper but far more durable – wiped clean after use and stored flat, this material will last years.

Another useful item when making cream- or mousse-filled cakes and gâteaux is a strip of rigid, clear plastic film – the kind used with an overhead projector – to form an easy-wipe case or mould. Cut the sponge cake base to your desired size and place on a flat cake board, wrap the plastic film strip around the cake to provide a vertical support for the cake, overlap the ends and secure with tape. Then fill accordingly. Chill the cake until the cream is set, then carefully remove the plastic strip.

Griddle

A flat metal griddle is useful if you often make Scotch pancakes and Welsh cakes, though a wide, heavy-based frying or pancake pan works equally well.

Pastry board

If need be, pastry can be rolled out on a clean, laminate work surface – and there are even rectangular plastic or fabric covers to prevent the dough from sticking, if you wish. But I prefer to use a large wooden board that is reserved for pastry. Not only is wood a sympathetic surface to work on; the board is portable, enabling you to move or turn it with the rolled out pastry in place. A handy tip is to mark a measuring scale down one or two sides of the board with an indelible pen. This makes checking the size of a cake tin, for instance, quick and easy. And, if you bake lots of tarts and pies, marking a series of concentric circles in the centre of the board to act as a guide saves time when rolling out pastry to specific sizes.

Rolling pin
Again, I prefer wooden rolling pins, either a long solid cylinder or one with a rotating handle – it's a matter of which kind you find most comfortable to use.

Pastry cutters
I confess to owning far more pastry and cookie cutters than anyone could ever need in a domestic kitchen. All of them, though, are hugely popular with my grandchildren when we make pastry, biscuits, and marzipan together. However, the ones I use most often are two sets of circular cutters – one fluted, the other plain – in different sizes, for making scones, biscuits, cookies and tarts. My French friends use an upturned wine glass as a pastry cutter, but a metal shape works better and quicker. If you bake for or with children, then a gingerbread man, possibly a Paddington Bear, and an assortment of Christmas cutters are also a good idea.

Pastry brush
Use either a nylon bristle pastry brush from a kitchenware shop, or a brand-new paint brush, for applying a thin layer of beaten egg or milk to pastry, or for brushing sieved jam or jelly over a cake.

Wooden or plastic ruler
A cheap wooden or plastic ruler is needed for measuring pastry and cakes – and for checking the sizes of rolled-out pastry, biscuit dough and cake tins.

Cooling rack
An essential item, so that cakes can cool with air circulating around them –

two racks are ideal so that you can turn the cake out of the tin on to one, then use the other to turn it right way up.

Icing set and piping-bags
A stainless steel or plastic icing-tube set with nozzles in different patterns is used for delicate work when writing names or a message on a cake with royal icing and glacé icing. Larger nylon piping-bags with a range of screw-in nozzles are more versatile and are useful for piping éclairs, meringues, whipped cream and butter icing.

Oven glove, cloth and apron
This is vital protective clothing – and if you need to reach into the back of the oven, do protect bare arms by covering them with a dry cloth or wear a long-sleeved shirt. And *always* handle hot objects with a dry cloth, never a wet one, since dry fabric provides better insulation.

Oven thermometer
Even though your oven may have its own thermometer, it may not be accurate or the temperature may vary depending on the position of the shelves. A good oven thermometer can offer reassurance. Placed on the baking shelf, it will indicate the actual temperature that your oven has reached at that point and show any changes during the baking time, enabling you to make a correct judgement of when a cake is baked.

Sugar thermometer
Essential for checking the temperature of a boiled sugar syrup, and the thermometer is also useful when making jam. A good sugar thermometer has a clearly marked scale which is easy to read at a glance.

Useful temperatures when making a sugar syrup:
Short thread, 110°C / 220°F.
Soft ball, 116°C / 240°F.
Firm ball, 120°C / 250°F.
Hard ball, 126°C / 260°F.
Caramel, 174°C / 345°F.

Tablespoon, knife, fork and teaspoon
It saves time if you set aside some cutlery to be used only for baking; other useful items are a finely serrated bread knife for cutting a cake into layers and a sharp knife with a long blade for cutting pastry dough and for dividing baked cakes into neat portions.

Wooden or metal skewer
A slim wooden brochette stick or flat metal skewer is helpful when testing whether a cake is correctly baked. Carefully lower the clean, dry skewer into the centre of the cake and remove it slowly. If cake mixture adheres to the skewer, bake the cake for longer. If the skewer comes out clean then the cake is cooked.

Grater and zester
A stainless steel box grater is needed for removing the oily aromatic peel, or zest, of citrus fruit in narrow short pieces. A citrus zester enables you to remove long slim shreds of lemon and orange peel, which can be blanched then dredged with caster sugar for decorating a cake.

Lemon squeezer
A traditional lemon squeezer, made in glass, china, stainless steel or plastic with strainer and pouring dish, catches the juice of all kinds of citrus fruit.

Oven
The conventional enclosed oven with thermostat, heated by electricity, gas or solid fuel, is a fairly recent introduction in the history of baking. For centuries cooks baked over an open fire or in the slowly falling heat of a clay or stone bread oven. In Britain, the industrial revolution brought large-scale smelting and cheaper iron. By the time of Isabella Beeton in the nineteenth century, black cast-iron stoves and cookers equipped with one or even two ovens were being installed in domestic kitchens. Although still heated by burning coal, wood or peat and vulnerable to the vagaries of the wind in the chimney, a metal oven with a hinged door presented new possibilities to the home cook. A wide range of cakes, biscuits, buns and pastries were now achievable and recipe books of the time reflect this shift in the scope of domestic baking.

However, for all the labour-saving advantage of the modern oven, each appliance has its own characteristics such as speed of heating and temperature profile, even hot or cold spots. Although you gradually acquire a sound working knowledge of your own oven and its foibles, it's a wise cook that uses an oven thermometer as well as the thermostat gauge fitted to the outside of the door to verify the oven temperature.

My own preferred oven is electric, with heating elements fitted into the sides, or the top and floor, and equipped with a fan that can be brought into use when required. A fan oven distributes the heat more evenly and allows you to lower the temperature setting by 10–20 degrees from that stated in the recipe. Furthermore, the baking time is often reduced by 5–10 minutes in each hour. That said, don't forget that however reliable your recipe, a watchful eye is helped by an oven light, a glass oven door, and a slim wooden skewer as aids to judging when a cake is baked to perfection.

Kitchen notebook
A notebook works better than odd scraps of paper for jotting down ideas, recipe adaptations and baking tips, and it can provide a satisfying record of your work.

Cookery bookstand
Not essential to baking, but this is an item that makes life a little easier and also frees some of the work surface. Though, of course, whether placed vertical or horizontal, a good cookery book will inevitably reveal the honourable stains of frequent use and its own store of memories.

Serving plates
Large cakes served at home need a flat surface for cutting neatly with the minimum of wasted crumbs, so it's worth looking out for flat cake plates in charity shops. Long narrow plates are perfect for Swiss rolls, biscuits and cookies. Plain cakes look fine on a wooden bread board, but layered confections and iced cakes deserve a flat cake plate with a stand. The renewed enthusiasm for cakes has prompted the production of copies of Victorian glass and china cake stands which are now widely available.

MAKING THE MOST OF YOUR TIME

What to bake? Requests from family and friends, a special occasion like a birthday or anniversary, or just afternoon tea on a wintry weekend, all prompt us towards particular treats. Many home bakers have their own specialities which everyone enjoys – for who makes a cake just for themselves? It's a generous act to spend time in the kitchen producing a cake that will bring pleasure to others. These notes have as much relevance for the family cake-maker as they do for someone who might be tempted to bake cakes for sale to the general public, as described in the next section.

You'll already know how much time you have – 1 hour, 2 hours, all day or evening – to devote to mixing and baking. Remember, though, that while scones and pancakes can be turned out in 30 minutes, having to stay awake while a rich fruit cake slowly cooks can be tiresome. So, even before turning on the oven, read the recipe carefully, if in doubt read it again, then check that you have all the ingredients, equipment and time required.

Ideally, I prefer not to bake just one cake at a time. It's only sensible to utilize the heat and space of the oven by sliding in an extra tray of flapjack or a few cup cakes. And if you plan to bake for some hours, it's often a good idea to prepare several sheets of cookie or biscuit mixture that won't spoil while waiting for oven space. To avoid wasting the heat of an empty oven, I recommend a roll of ready-to-bake refrigerator cookie mixture (see p. 225) that can be sliced on to a baking sheet and popped into the oven before you can say Eliza Acton.

Cakes not needed on baking day can easily be stored: rich fruit cakes should be wrapped in greaseproof paper and placed in a lidded plastic container. If you want to store the fruit cake for some weeks, its flavour is enhanced if you make a few small holes in the base and dribble in a tablespoon or so of brandy, sherry or whisky, repeating the procedure every fortnight.

Sponge cakes and other cakes which stale quickly are best stored in the freezer in a plastic box or sealed bag. Defrost iced and cream-filled cakes in the fridge until ready to serve.

Tarts and cup cakes should also be frozen to maintain their newly-baked flavour – I find these store well if arranged in layers separated by greaseproof paper in lidded plastic boxes.

Meringues will keep quite well for a week or so in an air-tight container in a cool place, though cream-filled meringues and meringue layer cakes need to be stored in the freezer.

An orderly kitchen is clearly an advantage when cooking – having to rummage through drawers looking for a particular implement is tedious and time-consuming, and I speak as an experienced rummager. If, however, you are baking to supply a cake stall then a well-organized kitchen is essential: plenty of work surface is vital, open shelving is often more convenient than cupboards, jugs of wooden spoons and implements make each one easy to grab, and all ingredients and equipment should be to hand and arranged in a logical sequence to help you save time. Many experienced chefs work in quite small spaces and I now understand why.

If possible, it makes sense to minimize the time spent shopping for supplies, so bulk-buying is an advantage and large catering packs can be useful. Free delivery is an offer I never refuse.

Baking cakes all day and everyday calls for a disciplined approach: take regular rest times and don't work too late – better to rise early and work more effectively with fewer mistakes.

Batch baking where you mix and bake several of the same cake at one time is both efficient and economical, though you may need to acquire more cake tins. If you are baking to sell, the results must be consistent – each cake of the same type should be the same size and weight. This is not as difficult as it sounds. Just keep to the recipe, weigh everything carefully, and use identical tins. Mix the ingredients in a really large bowl then spoon it into the prepared cake tins. Check the weight of each filled cake tin by placing it on the scales and adjust accordingly by adding or removing some of the mixture. Keep a record of the weight of each cake tin plus mixture in your notebook or against the recipe – this saves time when you make the next batch. And jot down the larger quantities of ingredients needed to mix several cakes at the same time in a column beside the original recipe – this helps to prevent simple arithmetical mistakes in the future.

Recipes should list the ingredients in the order of use in the method, but to save time I usually line the scale pan with a sheet of kitchen paper which cuts down the washing up, then I weigh a dry ingredient such as caster sugar, adding a messy ingredient like butter or syrup on top – adjusting the combined weight accordingly. Then whoosh, both ingredients are tipped into the mixing bowl together. Similarly, it's sometimes easier to put, for instance, a tin of treacle or cocoa on the scales, note the weight, and spoon out what you need until the weight has fallen by the required amount.

Deciding which recipes save you most time depends on the method involved and whether any filling or frosting is called for – cake decoration, though often enjoyable to do, should be quick if you are baking to sell your produce. Cakes that depend on rubbing in and quick-mix methods plainly save time and are usually dependable. And if you are running a cake stall you don't want baking failures – even though they disappear fast when hungry children are around.

Specially-shaped cakes, such as those cut into a letter or numeral, usually produce perfectly edible cake trimmings. These should be saved in a plastic bag in the freezer for adding to a trifle or for turning into cake crumbs. Or try sprinkling with rum and spooning the mixture into small chocolate cases (see the recipe for Chocolate Dreams on page 198 and substitute the crumbs for the made-to-order sponge mixture). And don't discard small amounts of surplus icing and frosting – use them to sandwich biscuits or sweeten stewed fruit and baked puddings.

I always start a baking session with the cakes that need the highest temperature and the shortest baking time, such as scones, continue with sponge cakes and teabreads, and finish with fruit cakes and meringues, which need both a lower temperature and a longer time yet do not require your constant presence in the kitchen.

Always have a kitchen notebook to hand, for jotting down baking times and temperatures of cakes and biscuits, or variations or changes that have improved the original recipe. One always hopes to remember these things, but on a busy day other priorities soon crowd them out of the memory.

Finally, after all your hard work it's important to keep your cakes looking their best as they travel to market: all your baked goods should be carefully wrapped and placed in crush-proof trays or containers that ideally are stackable and easy to carry, then stored in a cold, dry place until required.

SELLING CAKES

I began to sell cakes when I was very young, helping my mother with cake stalls at fund-raising events such as school fêtes, church bazaars, and charity sales. We sold not only her own baking but also other people's. You probably know how popular home-made cakes are and have seen how quickly the stall sells out at these functions.

So when I launched my own cake stall at Tiverton Pannier Market in Devon, I felt confident that as long as I produced high-quality home-baked cakes and biscuits at the right price they would sell. When I told my mother of the proposed project, she was immediately enthusiastic and offered to help, baking her own contribution of Harvest Cake, Congress Tarts and a range of pies – some of them, it turned out, still warm from the oven.

Sure enough, just as I'd hoped, the cake stall was an immediate success and I soon discovered we could hardly keep up with demand. It may be that even if every local market had a reputable home-baking stall, the call for good cakes would still not be satisfied. And so, a generation after I wrote my first book, *Cake Stall* (published in 1980), there still appears to be great scope for a cake stall of your own.

In some parts of the country, the Women's Institute run their Country Market stalls selling home-baked cakes, jam and preserves. What a blessing these enterprises are, with their freshly laid eggs, vegetables and bunches of garden flowers brought into the market that morning by a band of keen volunteers! Any members of the Women's Institute looking for new recipes for their stalls will find lots of ideas in this book.

If, though, you plan to launch a cake stall in your own name, it is important to set about it the right way. You'll certainly need to know the legal position involved in producing food at home for selling to the general public. A telephone call to your local environmental health officer is essential. This department will be able to advise you on your scheme, and provide up-to-date information on the requirements under the most recent Food and Drugs Act. Environmental health officers can offer practical information which it would be foolish to ignore, and an official visit to your premises can result in much helpful advice. To conform with trading standards regulations, every cake or packet of biscuits must be labelled with your name and address or contact details, the 'best before' date or, if the cake contains fresh cream, the 'use by' date, and the ingredients must be listed in descending order. You will also need to take out comprehensive insurance and to keep accurate records of your finances.

Once you have established that your home is an acceptable workplace and completed the necessary paperwork, it is then a matter of considering where to sell your cakes. If you are principally interested in baking to raise funds for charity – and every good cause needs support – then the location of the stall is often already decided, A hospital's League of Friends normally sells its cakes near the entrance to the building itself, whereas the Macmillan Cancer Charity coffee mornings are usually held in private houses. Other fund-raising events happen in school halls, the village square or even in a busy street on a Saturday morning. But if you plan to raise funds for yourself by trading at a profit, then you need to choose the ideal location. If you live on a farm it may be possible to sell at the farm gate. Or perhaps a mobile cake stall run from a small van would be feasible.

The simplest solution may be to take advantage of your local market, but first pay a visit to chat to the stallholders. I chose the large covered market at Tiverton. This fine building with its double hall is run by the local council and the market superintendent was most helpful: he told me which days of the week the market functioned and the daily charge for a table of a certain size. He even suggested an advantageous position for it! I was lucky that Tiverton had a vacancy, since I knew that some markets had long waiting lists. If you have a choice between a site in the open air or one indoors, then I would advise the latter – simply to be protected from the wind and rain and to keep your cakes looking pristine. That said, the outdoor Gloucester Green market in Oxford, where I now live, offers a flourishing weekly outlet at a lower cost per day per stall than in the well-known Covered Market nearby with its lock-up shops and kiosks open six days a week.

Another excellent development since I wrote the first *Cake Stall* is the arrival of farmers' markets held in towns, villages and cities all over the country. Now numbering upwards of five hundred, more information can be found at www.farmersmarkets.net. You can also consult www.lfm.org.uk for farmers' markets in London. Depending on local demand, farmers' markets are held weekly, fortnightly or monthly. Along with others in the Thames Valley, Oxford's farmers' market, held fortnightly in Gloucester Green, is administered by a local association that readily provides information and advice on how to take part. One of the requirements of a farmers' market is that the produce comes from the locality – usually within a radius of 25 miles.

My Tiverton cake stall was twelve miles from my kitchen and it usually took half an hour to get there along the narrow Devon lanes. I still remember the excitement of setting out with my small yellow car crammed with goodies, many of them ordered a week earlier by regular customers. And I also recall the pleasure of driving home, fairly tired but with all the cakes sold, the money jingling in the cash-box.

Slow Food markets have also recently appeared as a variant on a farmers' market. Again, these markets are held in public places such as city streets and squares. The Topsham Slow Food Market, near Exeter, is a fine example: in the village hall there are stalls selling local food – meat, cheese, bread, pies and cakes, with tastings and samples available and even some chairs with tables for visitors to eat a light meal or a just gaze at the proceedings. Consult www.slowfooduk.org for information on your nearest Slow Food market and your local group.

Food fairs and food festivals also offer possibilities for a cake stall. Though held less frequently than regular markets, these seasonal events provide an excellent shop window for your particular baking speciality. Information about local food fairs can be found at tourist offices and on the events pages of newspapers and food magazines. Websites such as Henrietta Green's FoodLoversBritain.com ares full of valuable details on local foods and fairs.

When I gave up my Tiverton market stall, a friend in the village took it over. She was so successful that after a few years, she rented premises in the town and opened a tea-shop. The back of the shop was fitted with ovens for baking and the front was filled with polished wooden tables and an assortment of chairs, where customers enjoyed a pot of tea or coffee along with her freshly-baked cakes. Before leaving, many people bought a few more to take home. All over the country, the traditional English tea-room is flourishing, popular with people of all ages. And what marks out a good one is the quality of its baking.

Selling directly to your customers is one of the attractions of running your own cake stall or tea-shop. Not only do you dispense with an intermediary – who has to be paid – but you also benefit from your customers' opinions and preferences, which enable you to tailor your baking programme to their requirements. I used to relish the chats with my customers, discussing the merits of one cake over another or discovering a long-felt want for, say, a Victorian caraway seed cake or old-fashioned Easter biscuits. Fulfilling these requests helps to broaden your repertoire.

For those with a passion for baking but not a lot of time, then supplying cakes to friends and neighbours is also a possibility – not everyone likes or has time to bake. A small ad in the local paper or post-office will probably set your phone ringing. And, of course, nothing beats a recommendation by word of mouth.

If, though, you prefer to concentrate on the baking rather than the selling, then supplying your cakes to a retail outlet might well appeal. A local restaurant or delicatessen may be interested in your high-quality home-baked cakes – usually the best way of initiating such a scheme is by bringing in some tempting samples.

Nowadays it's possible to run a cake business via the internet. An attractive website with photographs of your cakes and cookies, and details of a reliable mode of delivery, could be a perfect way in which to run a cake stall from home. If you do this, you may decide to specialize in fruit cakes or rich choco-late cakes to give yourself a market edge. Or you could offer a baking version of the vegetable-box scheme, with a selection of cakes, biscuits, cookies and scones. Some of my Tiverton customers who lived a couple of hours from the market would buy a supply of cakes and store half of them in the freezer, returning two or three weeks later when they'd all been eaten.

Whatever method you adopt for selling your cakes, how you present them is of cardinal importance. All the cakes and biscuits must be wrapped attractively – clear cellophane is ideal, secured with ribbon or raffia. Cake boxes (check in Yellow Pages for a local supplier) are useful for delicate gâteaux and highly decorated cakes since they protect them while travelling. Adopt a particular colour scheme so that your cake wrapping is readily identifiable. I used a pretty pink and white Liberty fabric to cover the stall and for our aprons, continuing the pink and white theme through to the packaging with white boxes and pink ribbon and paper string. Grander cakes and those intended as gifts should be wrapped luxuriously in see-through film with plenty of billowing ribbons and a small card. Cake boards, from kitchenware shops and some stationers, help to keep a cake in place and they make wrapping it easier. Baking cakes in paper cases – both large and small – not only keeps a cake fresh but also helps when transporting them. And it cuts down on the washing up of cake tins – hardly the most glamorous task.

Since a cake stall attracts a wide range of customers, another popular idea is to offer a selection of small cakes on paper plates – large and small sizes. Square and rectangular cakes are easily cut into portions; arrange a few on a plate with a couple of cup cakes and cookies or scones and wrap in food film. Elderly people and those living alone particularly like this idea since it provides variety. And remember to offer single portions of cake, individual cup cakes, separate gingerbread people, or coconut macaroons that even children can afford.

When it comes to deciding what to charge for your cakes, I found a fairly reliable guide was to check the prices of the best-quality manufactured cakes on offer and charge at least that price and preferably rather more. After all, your cakes should be better in every way, freshly baked at home with the highest quality ingredients, often to recipes that are unusual and exclusive or are not viable for a commercial bakery.

If you are selling cakes for charity it is possible to charge a higher price than normal, since the proceeds go to a good cause. It's worth explaining this to your customers or to have a sign saying so, pointing out that you and all your contributors have donated their time and materials so that the stall's total takings go straight to the charity in question. Once people understand this, they are then often wonderfully generous.

Every week on my cake stall I would introduce new kinds of cake and different biscuits to give variety, offering samples for tasting. And as the seasons and festivals arrived throughout the year, the baking reflected them: Simnel Cakes for Easter, fresh fruit cakes and open tarts during the summer, while in December the stall was decorated with greenery and ribbon as a backdrop to the joys and excitement of Christmas baking – brandy snaps and mince pies, rich fruit cakes and chocolate logs or Bûches de Noël were available. I like baking a very wide range of cakes but I would advise anyone with a cake stall to bake the particular cakes they most enjoy. Not only will you put your heart into the task – it then never becomes a chore.

I hope that this book will encourage you to bake a true cornucopia of cakes, biscuits and cookies, and relish the challenges and pleasures. If your family and friends are the recipients, how fortunate they are! And if you are also attracted by the idea of selling your baking, I wish you good luck and great success in your venture.

CHAPTER TWO

Scones, Teabreads, Muffins and Waffles

THE CONTENTS OF THIS CHAPTER

Northern, 23, male, graduate, stuck in London, seeks clever girl in similar predicament, brunette, 20–23 with good recipe for scones and life in general. Box No. ...

Private Eye, 1986, advertisement

A batch of scones straight from the oven is a tempting – even seductive – prospect with an appetizing fresh-baked bread aroma, the thin golden crust hiding the soft creamy crumb inside. Served straight away with strawberry jam and clotted cream, scones are the stars of the traditional cream teas of Devon and Cornwall.

I add butter and eggs to my scones, which lighten the mixture and enrich the flavour. And I prefer to use a small crinkle-edge cutter to produce scones that are deep enough to be pulled apart or split easily. Although at their best when freshly baked, scones made a few hours ahead can be revived quite well in a hot oven. But yesterday's scones are better halved and toasted, then spread with sweet butter and jam or jelly.

Originally made on a griddle or hearth-stone using an open fire, scones are one of the oldest examples of home baking. Some versions of drop scones such as Welsh teacakes are still baked on a flat metal plate over high heat, though baking scones in a hot closed oven is an easier alternative.

Teabreads are a splendid example of traditional British baking. The yeast-leavened type are more often produced by commercial bakers, those made with baking powder are usually the province of the home baker. Baked in loaf tins, teabreads are often enriched with sugar, spices, dried fruit or even chopped nuts. Alan Davidson describes such teabreads as the forerunners of today's fruit cakes. A light, rich teabread mixture baked in a round flat shape is usually known as a teacake.

Unsweetened savoury versions of traditional teabreads are ideal for taking to a picnic or for adding to a lunch-box when served sliced and spread with nut butter or a soft cheese. Extra ingredients can include grated vegetables and olives. French home bakers have also taken to savoury teabreads, usually with a batter-base which produces a loaf with a coarser texture. Cut into narrow fingers and served warm, savoury teabreads go well with an aperitif.

Leisurely weekend breakfasts are the time for muffins and waffles. Tasting their best when freshly made, these are also good items for children to prepare, provided help is at hand. Our present-day waffles are related to the wafers of Chaucer's time, still made by cooking a mixture of eggs, milk and flour between two hot metal plates until the mixture has set in the centre under a crisp golden crust. An electric waffle iron makes producing a basket of waffles a simple and easy operation.

High-domed, cushiony muffins baked in paper cases and leavened with baking powder originated in America. Usually sweetened and flavoured with fruit or nuts such as blueberries and pecans, muffins have become popular in Britain and are excellent served warm at breakfast and brunch.

PLAIN SCONES

By some people's reckoning these are not totally plain scones since I include butter, sugar and eggs in my recipe. The result, however, is so much more delicious than the all-too-solid, floury versions often encountered that I've long preferred this version.

Oven: 220°C/425°F/gas mark 7 ♦ Baking time: 12–15 minutes
Equipment: 5 cm/2 in. fluted pastry cutter; baking sheet – lightly floured
Makes: about 12 scones

230 g/8 oz self-raising white flour ♦ 1 tsp baking powder
good pinch salt ♦ 45 g/1½ oz caster sugar ♦ 60 g/2 oz butter
1 egg lightly whisked with milk to make 150 ml/5 fl oz

glaze: egg yolk blended with a little cream or milk

Sift the flour, baking powder, salt and sugar into a mixing bowl. Add the butter in pieces and rub in with the fingertips until the mixture resembles breadcrumbs. Add the egg and milk while mixing with a knife to form a wet, sticky dough.

Turn the dough on to a well-floured board and knead lightly into a flat, round shape. Dust a little flour over the dough and pat or gently roll out until 1 cm/½ in. thick. Dip the pastry cutter into some flour and using a firm downward movement, cut out as many scones from the dough as you can. Knead together the trimmings and cut out more circles. Place the scones on the prepared baking sheet and brush the tops with the egg yolk glaze.

Bake in the preheated oven until well risen with a golden-brown crust. Cool on the baking sheet for 2 minutes then transfer to a cloth-lined plate or basket and serve while still hot.

FRUIT SCONES

Add 60 g / 2 oz seedless raisins or sultanas to the dry ingredients in the recipe for Plain Scones, then follow the same method, allowing an extra 1–2 minutes in baking time.

WHOLEMEAL FRUIT SCONES

These excellent scones are adapted from a recipe originating at Bateman's Mill, the flour mill in the grounds of Rudyard Kipling's house in Sussex.

Oven: 220°C / 425°F / gas mark 7 ♦ *Baking time: 20 minutes*
Equipment: baking sheet – lightly floured ♦ *Makes: 8 scones*

120 g / 4 oz self-raising white flour ♦ 2 tsp baking powder
60 g / 2 oz light muscovado sugar ♦ 120 g / 4 oz wholemeal flour
60 g / 2 oz butter ♦ 100 g / 3½ oz mixed dried fruit
milk to mix ♦ 1 tbs sesame seeds

Sift the white flour, baking powder and sugar into a mixing bowl and stir in the wholemeal flour. Rub in the butter and mix in the dried fruit and sufficient milk to make a soft dough. Shape the dough into a 15 cm / 6 in. circle and place on a floured baking sheet. Mark the dough into 8 wedges cutting halfway through. Brush the top with milk and sprinkle with sesame seeds.

Bake in the centre of the preheated oven until well risen and golden-brown. Transfer to a wire rack to cool slightly. Serve warm with butter or clotted cream.

WHOLEMEAL OAT SCONES

An attractive scone with a crumbly texture and delicate nutty flavour. Serve the scones warm with bramble jelly and clotted cream.

Oven: 220°C/425°F/gas mark 7 ♦ Baking time: 15 minutes
Equipment: 5 cm/2 in. fluted pastry cutter (optional);
baking sheet – lightly floured
Makes: about 20 scones

175 g/6 oz self-raising white flour ♦ 2 tsp baking powder
1 tsp ground ginger ♦ ¼ tsp salt
175 g/6 oz wholemeal plain flour ♦ 100 g/3½ oz buttermilk
60 g/2 oz rolled oats ♦ 4 tbs honey
1 egg whisked with milk to make 200 ml/7 fl oz

Sift the white flour, baking powder, ground ginger and salt into a mixing bowl. Stir in the wholemeal flour, cut and rub in the butter until the mixture resembles breadcrumbs, then mix in the rolled oats. Blend the honey with the egg mixture and pour on to the dry ingredients. Mix together to make a soft sticky dough.

Turn on to a floured board and pat or roll until 1 cm/½ in. thick. Use either the pastry cutter to cut as many scones as possible or use a sharp knife to divide the dough into triangular pieces. Place the scones on the prepared baking sheet. Bake in the preheated oven for 15 minutes until well-risen and golden-brown. Cool the scones on the baking sheet for 2 minutes then serve straight away.

WHOLEMEAL PECAN NUT SCONES

The recipe for these deliciously nutritious scones comes from Elizabeth Guy, a friend and a talented cook.

Oven: 220°C/425°F/gas mark 7 ♦ *Baking time: 10–15 minutes*
Equipment: large baking sheet – buttered and lightly floured
Makes: 12 scones

230 g / 8 oz wholemeal self-raising flour
pinch of salt ♦ 90 g / 3 oz butter
30 g / 1 oz pecan nuts, chopped ♦ 1 egg
100 ml / 3½ fl oz milk, buttermilk or yoghurt
12 pecan nut halves

Sift the flour and salt into a bowl then tip in the bran left in the sieve. Rub in the butter then stir in the chopped nuts. Beat the egg with the milk, reserve a little for brushing the tops of the scones and stir the rest into the mixture to make a soft dough.

Turn out on to a floured board and pat or gently roll into an oblong shape about 2 cm / ¾ in. thick. Use a palette knife to cut into 12 rectangular scones. Brush the tops with the reserved egg mixture and press a pecan nut on to each one.

Bake in the preheated oven until golden-brown. Transfer to a wire rack to cool.

SAVOURY SCONE RING

Fresh herbs and a hint of cheese make these scones a good partner to soup or a salad.

Oven: 200°C/400°F/gas mark 6 ◆ Baking time: 15–17 minutes
Equipment: 5 cm/2 in. fluted pastry cutter; baking sheet – lightly floured
Makes: two small or one large scone ring or rings

120 g/4 oz self-raising white flour
120 g/4 oz self-raising wholemeal flour
1 tsp baking powder ◆ ¼ tsp salt
pinch of celery salt (optional) ◆ 60 g/2 oz butter
2 tbs chopped fresh herbs: chives, oregano, rosemary, sage
60 g/2 oz English cheese, Cheshire or Red Leicester, grated
1 egg mixed with milk to make 150 ml/5 fl oz
a little extra milk

Stir the flours in a mixing bowl with the baking powder and salt(s). Cut then rub in the butter until the mixture resembles breadcrumbs. Set aside one quarter of the herbs and the cheese and stir in the rest with the egg liquid to form a soft dough.

Turn the dough on to a floured board and gently knead for one minute. Roll out the dough until 1 cm/½ in. thick. Use the pastry cutter to cut out 14 scones in all. Arrange the scones, their sides touching, in one or two circles on the baking sheet. Brush the tops of the scones with the extra milk and sprinkle with the reserved grated cheese and chopped herbs.

Bake towards the top of the preheated oven until well-risen and golden-brown. Cool slightly then transfer to a wire rack or a cloth-lined basket for serving straight away.

SCOTCH PANCAKES

A light and delicious version of the well-known girdle or griddle scones. Scotch pancakes are nicest when freshly made and served straight away with sweet butter or cinnamon honey.

Hotplate or hob on medium heat ♦ Baking time: about 4–6 minutes each
Equipment: griddle or heavy-based frying pan ♦ Makes: 12 pancakes

120 g / 4 oz self-raising white flour
60 g / 2 oz caster sugar ♦ ¼ tsp salt
30 g / 1 oz butter, softened
1 egg ♦ 5 tbs milk
a little sunflower oil for cooking

Sift the flour, sugar and salt into a mixing bowl. Add the butter to the bowl and cut into small pieces. Pour in the egg mixed with the milk and beat for 1–2 minutes until the batter is smooth.

Heat the griddle, though you don't want it too hot – Scotch pancakes are baked not fried – and brush lightly with sunflower oil using a pastry brush or a wad of crumpled kitchen paper. Drop tablespoons of the batter on to the hot surface. Slightly flatten each pancake with the back of a spoon and bake for about 3 minutes on each side until golden. Transfer to a cloth-lined basket and cook the remaining pancakes.

TREACLE AND RAISIN GIRDLE SCONES

This version of Scotch pancakes is dark and spiced. As an alternative to butter, try spreading them with clotted cream or cream cheese.

Hotplate or hob on medium heat
Baking time: 5–6 minutes for each scone
Equipment: griddle or heavy-based frying pan
Makes: 12 scones

120 g / 4 oz self-raising flour ♦ ¼ tsp salt
freshly grated nutmeg ♦ 2 tsp caster sugar
30 g / 1 oz butter ♦ 1 egg
1 tbs black treacle ♦ 5 tbs milk
60 g / 2 oz seedless raisins
clarified butter or sunflower oil

Sieve the flour and salt into a bowl, grate in some nutmeg and stir in the sugar. Cut the butter into the flour until very fine, then mix in the egg, treacle and milk. Beat to a smooth batter.

Heat the girdle or griddle and smear with a little sunflower oil. Drop 2 or 3 tablespoons of the batter on to the griddle, spacing them well. When the bubbles begin to form, sprinkle a few raisins on each scone. After 2–3 minutes the underside of the scones should be cooked. Flip over each one to bake the other side for about 3 minutes. Transfer to a cloth-lined basket and keep warm while you make the rest of the scones.

WELSH TEACAKES

These spiced and fruited scones are rolled out and cut before baking on the griddle. Serve them warm with jam or honey.

Hotplate or hob on medium heat ♦ Baking time: about 6 minutes each
Equipment: 6.5 cm / 2½ in. plain pastry cutter;
griddle or heavy-based frying pan
Makes: about 15 teacakes

230 g / 8 oz self-raising flour
½ tsp salt ♦ ½ tsp grated nutmeg
90 g / 3 oz caster sugar ♦ 120 g / 4 oz butter
90 g / 3 oz seedless raisins or sultanas
1 egg, beaten
a little sunflower oil

Sift the flour and salt into a mixing bowl. Stir in the nutmeg and sugar, cut the butter into the mixture in small pieces and mix in the raisins with the egg to make a soft dough.

Turn the dough on to a floured board and roll out until 5 mm / ¼ in. thick. Use the pastry cutter to cut out as many scones as you can. Knead the trimmings, roll again and cut out the rest.

Lightly oil the griddle or frying pan and bring to medium heat on the hob. If the griddle is too hot the scones may burn. Place scones on the hot surface and after 30 seconds shake the griddle to make sure they are not stuck to the base.

Bake the teacakes for about 3 minutes on each side when they should have a crisp crust and be soft and cooked inside. Transfer to a wire rack and bake the remaining teacakes.

IRISH SODA BREAD

When made with freshly-milled organic wholemeal flour, soda bread has an excellent flavour. I like the loaf cut in thick slices when still warm from the oven. But if you wait until the following day, the bread can be sliced thinly. This version with rolled oats in the mixture has a slightly more open texture than an entirely wholemeal loaf.

In Ireland, soda bread is traditionally mixed with buttermilk – the liquid produced when churning cream into butter. However, it's worth noting that diluted natural yoghurt – made from equal quantities of yoghurt and cold water – can replace buttermilk perfectly well. Alternatively, use soured milk, either allowed to sour naturally or by stirring 2 tablespoons of lemon juice into 300 ml / 10 fl oz fresh milk.

Oven: 220°C/425°F/gas mark 7 ◆ Baking time: 45 minutes
Equipment: baking sheet – floured; and two cake tins for covering the dough
Makes: 2 small loaves

450 g / 1 lb wholemeal flour ◆ 100 g / 3½ oz rolled oats
3 tsp salt ◆ 1½ tsp bicarbonate of soda
300 ml / 10 fl oz buttermilk, soured milk, or diluted yoghurt
4–6 tbs warm water

Measure the flour and oats into a mixing bowl. Sift the salt and soda together and mix in well. Add the buttermilk and water and quickly blend together until you have a soft dough. Try not to over-mix – soda bread should be made quickly and with a light hand.

Divide the dough in two and shape each piece into a round loaf about 13 cm / 5 in. across. Place the bread on the prepared baking sheet and cover each loaf with an upturned cake tin or saucepan.

Bake in the preheated oven for 30 minutes. Remove the covers from the loaves and bake for a further 15 minutes until golden and crusty. The bread is cooked when each loaf sounds hollow when tapped on the base. Cool on a wire rack.

DATE AND WALNUT LOAF

A single-mix teabread, easy enough for children to prepare. Serve sliced with butter or soft cheese.

Oven: 190°C/375°F/gas mark 5 ♦ Baking time: 50–60 minutes
Equipment: 0.5 kg/1 lb loaf tin – buttered and base-lined
Makes: a 10–12 slice loaf

120 g/4 oz self-raising white flour
120 g/4 oz self-raising wholemeal flour
60 g/2 oz dark muscovado sugar
60 g/2 oz butter, softened
2 tbs honey ♦ 90 g/3 oz chopped dates
90 g/3 oz chopped walnuts or pecan nuts
1 egg ♦ 5–6 tbs milk

Measure all the ingredients into a mixing bowl and stir for 1–2 minutes until well combined. Spoon the mixture into the prepared tin and smooth level.

Bake in the preheated oven until a wooden skewer comes out clean from the centre. Cool the loaf in the tin for 5 minutes then turn on to a wire rack.

BARA BRITH

One of my mother's recipes, this fat-free Welsh teabread is usually served sliced and spread with butter though I prefer cream cheese or crème fraîche, both of which complement the fruity sweetness of the loaf. Note that the dried fruit is first steeped in tea for 6–8 hours.

Oven: 180 °C/350 °F/gas mark 4 ♦ Baking time: 55–60 minutes
Equipment: 0.5 kg/1 lb loaf tin – buttered and base-lined
Makes: 8–10 slice loaf

150 g/5 oz sultanas ♦ 150 g/5 oz seedless raisins
120 g/4 oz dark muscovado sugar
150 ml/5 fl oz freshly-brewed Indian tea
230 g/8 oz self-raising flour
1 tbs honey or golden syrup
1 egg ♦ 2 tbs milk

Measure the dried fruit and sugar into a mixing bowl and pour over the hot tea. Stir well and set aside for 6–8 hours or overnight. Add the remaining ingredients to the mixing bowl and stir until well combined. Pour the mixture into the prepared loaf tin.

Bake in the preheated oven until a wooden skewer comes out clean from the centre. Cool in the tin for 5 minutes then turn on to a wire rack.

CELERY, CHIVE AND BRAZIL NUT TEABREAD

Slices of a savoury teabread spread with soft cheese or olive *tapenade* are first-rate for picnic lunches and portable meals. The brazil nuts in the recipe can be replaced by hazelnuts, cashews or almonds if you prefer.

Oven: 180°C/350°F/gas mark 4 ◆ Baking time: 50–60 minutes
Equipment: 0.5 kg/1 lb loaf tin – buttered and base-lined
Makes: a 10–12 slice loaf

150 g/5 oz self-raising wholemeal flour
150 g/5 oz self-raising white flour
½ tsp salt (optional)
100 g/3½ oz butter
2 sticks celery, washed and finely chopped
1 tbs chopped chives
100 g/3½ oz brazil nuts, roughly chopped or sliced
1 egg
150 ml/5 fl oz milk

Measure the flours and salt into a mixing bowl and add the butter cut into pieces. Rub the mixture together until it resembles breadcrumbs. Stir in the celery, chives and most of the nuts reserving some for the top of the loaf. Mix the egg with the milk and stir into the mixture. Knead the dough lightly in the bowl then shape roughly to fit the prepared tin. Gently press the reserved nuts on top of the loaf.

Bake in the preheated oven until a wooden skewer comes out clean from the centre of the loaf and it is starting to shrink from the tin. Cool in the tin for 5 minutes then turn out to cool on a wire rack.

HAZELNUT, CRANBERRY AND BANANA LOAF

An excellent fruit and nut loaf made with half wholemeal and half white flour.

Oven: 180°F/350°C/gas mark 4 ♦ Baking time: 50–60 minutes
Equipment: 0.5 kg/1 lb loaf tin – buttered and base-lined
Makes: a 10–12 slice loaf

90 g/3 oz butter
90 g/3 oz light muscovado sugar
1 egg
100 g/3½ oz self-raising wholemeal flour
100 g/3½ oz self-raising white flour
¼ tsp ground cinnamon
2 large ripe bananas, peeled and sliced
60 g/2 oz dried cranberries
90 g/3 oz coarsely chopped toasted hazelnuts

Cream the butter with the sugar until light and fluffy. Beat in the egg and stir in the remaining ingredients. Spoon the mixture into the prepared loaf tin and spread level.

Bake in the preheated oven until the loaf is firm but just starting to shrink from the tin. Cool in the tin for 5 minutes then turn out on to a wire rack.

DEVONSHIRE SAFFRON LOAF

Bright daffodil-yellow saffron with its bewitching scent and taste is characteristic of West Country baking, particularly in yeast-risen bread, buns and cakes. The dried stigmas of the lilac-flowered *Crocus sativa*, harvested by hand mainly in Spain and Iran, produce the world's costliest spice. Soak the saffron threads overnight to obtain the deepest flavour and colour. If you prefer to make a plain fruit Devonshire tealoaf, simply omit the saffron from the recipe.

Oven: 200°C/400°F/gas mark 6 ♦ Baking time: 45–50 minutes
Equipment: two 0.5 kg/1 lb loaf tins – buttered and base-lined
Makes: two 500 g/1 lb loaves

¼ tsp dried saffron threads ♦ 60 ml/2 fl oz warm water
500g/1 lb 2 oz plain flour ♦ 7 g/¼ oz fast-action dried yeast
½ tsp ground nutmeg ♦ 60 g/2 oz caster sugar
300 g/10 oz dried mixed fruit and candied peel ♦ 60 g/2 oz butter
300 ml/10 fl oz warm milk ♦ extra warm water for mixing
½ tsp clear honey

Measure the dried saffron into a cup and add the warm water. Stir well and leave overnight.

In a large bowl, mix together the flour, yeast, nutmeg, sugar and dried fruit. Melt the butter in the milk and add the saffron liquid with the threads. Pour on to the flour mixture and add enough warm water to mix to a sticky dough. Mix well for 3–4 minutes. Cover the bowl with a clean cloth and leave in a warm place for 1–2 hours or until the mixture has doubled in size.

Transfer the dough to a lightly floured board and knead lightly for 1–2 minutes. Divide in half, knead each piece into an oval shape and place in the prepared loaf tins. Leave the leaves to prove in a warm place for 1 hour or until the tops of the loaves are above the edge of the tins.

Bake in the preheated oven until golden brown and the bottom of each loaf gives a hollow sound when tapped. Cool the loaves on a wire rack and brush the honey over the top crust.

APÉRO CAKE

A recipe from a French friend for a savoury cake to accompany drinks or an apéritif. The batter-based cake is studded with green olives, red peppers, ham and cheese. Serve the cake straight from the oven, cut into narrow fingers.

Oven: 200°C/400°F/gas mark 6 ◆ Baking time: 35–40 minutes
Equipment: 23 cm/9 in. tin – buttered and base-lined
Makes: 18-portion cake

265 g/9 oz plain flour ◆ 2 tsp baking powder
4 eggs ◆ 100 ml/3½ fl oz olive oil
100 ml/3½ fl oz dry white wine
175 g/6 oz green olives, stones removed
100 g/3½ oz Gruyère or Emmental cheese, grated
1 red pepper, grilled, skinned and diced
2 slices *jambon cru* or back bacon, diced
1 tsp dried *herbes de Provence*

Measure the flour and baking powder into a bowl. Add the eggs, olive oil and white wine and mix to a smooth batter with an electric beater. Stir in the olives, cheese, red pepper and *jambon cru* with the herbs. Pour the batter into the prepared cake tin.

Bake in the centre of the preheated oven until cooked and the cake is starting to shrink from the tin. Turn out on to a wooden board and serve straight away or while still warm.

BLUEBERRY CORNMEAL MUFFINS

These North American classics have now become popular in Britain. Muffins are quick and easy to make and are nicest served hot with sweet butter, maple syrup or thick cream.

Oven: 200°C/400°F/gas mark 6 ♦ Baking time: 20 minutes
Equipment: 12-cup muffin tray – lined with paper cases
Makes: 12 muffins

300 ml / 10 fl oz buttermilk or plain yoghurt ♦ 2 eggs
3 tbs mild-tasting vegetable oil – sunflower or grape seed
few drops vanilla essence ♦ 60 g / 2 oz caster sugar
230 g / 8 oz fine-ground yellow cornmeal
100 g / 3½ oz plain flour ♦ 1 tbs baking powder
120 g / 4 oz blueberries or cranberries, fresh or frozen

Use a balloon whisk or electric beater to mix together the buttermilk or yoghurt with the eggs, oil and vanilla essence. Gradually whisk in the sugar, cornmeal, flour and baking powder to make a smooth batter. Spoon into the prepared muffin tins. Divide the blueberries or cranberries between them gently pressing the fruit into the mixture.

Bake in the preheated oven until the centres of the muffins are springy to the touch. Remove from the oven and serve straight away.

DOUBLE CHOCOLATE CHIP MUFFINS

These small rolled-oat muffins crammed with white and dark chocolate chips are nicest served warm for breakfast or brunch, though they can be reheated in a microwave oven.

Oven: 200 °C / 400 °F / gas mark 6 ♦ *Baking time: 15–20 minutes*
Equipment: 12 small-cup muffin tray – lined with paper cases
Makes: 18 small muffins

300 ml / 10 fl oz milk, buttermilk or plain yoghurt ♦ 2 eggs
3 tbs mild-tasting vegetable oil – sunflower or grape seed
¼ tsp vanilla essence ♦ 90 g / 3 oz dark soft brown sugar
175 g / 6 oz self-raising flour
2 tsp baking powder ♦ 120 g / 4 oz rolled oats
60 g / 2 oz white chocolate chips
100 g / 3½ oz plain chocolate chips

Use an electric mixer or balloon whisk to mix together the yoghurt, eggs, oil and vanilla essence. Mix in the sifted sugar, flour and baking powder until the mixture is smooth. Stir in the rolled oats, white chocolate chips and almost all of the plain ones. Spoon the mixture into the prepared muffin tins and sprinkle the extra chocolate chips on top.

Bake in the preheated oven until the centres of the muffins are springy to the touch. Remove from the oven and serve while still warm.

CANADIAN CRULLERS

A recipe that illustrates the Scottish heritage of some Canadian cooking. These deep-fried pastries are flavoured with mace, a beautifully aromatic spice made from the lacy husk of a nutmeg.

Equipment: electric deep fryer or large pan containing 600 ml / 1 pint sunflower oil
Makes: 24–30 pastries

230 g / 8 oz flour ♦ 1 tsp baking powder
30 g / 1 oz caster sugar, ideally vanilla-flavoured
¼ tsp ground mace
grated zest of half a lemon ♦ 60 g / 2 oz butter
2 eggs ♦ vanilla sugar for dredging crullers

Sift the flour, baking powder, sugar and ground mace into a bowl and stir in the grated zest of lemon. Add the butter in pieces and rub the mixture together with your fingertips. Stir in the beaten eggs and mix to a stiff dough. Turn the dough on to a floured board and roll out until about 1 cm / ½ in. thick. Use a sharp knife to cut out crescent shapes or short narrow strips that can be twisted.

Heat the oil to 190°C / 375°F or until a cube of white bread fries to a golden colour in 1 minute.

Deep-fry the pastries, three or four at a time, until they are golden-brown and cooked right through. Lift out the crullers with a slotted spoon or a fish slice and drain on kitchen paper. Transfer to another sheet of kitchen paper and dredge with the vanilla sugar. Serve the crullers warm.

GERMAN VANILLA WAFFLES

When *Cake Stall* was published, the launch party was held in Tiverton's Angel Bookshop run by my friends Frances and Patrick Hutchinson with their two Burmese cats. I suggested making these waffles with my portable electric iron for the guests, who were mainly my cake-stall customers from the Pannier Market around the corner. A table selling made-to-order vanilla-scented waffles is a reliable way of raising funds at a fête or bazaar.

Equipment: electric waffle iron
Makes: approximately 30 waffles of the 5-heart shape design

265 g / 9 oz butter, softened
175 g / 6 oz caster sugar
1 tsp vanilla essence
2 tbs Jamaican rum (optional)
6 eggs
300 g / 10 oz self-raising flour ♦ 175 g / 6 oz plain flour
500 ml / 18 fl oz milk

for serving:
sieved raspberry jam, bramble jelly, honey, or chocolate spread
soured cream or crème fraîche

Cream the butter with the sugar, vanilla essence and rum. Beat in the eggs one at a time alternately with the flour and the milk.

Heat the waffle iron and place 2–3 tablespoons of mixture on the base plate. Lower the lid and cook the waffle – usually for 2–3 minutes – until the outside is crisp and the inside is done. Transfer the waffle to a wire rack and serve straight away while still warm. Accompany with the jam or honey and cream.

CHOCOLATE WAFFLES WITH CHOCOLATE SAUCE

Another of my mother's recipes that my grandchildren enjoy making – just as their parents did. Under the heading 'Waffles on the Electric Table Grill', my mother's copy of the 1929 *Anyone Can Bake* cookery book includes a photograph of an electric waffle iron in use. My first electric waffle iron came from Germany but nowadays these kitchen aids are available in Britain.

Equipment: electric waffle iron
Makes: 10 large or 50 small heart-shaped waffles

45 g / 1½ oz cocoa powder ♦ ¼ tsp ground cinnamon
175 ml / 6 fl oz hot water ♦ 90 g / 3 oz butter, softened
90 g / 3 oz caster sugar ♦ 2 eggs, separated
120 g / 4 oz self-raising flour

chocolate sauce:
175 g / 6 oz plain dessert chocolate ♦ 6 tbs hot black coffee or milk
a splash of rum or brandy (optional)
thick cream or vanilla ice-cream (optional)

Blend the cocoa and cinnamon with the hot water in a large mixing bowl. Add the butter, sugar and egg yolks with the sifted flour. Mix until smooth then beat for 2 minutes. Whisk the egg whites until stiff and fold into the mixture.

Heat the waffle iron and when hot place 2 rounded tablespoons of the mixture on the lower half. Close the lid and cook the waffle for 2–3 minutes until crisp on the outside and cooked through. Transfer the waffles to a clean cloth and keep warm while making the remainder.

To make the chocolate sauce: break the chocolate into pieces and melt in a heat-proof bowl in a microwave oven or by placing the bowl over simmering water. Gradually stir in sufficient coffee or milk and add rum or brandy, if desired, to make a pouring sauce. Serve with the warm waffles and, if preferred, the cream or ice-cream.

Sponge Cakes

THE CONTENTS OF THIS CHAPTER

Whether cake making is to be a handicraft for profit or pleasure, the aim should be perfection, and a divine discontent cherished until that end is reached.

Helen Jerome, *Concerning Cake Making*, 1932

Nothing captures the magic of baking quite so vividly as a sponge cake. The simple ingredients – eggs and sugar whisked until as light as snow then dusted with flour, perhaps enriched with a trickle of melted butter – are transformed in the heat of the oven into a fine textured cake with a pale amber crust and springy crumb.

When I ran my cake stall, there were more queries about how to make a good sponge cake than for any other recipe. Small wonder perhaps that village produce shows still give prizes for the best sponge cake exhibited.

Three types of sponge cake are favoured in the English kitchen:

The *Fat-free Sponge Cake* is the lightest type because it contains no butter at all. Whole eggs and sugar are whisked together for several minutes until pale and foamy. In the past this was done by hand but today an electric mixer or hand-held electric beater reduces the time and effort needed for a satisfactory result. When the egg foam is firm enough for the whisk to leave a trail across the surface, plain flour is sifted over the top and gently folded in. Then the mixture is poured into a sponge cake tin and baked.

The *Genoese Sponge Cake* includes melted butter, which adds flavour to the cake and improves its moistness and keeping quality. I find that halving the quantity of butter given for a classic Genoese works well and makes the mixture easier to handle. Sifted plain flour is folded into the egg foam alternately with the melted butter, then the mixture is baked.

The *Victoria Sponge Cake* is a butter-rich mixture with an equal weight of butter, sugar and flour. This cake is the easiest sponge cake to make since no whisking is called for. The butter and sugar are blended together until pale and creamy, then whole eggs are beaten in and finally sifted plain flour is gently folded into the mixture.

A modern variation of the classic version is the *Quick-mix Victoria Sponge Cake* which employs an all-in-one-mix method with softened butter and self-raising flour. I recommend this cake to novice bakers since it is easier, speedy and virtually foolproof.

In home-baking the Victoria Sponge Cake is the mother recipe to hundreds of adaptations. A certain amount of extra flour can be added to the mixture though this will, of course, affect the flavour of the cake and reduce the fine springy nature of the crumb in the original recipe. However, the addition of more flour produces a mixture that will support other ingredients such as fruit and nuts.

Further variations on all three types of sponge cake are possible if you separate the eggs, adding the yolks and stiffly whisked egg whites at different stages. In fact, the egg yolks are omitted altogether in a pure white Angel Cake while only yolks are included in the mixture for a Golden Cake.

A well-made sponge is the basis of numerous cakes and gâteaux; try adding lemon or orange zest, or strong black coffee, or use muscovado sugar rather than golden caster to produce a range of different sponge cakes from the same basic recipe. Or simply adapt a basic recipe by changing the filling, icing or frosting of one cake for another to broaden your repertoire.

The aim is to produce a sponge cake with the two elements of the cake and the filling or frosting in harmony. If, for instance, I plan to use a cake filling of whipped cream, possibly enlivened with liqueur, I usually prefer to bake a fat-free sponge cake rather than a Victoria sponge since it is a better foil for the rich high-fat cream. For a Swiss roll, for example, which contains a high proportion of filling to cake, the best choice is usually a fat-free sponge cake. But of course there are always exceptions when, say, a buttery cake supports an even richer filling and is for serving in small portions at the end of a meal.

SPONGE CAKES

FAT-FREE SPONGE CAKE

Possibly the earliest form of sponge cake, known in France as *biscuit de Savoie*. At its best when served freshly baked, this cake is popular just sandwiched with jam and thick cream. Omit the cream if you wish the cake to remain fat-free.

Oven: 180°C/350°F/gas mark 4 ♦ Baking time: 20–25 minutes
Equipment: two 18–19 cm/7–7½ in. sponge sandwich tins
– buttered and base-lined
Makes: 8-portion cake

4 eggs ♦ 120 g/4 oz caster sugar
½ tsp vanilla essence (optional) ♦ 120 g/4 oz plain flour

filling:
2 heaped tbs raspberry jam, sieved
150 ml/5 fl oz whipping or double cream ♦ 2 tsp caster sugar

Whisk the eggs with the sugar and vanilla essence until thick and foamy and the whisk leaves a trail over the mixture. This is achieved most easily in a food mixer or using a hand-held electric beater. If you are making the cake by hand, using a balloon whisk or an egg beater, it is helpful to place the mixing bowl over a pan of simmering water while you whisk the mixture, then remove the bowl from the heat.

Place the flour in a large sieve and tap the side to give a dusting of flour over the top of the egg foam. Use a balloon whisk to fold in the flour gently. Repeat until all the flour has been incorporated.

Divide the mixture between the prepared cake tins. Bake in the preheated oven until the cakes are golden-brown and just starting to shrink from the tins. Cool the cakes in their tins for 2 minutes then turn out on to a wire rack and peel off the baking paper.

When the cakes are cold, spread the sieved jam in one layer. Whisk the cream until thick and glossy and spoon over the jam. Place the other cake on top and sprinkle with caster sugar. Set the cake in a cool place until ready to serve.

GENOESE SPONGE CAKE FILLED WITH LEMON CURD

Although this modified Genoese sponge cake includes slightly less butter than the classic version, its flavour and keeping quality still prevail. I recommend the lemon curd filling: home-made fruit curd such lemon or passion-fruit can be prepared a day or so before baking the cake, provided the mixture is stored covered, in a small bowl in the fridge, until needed.

Oven: 180°C/350°F/gas mark 4 ♦ Baking time: 25 minutes
Equipment: two 18–19 cm/7–7½ in. sponge sandwich tins
– buttered and base-lined
Makes: 8-portion cake

4 eggs ♦ 120 g/4 oz caster sugar
120 g/4 oz plain flour ♦ 60 g/2 oz butter, melted

lemon curd filling:
1 large lemon ♦ 60 g/2 oz caster sugar ♦ ¼ tsp cornflour
1 egg ♦ 30 g/1 oz butter ♦ 1 tsp caster sugar

Use an electric mixer or beater to whisk the eggs with the caster sugar until foamy and thick enough for the whisk to leave a trail across the top of the mixture. If whisking by hand, place the mixing bowl over a pan of simmering water. Whatever method you use, whisking usually takes 5–10 minutes. Measure the flour into a sieve and dust the top of the mixture with a thin layer then fold in with a balloon whisk, repeat 2–3 times then add the flour alternately with a trickle of melted butter. Fold in really gently to lose the minimum amount of air from the mixture. When the flour and butter have been incorporated, divide the mixture between the prepared cake tins.

Bake in the preheated oven until the cakes are golden brown and just starting to shrink from the tin. Cool in the tins for 3 minutes then turn out on to a wire rack and peel off the lining paper.

Sandwich the sponge cakes with the lemon curd and dust the top of the cake with the caster sugar. Leave the cake in a cool place until ready to serve.

To make the lemon curd: wash and dry the lemon and grate the zest into the ceramic top half of a double-boiler or use a small bowl balanced over a pan of hot water. Add the strained juice of the lemon, the sugar, cornflour and egg. Cook, stirring all the time, over simmering water for 5–7 minutes or until the mixture thickens. Remove the bowl from the heat and stand in cold water to cool the mixture. While the curd is still warm beat in the butter in small pieces. Set aside until cold.

VICTORIA SPONGE CAKE WITH PASSION-FRUIT CURD

A butter-rich, creamed not whisked, sponge cake dating from the time of Queen Victoria. This type of sponge is the basis for dozens of variations and is justly popular with home bakers; the filling for the cake can be as you wish, just sieved jam or a fruit jelly, or the passion-fruit curd that I give below.

Oven: 180 °C / 350 °F / gas mark 4 ♦ Baking time: 30 minutes
Equipment: two 18–20 cm / 7–8 in. sponge sandwich tins
– buttered and base-lined ♦ Makes: 8–10-portion cake

175 g / 6 oz butter, at room temperature ♦ 175 g / 6 oz caster sugar
3 eggs ♦ ¼ tsp vanilla essence ♦ 175 g / 6 oz self-raising flour

passion-fruit curd:
4 large ripe passion-fruit ♦ 2–3 tbs caster sugar ♦ ¼ tsp cornflour
1 egg, beaten ♦ 45 g / 1½ oz butter ♦ 1 tsp icing sugar

Cream the butter with the sugar until the mixture is pale and fluffy. Add the eggs one at a time, beating them in well. Mix in the vanilla essence. Gradually fold in the sifted flour. Divide the mixture between the two prepared cake tins and smooth level.

Bake the cakes in the preheated oven until golden brown and just starting to shrink from the cake tin. Cool in the tins for 2 minutes then turn out the cakes to cool on a wire rack.

Sandwich the cakes with the passion-fruit curd, dust the top of the cake with icing sugar and set aside until ready to serve.

To prepare the passion-fruit curd: wash each fruit and cut in half, use a teaspoon to scrape out the flesh, juice and pips – if you prefer to remove the pips press the mixture through a sieve at this stage – into the ceramic top of a double-boiler, or into a small heat-proof bowl placed over a pan of simmering water. Add the sugar, cornflour and beaten egg and blend together with a wooden spoon. Cook the mixture for 5–7 minutes stirring all the time until thickened. Remove from the heat and cool the curd by standing the top half of the double-boiler, or the bowl, in cold water. When almost cool, gradually beat in the butter.

QUICK-MIX VICTORIA SPONGE CAKE
WITH MASCARPONE AND MANGO

For the novice or experienced cook, this is one of the easiest cakes to make using the all-in-one method. The ingredients should be at room temperature and using an electric mixer, beater or processor, mixing the cake takes only a couple of minutes. The freshly-baked cake is excellent served quite plain or it could be enhanced with mascarpone cheese and fresh mango. Since this cake can also be made perfectly well by hand, and by children, I give an alternative version with chocolate chips.

Oven: 180°C/350°F/gas mark 4 ◆ Baking time: 30–35 minutes
Equipment: 20 cm/8 in. spring-clip tin – buttered and base-lined
Makes: 8–10-portion cake

175 g/6 oz butter, at room temperature ◆ 175 g/6 oz caster sugar
3 eggs ◆ 175 g/6 oz self-raising flour ◆ 1 tsp baking powder

for serving:
150 ml/5 fl oz mascarpone cheese ◆ 1 ripe mango

Measure all the ingredients into a mixing bowl and beat together until the mixture is smooth. Spoon the mixture into the prepared cake tin and spread it level. Bake in the preheated oven until golden brown and the cake is just starting to shrink from the tin. Cool in the tin for 2 minutes then open the clip and remove the side of the tin and slide the cake on to a wire rack to cool.

Place the cake on a flat serving plate and spread the mascarpone cheese over the top. Wash and peel the mango and cut the flesh into long, slim slices. Arrange the mango over the mascarpone then set the cake aside in a cold place until ready to serve.

QUICK-MIX CHOCOLATE CHIP VICTORIA SPONGE CAKE

Prepare the cake as above, using a wooden spoon or an electric hand-held beater to mix until smooth. Stir in 100 g/3½ oz chocolate chips. Bake the cake as above and turn it out to cool on a wire rack. Serve the cake plain or dusted with caster sugar.

COFFEE SWISS ROLL FILLED WITH MARSALA CREAM

A Swiss roll is made by folding a thin layer of light sponge cake around a well-flavoured filling. To make a Swiss roll with several turns, the sponge cake should be the correct thickness for its size – a very thick layer of cake either cracks as you roll it, or has to have such a thick filling that the whole charm of the cake is lost. For a plain Swiss roll, replace the coffee with warm water; the filling can be raspberry or strawberry jam, though a nicely judged wine cream makes the cake more distinctive.

Oven: 200°C/400°F/gas mark 6 ♦ Baking time: 12–15 minutes
Equipment: 30 x 20 cm/12 x 8 in. Swiss roll tin – buttered and base-lined; tea cloth ♦ Makes: 10–12-portion cake

60 g / 2 oz plain flour ♦ a pinch of baking powder
2 large eggs ♦ 1 tbs strong black coffee or warm water
60 g / 2 oz caster sugar ♦ a little extra caster sugar

filling:
300 ml / 10 fl oz double or whipping cream ♦ 2–3 tbs marsala wine
pinch of ground cinnamon ♦ 1–2 tbs caster sugar
1 tbs icing sugar

Sieve the flour and baking powder twice on to a sheet of paper. Whisk the eggs with the coffee or water and sugar, in an electric mixer or in a bowl set over simmering water using an electric beater, until the mixture is pale and foamy and the whisk leaves a trail over the surface. Use a balloon whisk to gently fold the flour into the mixture retaining as much air as possible. Pour the mixture into the prepared cake tin and spread evenly.

Bake in the preheated oven until the cake is springy to the touch in the centre. Cool in the tin for 2 minutes then turn out on to the teacloth sprinkled with the extra caster sugar. Peel off the lining paper and use a sharp cook's knife to trim the crusty edges. Holding the cloth, gently roll up the cake from the short side, allowing the cloth to take the place of the filling, and leave wrapped in the cloth while you prepare the cream.

Whisk the cream until thick and glossy. Mix in the wine, cinnamon and sugar to taste. When the cake is cold, unroll carefully and spread the cream evenly on top. Carefully re-roll the cake and dust with sifted icing sugar. Chill until ready to serve. To cut the cake into slices, use a fine-toothed bread knife and a gentle sawing action – this tip from my mother helps to keep the cake in shape and produces attractive slices.

Variation: try adding finely grated zest of lemon, orange or tangerine to the raw mixture, and enhance the filling in the same way.

LEMON OR ORANGE DRIZZLE CAKE

Until I discovered a French handwritten recipe from the 1930s, I hadn't appreciated that the cake we now call a Drizzle Cake had been around for so long. The French recipe includes white rum in the fruit syrup though it's not essential. This popular cake is recommended for a fund-raising stall.

Oven: 180 °C / 350 °F / gas mark 4 ♦ Baking time: 30–35 minutes
Equipment: two 0.5 kg / 1 lb loaf tins,
or a 30 x 23 x 4 cm / 12 x 9 x 1½ in. baking tray – buttered and base-lined
Makes: two loaf cakes or 20 square portions

Victoria Sponge Cake recipe ♦ 2 lemons or oranges
100 g / 3½ oz golden granulated sugar ♦ 2 tbs white rum (optional)

Prepare the Victoria Sponge Cake recipe using the classic creaming method or the quick-mix method – see recipes on pages 76–7.

Spoon the cake mixture into the cake tin(s) and smooth level. Bake in the preheated oven until the cake is just shrinking from the tin.

Meanwhile, grate the zest of the lemons or oranges into a bowl, add the strained juice of the fruit and stir in the granulated sugar. If you wish, add the white rum.

Remove the cake(s) from the oven and gradually spoon the fruit syrup over the top in a trickle or drizzle allowing the liquid to seep into the crust. Cool the cake(s) in the tin for 30 minutes then transfer the loaf cakes to a wire rack, though it's better to cut the tray cake into portions while still in the tin. When possible, I prefer to serve this cake warm.

WHOLE-WHEAT SPONGE CAKE WITH FUDGE FILLING

A nicely flavoured sponge cake from my friend Doreen Chetwood, a life-long champion of baking with wholemeal flour.

Oven: 160°C/325°F/gas mark 3 ♦ *Baking time: 30–35 minutes*
Equipment: two 20 cm/8 in. sponge sandwich tins – buttered and base-lined
Makes: 8-portion cake

90 g/3 oz light muscovado sugar ♦ 1 tbs clear honey
¼ tsp vanilla essence ♦ 4 eggs, separated
4 tbs hot water ♦ 120 g/4 oz plain whole-wheat flour

fudge filling:
60 g/2 oz butter ♦ 120 g/4 oz light muscovado sugar
1 tbs single cream ♦ 1 tsp icing sugar

Measure the sugar, honey, vanilla essence, egg yolks and hot water into a bowl. Whisk until light and foamy with an electric beater or food mixer. In a separate bowl, whisk the egg whites until stiff, then fold into the yolk mixture. Tip the flour into a sieve and shake a fine layer over the mixture. Fold in gently and repeat until only bran remains in the sieve. Fold in half the bran and return the remainder to the flour bag. Divide the cake mixture between the prepared tins and smooth level.

Bake in the preheated oven until the cakes are well-risen and springy to the touch. Cool in the tins for 2 minutes then turn the cakes on to a wire rack to cool.

For the filling, melt the butter in a pan over moderate heat, stir in the sugar and cream until dissolved. Bring the mixture to the boil and cook for 2 minutes. Remove from the heat and cool the pan by standing it in cold water for 2–3 minutes. Beat the filling until it is thick but still spreadable. Pour the filling over one cake and place the other on top. Lightly dust the cake with sieved icing sugar and leave until the filling is set.

ITALIAN SPONGE CAKE FILLED WITH RASPBERRIES AND CREAM

This is a particularly good fat-free sponge cake with a fine texture, though you will need two mixing bowls. The cake recipe came from my mother, yet I see that my friend Anna del Conte uses the same technique for her fatless sponge cake, *pan di spagna*, so the method may originate in Italy. The cake goes well with raspberry cream and looks particularly attractive assembled in this way.

Oven: 180 °C / 350 °F / gas mark 4 ♦ Baking time: 25 minutes
Equipment: two 20 cm / 8 in. sponge sandwich tins – buttered and base-lined
Makes: 8-portion cake

4 eggs, separated ♦ ¼ tsp vanilla essence
120 g / 4 oz caster sugar
120 g / 4 oz plain flour

filling:
120 g / 4 oz ripe raspberries ♦ 150 ml / 5 fl oz double cream
1 tbs caster sugar ♦ 1 tsp icing sugar

Use a hand-held electric beater to whisk the egg white until stiff, whisk in the vanilla essence with half the sugar and continue whisking for half a minute. Transfer the beater to a mixing bowl containing the egg yolks and the rest of the sugar, whisk until pale and foamy and thick enough for the whisk to leave a trail across the surface. Tip the flour into a sieve. Using a balloon whisk gently fold one third of the whisked egg white into the yolks, then sift one-third of the flour over the top of the mixture and gently fold in. Repeat until all the ingredients are incorporated.

Divide the mixture between the prepared cake tins. Bake in the preheated oven until the cakes are golden brown and just starting to shrink from the tin. Cool in the cake tins for 2 minutes then turn on to a wire rack to cool and peel off the paper lining.

To make the filling: set aside a tablespoon of the raspberries for decoration. Whisk the cream until stiff but still glossy. Tip the remaining raspberries into a sieve balanced over the cream bowl. Use a wooden spoon to press the fruit through the sieve so that the purée falls on to the cream. Add the caster sugar and gently mix together to make the raspberry cream.

To assemble the cake: place one cake on a flat serving plate and spread a little raspberry cream over the top. Arrange a small saucer (10 cm / 4 in. across) upside down in the centre of the other cake. Use a small serrated knife to cut vertically around the saucer and remove the circle of cake beneath it. This calls for a certain amount of dexterity but if you do it slowly, you will manage perfectly. Place the outer ring of cake on top of the layer of raspberry cream. Spoon the remaining cream into the centre of the cake. Now use a sharp knife to divide the small inner disc of cake into 8 wedge-shaped portions and arrange them on top of the cream, each piece slightly angled but with the pointed ends dipping into the cream. Sprinkle the reserved raspberries over the top and dust with the icing sugar. Serve straight away or within a hour or so.

BRIOCHE-STYLE SPONGE CAKE WITH SHERRY SABAYON

An ideal stand-by cake that's excellent for a weekend lunch. Store the fat-free cake in the freezer until needed and defrost in a warm oven or a microwave. Prepare the sauce, pour over the warm cake and serve straight away.

Oven: 180°C/350°F/gas mark 4 ♦ *Baking time: 25–30 minutes*
Equipment: 22 cm/8½ in. fluted brioche tin
– buttered and dusted with caster sugar
Makes: 8–10-portion cake

4 eggs ♦ 120 g/4 oz caster sugar
½ tsp vanilla essence
120 g/4 oz plain flour

sherry sabayon sauce:
2 egg yolks ♦ 30 g/1 oz caster sugar ♦ 75 ml/2½ fl oz cream sherry
75 ml/2½ fl oz double cream

Whisk the eggs with the sugar and vanilla essence until thick and foamy so that the whisk leaves a trail over the mixture. This is achieved most easily in a food mixer or using a hand-held electric beater. If you are making the cake by hand, using a balloon whisk or an egg beater, it is helpful to place the mixing bowl over a pan of simmering water while you whisk the mixture then remove the bowl from the heat.

Place the flour in a large sieve and tap the side to give a dusting of flour over the top of the egg foam. Use a balloon whisk to fold in the flour gently. Repeat until all the flour has been incorporated.

Pour the mixture into the prepared cake tin. Bake in the preheated oven until the cake is golden-brown and just starting to shrink from the tin. Cool the cake in the tin for 5 minutes then turn out on to a wire rack.

To make the sauce: measure all the ingredients into a heat-proof bowl and place it over a pan of simmering water. Use a hand-held electric beater to whisk the mixture for 5–6 minutes until thick and frothy. Ladle some of the warm sauce over the sponge cake and pour the rest into a serving bowl. Serve the cake straight away with the extra sauce for spooning over each portion.

COFFEE CREAM SPONGE CAKE

Every week, I would bake more and more coffee cakes for the stall – they were one of the first cakes to sell every morning. Their appeal depends on the contrast of a plain coffee sponge cake with the rich French butter cream. This cake makes an excellent pudding partnered with a warm dish of fresh apricots baked with brown sugar, a splash of vermouth and some curls of butter.

Oven: 180°C/350°F/gas mark 4 ♦ Baking time: 25 minutes
Equipment: two 23 cm/9 in. spring-clip tins – buttered and base-lined
Makes: 12–16-portion cake

6 eggs, separated ♦ 90 g/3 oz caster sugar ♦ 90 g/3 oz light brown sugar
1 tbs strong black coffee or 1 tsp coffee essence
175 g/6 oz plain flour

coffee butter cream:
2 egg yolks ♦ 90 g/3 oz caster sugar ♦ 3 tbs water
150 g/5 oz butter ♦ 2 tbs strong black coffee or 2 tsp coffee essence
chocolate coated coffee beans or toasted split almonds

Use an electric beater to whisk the egg whites until stiff, gradually whisk in the caster sugar. Move the same beater – there's no need to wash the whisks – to a large mixing bowl containing the egg yolks, light brown sugar and the coffee. Whisk until the mixture is pale and frothy and forms a trail across the top. With a balloon whisk fold one quarter of the egg whites into the yolks followed by one quarter of the flour, sifted over the surface of the mixture. Repeat until all the ingredients are incorporated. Divide the mixture between the prepared cake tins and smooth level.

Bake in the preheated oven until the cakes are golden brown and just starting to shrink from the tin. Leave the cakes to cool in the tins for 2 minutes, then open the clip and remove the sides of the tin. Gently turn the cakes on to a wire rack and peel off the baking paper. Use another wire rack to turn the cakes the right way up.

Sandwich the sponge cakes with the butter cream, and use a palette knife to spread the rest over the sides and top of the cake. Place in the refrigerator to chill slightly then decorate with the coffee beans or almonds, arranging them around the rim and base of the cake. Chill the cake until ready to serve. Alternatively freeze the cake, then wrap in plastic, and store for 1 month. To defrost, unwrap the cake and allow to thaw slowly in a refrigerator.

To make the butter cream: place the egg yolks in a medium size mixing bowl. Dissolve the sugar in the water in a small pan over low heat. Raise the heat, bring the syrup to the boil then cook steadily until it reaches 110°C / 220°F or the fine thread stage. Remove from the heat and cool slightly, whisk the egg yolks continuously using an electric beater while pouring in the sugar syrup in a thin thread. Continue whisking until the mixture is pale and foamy then gradually beat in the butter in small pieces until the cream is thick and smooth. Then beat in the coffee. The butter cream can be used straight away or can be covered and kept in a cold place for 24 hours.

ANGEL CAKE WITH ST CLEMENT'S CREAM

Pure white cakes are usually produced by aeration with just the white of egg. Though less common in Britain, Angel Cakes are popular in North America where they are baked in purpose-made deep ring moulds. To accompany this delicate, snow-white cake, I've devised a light citrus cream.

Oven: 160°C/325°F/gas mark 3 ♦ *Baking Time: 45–55 minutes*
Equipment: 25 cm/10 in. ring tin or 20 cm/8 in. spring-clip tin
– buttered and dusted with caster sugar
Makes: 12-portion cake

90 g/3 oz plain white flour ♦ 15 g/½ oz cornflour
175 g/6 oz caster sugar ♦ 6 large egg whites ♦ 1 tsp cream of tartar
1 tsp vanilla essence ♦ ½ tsp almond essence

orange and lemon cream:
1 orange ♦ ½ lemon ♦ 1 egg
60 g/2 oz caster sugar ♦ 300 ml/10 fl oz double cream

Sieve the flour with the cornflour and 120 g/4 oz of the sugar on to a sheet of paper. Whisk the egg whites with the cream of tartar in a wide bowl until stiff and fluffy but still a little moist – don't whisk until dry. Sprinkle the remaining sugar over the meringue and whisk in. Fold in the vanilla and almond essences. Sieve the flour mixture into the meringue, gently folding it in with a balloon whisk as you do so. Spoon the mixture into the cake tin and smooth level.

Bake in the preheated oven until the cake is just shrinking from the tin. Cool in the tin for 10 minutes then carefully loosen the cake with a flexible knife and turn out of the ring tin on to a wire rack to cool. Or unclip the side of the tin and slide the cake on to a wire rack.

To make the citrus cream: wash and dry the orange and remove one long strip of peel without the pith. Cut into fine shreds, then blanch in boiling water for 2 minutes, drain and cool. Grate the remaining zest of orange into a bowl and add the strained juice. Add the finely grated zest and strained juice of the lemon. Place the bowl over a pan of simmering water and whisk in the egg and sugar. Stir continuously until the mixture slightly thickens, then remove from the heat and stand the bowl in cold water to cool the custard.

Whisk the cream until thick but still glossy then fold in the custard. Spread the citrus cream thickly over the cake in swirling patterns. Decorate with the shreds of orange zest and set aside until ready to serve.

CHOCOLATE TIPSY CAKE

Noel Coward has told us how 'while adding some liquor to the Tipsy Cake,' Mrs Wentworth-Brewster discovered her life had just begun. In the eighteenth century, Tipsy Cake was another name for Brandy Trifle, and Eliza Acton states that 'the old-fashioned mode of preparing this dish was to soak a light sponge or Savoy cake in as much good French brandy as it could absorb.' For a traditional Tipsy Cake, use a plain sponge cake instead of the updated but good chocolate version here.

Oven: 190°C/375°F/gas mark 5 ◆ *Baking time: 40–45 minutes*
Equipment: 18–20 cm/7–8 in. ring tin or
22 cm/8½ in. fluted brioche tin – buttered
Makes: 10–12-portion cake

120 g / 4 oz caster sugar ◆ 120 g / 4 oz butter ◆ 2 large eggs
3 tbs cocoa powder ◆ 3 tbs strong black coffee
100g / 3½ oz self-raising flour

decoration:
150 ml / 5 fl oz French brandy or dark rum ◆ 150 ml / 5 fl oz double cream
1 egg white ◆ 1 tbs caster sugar
30 g / 1 oz chocolate curls or flakes (optional)

Tip a spoonful of the caster sugar into the buttered cake tin and tilt until lightly dusted with sugar. Return any surplus to the rest of the sugar in a bowl.

Add the butter and beat until light and fluffy. Beat in the eggs alternately with the cocoa blended with the coffee. Fold in the sieved flour. Spoon the mixture into the prepared cake tin and smooth level.

Bake in the preheated oven for 30–35 minutes or until the cake is springy in the centre and just starting to shrink from the tin. Cool in the tin for 2 minutes then turn on to a wire rack.

When the cake is cold, place upside down on a flat plate with a slight rim to catch any surplus liquid. Slowly spoon over the brandy so that the cake absorbs it gradually. Beat the cream until thick but still glossy. In a separate bowl whisk the egg white until stiff, whisk in the sugar and then fold into the cream. Spread the cream over the cake in a thick layer leaving a rough finish. Decorate if you wish with curls of chocolate and set aside in a cool place for 1–2 hours before serving.

BATTENBERG CAKE

Named after Prince Henry of Battenberg, this Victoria sponge cake is assembled with contrasting squares of pink and yellow and then wrapped in a thin layer of almond paste or marzipan.

Oven: 180°C/350°F/gas mark 4 ♦ Baking time: 35–40 minutes
Equipment: 28 x18 cm/11 x 7 in. tin; baking paper
Makes: 8–10-portion cake

175 g/6 oz butter ♦ 175 g/6 oz caster sugar ♦ 3 eggs
175 g/6 oz self-raising flour ♦ ¼ tsp vanilla essence
cochineal or pink food colouring ♦ ½ tsp rose-water
4 tbs apricot jam, sieved ♦ 350 g/12 oz marzipan (see page 291)

Prepare the cake tin by cutting a 28 x 28 cm/11 x 11 in. square of baking paper. Fold the paper in half and line the base of the buttered tin with the fold vertical lengthways to separate the two colours in the mixture while the cake bakes.

Cream the butter with the caster sugar and beat until light and fluffy. Beat in the eggs, one at a time, and then fold in the sifted flour. Mix the vanilla essence into one half of the mixture, and spoon into one side of the prepared cake tin. Add a drop or two of food colouring to the remaining mixture to colour it pink, mix in the rose-water and spoon into the other side of the cake tin. Smooth the mixture level.

Bake in the preheated oven until the cake is springy in the centre. Cool in the tin for 2 minutes then turn out on to a wire rack to cool. When cold, carefully peel off the paper to separate the two cakes. Trim the cakes to make them equal size and cut both in half lengthways. Spread apricot jam over the surface of each strip and sandwich them together to give alternating coloured squares.

Roll out the marzipan on a board lightly dusted with icing sugar to make a rectangle about 40 x 20 cm / 16 x 8 in. or large enough to wrap around the cake excluding the ends. Brush the marzipan with the rest of the jam and place the cake on top, bring the edges together and press together firmly. Trim the ends neatly if necessary. Turn the cake the right way up and crimp the top two edges with your finger tips as for pastry crust, then use a sharp knife to lightly mark a lattice pattern over the top. Wrap the cake in greaseproof paper and store in a lidded plastic box overnight before cutting.

ORANGE SPONGE CAKE WITH ORANGE COINTREAU CURD

The powerful aromas in the zest of citrus fruit such as sweet oranges, lemons or, nicest of all, tiny clementines, impart a delightful scent to a sponge cake. A Victoria Sponge works best here because the butter absorbs the fruit's essential oils, and the cake is filled with a traditional English fruit curd.

Oven: 180°C/350°F/gas mark 4 ◆ Baking time: 40–45 minutes
Equipment: 18 cm/7 in. tin or two 18 cm/7 in. sponge sandwich tins
– buttered and base-lined ◆ Makes: 8-portion cake

120 g/4 oz butter ◆ 120 g/4 oz caster sugar
1 orange or lemon, or 2 clementines, finely grated zest ◆ 2 eggs
120 g/4 oz self-raising flour ◆ 1 tsp icing or caster sugar (for dredging)

fruit curd filling:
1 orange, lemon, or 2 clementines, finely grated zest and strained juice
60 g/2 oz caster sugar ◆ 1 egg ◆ ¼ tsp cornflour ◆ 60 g/2 oz butter
2–3 tsp Cointreau liqueur

Cream the butter and sugar with the fruit zest in a mixing bowl until light and fluffy. Beat in the eggs separately, then fold in the sieved flour. Spoon the mixture into the prepared cake tin(s) and smooth level.

Bake in the preheated oven until golden brown and the cake is just starting to shrink from the tin. Cool in the tin for 3 minutes then turn out on to a wire rack. If you have one rather than two cakes, leave until cold then cut it carefully into two layers.

Sandwich the cake layers with the curd and sift icing or caster sugar over the top of the cake then set aside in a cold place before serving.

To make the fruit curd: use a glass or ceramic double-boiler or place a bowl over a pan of simmering water. Use a wooden spoon to mix together the fruit zest and juice with the sugar, egg and cornflour over moderate heat until thickened. Take care not to overcook or the curd will become granular with particles of cooked egg. As soon as it is cooked, remove from the heat and stand the pan or bowl in cold water to cool the mixture. When half-cooled, beat in the butter in small pieces until absorbed then stir in the Cointreau liqueur.

JANUARY LEMON CAKE

This buttery sponge, sandwiched and iced with lemon frosting is a lovely winter cake. Highly aromatic Primofiori lemons arrive from Italy in January, their fresh astringent flavour so welcome in the depths of winter. If possible, use wax-free, organic fruit.

Oven: 180°C/350°F/gas mark 4 ♦ Baking time: 30–35 minutes
Equipment: two 18 cm/7 in. sponge sandwich tins – buttered and base-lined
Makes: 8–10-portion cake

175 g/6 oz butter ♦ 175 g/6 oz caster sugar ♦ 1 small lemon
3 eggs ♦ 175 g/6 oz self-raising flour

frosting:
90 g/3 oz butter ♦ 1 small lemon ♦ 230 g/8 oz icing sugar, sifted

Cream the butter with the sugar and the finely grated zest of the lemon until light and fluffy. Beat in the eggs one at a time. Fold in the sifted flour with the strained juice of half the lemon. Divide the mixture between the prepared cake tins and smooth level.

Bake until golden brown and just beginning to shrink from the tins. Cool for 3 minutes then turn the cakes on to a wire rack to cool.

Meanwhile, use a zester to remove long strands from the peel of the lemon. Use a grater to remove the rest of the zest and set aside with the strands. Squeeze the juice from the lemon, add the juice of the remaining half-lemon from making the cake.

In a small glass or stainless steel pan, melt the butter with 3 tbs of the strained lemon juice. Bring to the boil, allow to bubble for 30 seconds, then remove from the heat and cool for 1 minute. Stir in the icing sugar and beat until smooth. Stand the pan in cold water for 1 minute to cool the frosting. When thick but still spreadable, pour half the frosting over the top of one cake. Place the other on top and pour the rest of the frosting over the top. Sprinkle the reserved strands and grated zest of lemon on top to decorate and add extra flavour to the cake. Set aside for the frosting to set before serving.

MADEIRA CAKE

There are few plain cakes more pleasing than a home-made Madeira Cake. Its name derives from the nineteenth-century custom of serving a slice, mid-morning, with a glass of Madeira wine. By tradition the top of a Madeira Cake is decorated with curling strips of candied citrus peel.

Oven: 180°C/350°F/gas mark 4 ♦ Baking time: 50–60 minutes
Equipment: 18 cm/7 in. tin – buttered and base-lined
Makes: 8-portion cake

150 g/5 oz butter ♦ 150 g/5 oz caster sugar ♦ 2 eggs
½ lemon or orange, finely grated zest ♦ 230 g/8 oz plain flour
1 tsp baking powder ♦ 3–4 tbs milk ♦ 2–3 strips candied citrus peel

Cream the butter with the sugar until pale and fluffy. Beat in the eggs separately with the grated zest. Sift the flour with the baking powder and fold into the mixture with the milk. Spoon the mixture into the prepared cake tin, smooth level and arrange the strips of candied peel on top.

Bake in the preheated oven until the top of the cake is springy and a wooden skewer comes out clean from the centre. Cool the cake in the tin for 5 minutes then turn out on to a wire rack.

COFFEE RUM RING

A Victoria Sponge Cake doused with rum and black coffee and decorated with whipped cream. Serve at tea-time or as a pudding.

Oven: 190°C/375°F/gas mark 5 ♦ Baking time: 40–45 minutes
Equipment: 18–20 cm/7–8 in. ring tin – buttered and dusted with caster sugar
Makes: 12-portion cake

175 g/6 oz butter ♦ 175 g/6 oz caster sugar ♦ 3 eggs
175 g/6 oz self-raising flour

decoration:
300 ml/10 fl oz strong black coffee such as espresso
75 ml/2½ fl oz dark rum or brandy ♦ 300 ml/10 fl oz double cream
1 tbs caster sugar ♦ 30 g/1 oz flaked almonds, toasted

Cream the butter with the sugar until light and fluffy. Beat in the eggs, one at a time. Fold in the sifted flour. Spoon the mixture into the prepared cake tin and smooth level.

Bake in the preheated oven until the cake is springy and is just starting to shrink from the tin. Cool in the tin for 4 minutes then turn out on to a wire rack.

When the cake is cold, replace it in the clean cake tin. Measure the coffee and rum into a jug and gradually pour the liquid over the cake, pausing at intervals to let it soak in. Whisk the cream with sugar until thick but still glossy. The cream can be spread over the cake with a palette knife or, if you prefer to pipe it on to the cake, spoon the cream into a nylon bag fitted with a 1 cm/½ in. star nozzle.

Carefully turn the cake out on to a serving plate – one with a stand looks pretty – and either spread or pipe the cream all over the cake. Decorate with the flaked almonds and set the cake in a cold place, preferably a refrigerator, until ready to serve.

RAINBOW RING CAKE

I devised this for a friend who loves rainbows – her clothes, shoes, car, and house are decorated with them. This is also a good cake to make with or for children since it is simply a marble cake based on a variation of Victoria sponge cake. The finished cake has all the colours of the rainbow – red, orange, yellow, green, blue, indigo and violet – though you only need small bottles of red, yellow and blue food colours to mix them.

Oven: 190 °C/375 °F/gas mark 5 ♦ *Baking time: 45 minutes*
Equipment: 18–20 cm/7–8 in. ring tin – buttered
Makes: 16–20-portion ring cake

175 g/6 oz butter, softened ♦ 175 g/6 oz caster sugar
3 eggs ♦ 200 g/7 oz self-raising flour ♦ 1½ tsp baking powder
red, yellow and blue food colours

icing:
175 g/6 oz icing sugar ♦ hot water
a few rainbow-coloured sweets such as Smarties

Measure the butter, sugar, eggs, and flour sieved with the baking powder into a mixing bowl or a food processor. Mix everything together until really smooth. Divide the mixture into 7 portions, each a little smaller than the one before. Colour them according to a rainbow, starting with red for the largest amount. Spoon the red mixture into the prepared cake tin and spread level. Continue with layers of the other rainbow colours in sequence.

For orange, mix red and yellow; for green, mix blue and yellow; for indigo, mix blue and violet; for violet, mix blue and red. When all the mixture has been spooned into the tin, smooth it level.

Bake in the preheated oven for 45 minutes. Cool in the tin for 5 minutes then turn out on to a wire rack.

Mix the sieved icing sugar with just enough hot water to give a smooth pouring consistency. Add 1 or 2 drops of blue food colouring to tint the icing a pretty sky blue. Pour the icing over the cake allowing it to run down the sides unevenly. Decorate with the coloured sweets if you wish. When you cut the cake, each piece should have all the colours of the rainbow.

RUSSIAN CAKE

One of the splendid cakes popularized a generation ago by Fuller's tea-shops. Though rarely seen today, Russian Cake appears in some Victorian cookery books; it is made from slivers of rich sponge cake macerated in rum syrup, sandwiched between layers of marzipan and covered with glacé icing. I remember that Fuller's Russian Cake was decorated with a pretty feathered design of chocolate on blossom pink; the cake is fairly rich and is nicest served in thin slices.

Oven: 190°C/375°F/gas mark 5 ♦ Baking time: 25–30 minutes
Equipment: 18 cm/7 in. square tin – buttered and base-lined;
0.5 kg/1 lb loaf tin – lined with cling-film
Makes: 10-portion cake

120 g/4 oz butter ♦ 120 g/4 oz caster sugar ♦ 2 eggs
120 g/4 oz self-raising flour ♦ 1–2 drops pink food colouring
1 tbs cocoa powder blended with 1 tbs hot water

filling:
2 tbs apricot or raspberry jam, sieved ♦ 230 g/8 oz marzipan (see page 291)
60 g/2 oz caster sugar ♦ 6 tbs water
2 tbs white rum or kirsch

glacé icing:
175 g/6 oz icing sugar ♦ hot water to mix
1 drop pink food colouring ♦ few drops rose-water
1 tsp cocoa powder

Cream the butter with the sugar until light and fluffy. Gradually beat in the eggs. Fold in the sieved flour. Spoon one third of the mixture into the prepared cake tin. Add a few drops of pink colouring to half the remaining mixture and spoon into the cake tin. Mix the blended cocoa into the rest of the mixture and add to the cake tin. Smooth the mixture level.

Bake in the preheated oven for 25–30 minutes until the cake is springy in the centre. Cool in the tin for 2 minutes then turn on to a wire rack.

To assemble the cake: roll out half the marzipan until large enough to line the base of the prepared loaf tin. Brush the sieved jam over the cake and cut into 5 mm / ¼ in. wide strips. Arrange the strips in a random fashion in the loaf tin. Dissolve the sugar in the water over moderate heat, bring to the boil and simmer for 5 minutes. Cool, then stir in the rum or kirsch. Spoon over the cake. Cover with the remaining marzipan rolled out to fit. Fit a piece of plastic-covered cardboard on top and weigh down lightly. Chill the cake overnight.

To ice the cake: turn the cake on to a wire rack. Blend the sieved icing sugar with sufficient hot water to make a thick pouring icing. Tint it pale pink with the food colouring and add rose-water to taste. Reserve a small amount of icing and blend in the cocoa. Pour the pink icing over the top and sides of the cake. Pipe or dribble fine lines of chocolate on top, and before it sets draw a fine skewer or needle through the lines first one way and then the other to produce a feathered effect. Set the cake aside until the icing is dry.

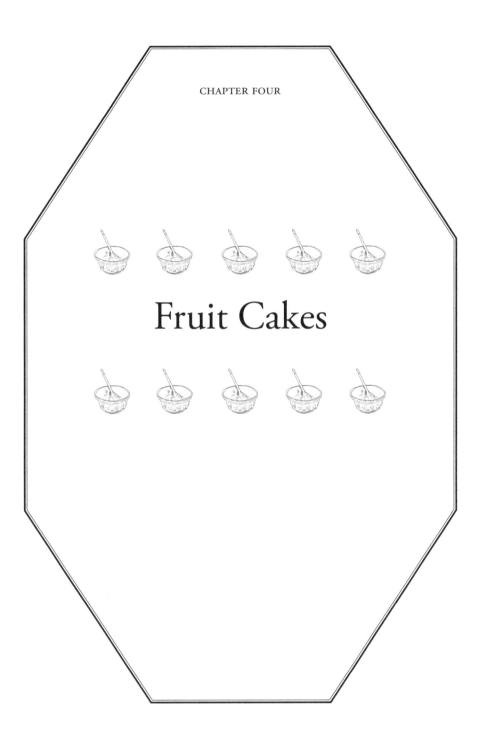

Fruit Cakes

THE CONTENTS OF THIS CHAPTER

The adjective 'home-made' is one which rings of the highest praise when used in connection with cakes... it conjures up many lovely pictures in our minds – the wonderful aroma in the kitchen while baking is in progress, the tea-table laden with good things – from the oven-fresh scones to the finger of plum cake, and finally the glamour of icing, and the iced cake.

Margaret Bates, *Talking About Cakes,* 1964

For centuries our fruit cakes have been prepared with dried vine fruits, usually raisins, sultanas and currants and possibly candied cherries and citrus peel too. This is the traditional British fruit cake, either dark, rich and moist such as a Christmas Cake, or lighter in colour and texture, maybe decorated with a layer of toasted almonds as in a Dundee Cake. The expense of the ingredients and the time taken to prepare and bake such cakes have ensured that they have acquired the status of a luxury, reserved for special occasions such as a marriage, a christening or an anniversary. Part of the pleasure in eating a slice of rich fruit cake is that it is not an everyday event.

Less heavily fruited cakes such as a Genoa have long been served through-out the year – at a weekend tea party or even at the end of lunch. 'It was fashionable at one time to have a good sultana cake on the luncheon table and it was eaten at the end of lunch. This habit still prevails in some old-fashioned houses in London and in the country,' wrote Mrs C.F. Leyel in *Cakes of England* (1936). Now that packed lunches have become popular, the custom of eating a slice of light fruit cake at the end of the meal is returning.

Cold winter days heighten the appeal of cakes made with dried fruits, their concentrated flavours an enduring reminder of summer harvests. Besides the well-known and popular dried vine fruits of the past there are now packets of dried pears, peaches, apricots, figs, prunes, banana, blueberries and cranberries to enliven our winter fruit cakes. Some fruit is labelled pre-soaked or ready-to-eat and can be added to a cake mixture without further preparation.

Dried fruit should be moist and flavourful, and tasty enough to nibble on its own. Fruit that has been stored too long tends to dry out and shrink. If the natural sugar has crystallized, the fruit benefits from a quick rinse in warm water. Drain well and dry the fruit on kitchen paper before adding to the mixture. When possible, I like to steep dried fruit in 2–3 tablespoons fruit juice or wine for a few hours. Cover the bowl and leave in a warm place for an hour or two until all the liquid has been absorbed by the fruit. Fresh orange juice, sherry or a liqueur all work well and contribute a delicate extra flavour to the cake.

When the warm balmy days of summer arrive, we are lured by the scent and flavour of oven-hot cakes oozing with juicy fresh fruit. Though apple cakes have been baked in West Country cider regions for generations, cakes rich with raspberries, apricots, peaches and figs are a welcome feature of home baking today. Many of these fresh fruit cakes are adapted from the *kuchen* and *galettes* of continental Europe and they often take the place of the traditional fruit pies and tarts of the English kitchen.

The simplest version of a fresh fruit cake is made with a layer of sweet shortcake pastry gently pressed into a shallow tart tin, covered with a thin layer of ground almonds or hazelnuts and topped with the prepared fresh fruit – halved figs, sliced nectarines, stoned cherries or whole raspberries. Sprinkle with powdered sugar and bake, then serve straight from the oven with thick cream or ice-cream. Perfect for pudding or tea-time.

HARVEST CAKE

Ever since I published my mother's recipe in *Cake Stall*, readers have written to tell me that this good, simple fruit cake has become such a firm favourite that it is now baked and appreciated in many other countries too.

Oven: 160°C/325°F/gas mark 3 ♦ *Baking time: 1½–1¾ hours*
Equipment: 20 cm/8 in. round or square tin – buttered and lined
Makes: 16-portion cake

230 g/8 oz butter, softened
230 g/8 oz caster or light muscovado sugar
4 eggs ♦ 350 g/12 oz plain flour ♦ 1 tsp baking powder
450 g/1 lb mixed dried fruit – seedless raisins, sultanas, currants
120 g/4 oz dried or glacé cherries, quartered
60 g/2 oz candied peel, quartered

Measure the ingredients into a warmed mixing bowl and stir well until you have a stiff mixture. That's all there is to it. Spoon the mixture into the prepared cake tin and smooth level.

Bake in the preheated oven until the cake is cooked, when it will be slightly firm to the touch and a wooden skewer comes out clean from the centre. Cool in the tin for 45 minutes then turn on to a wire rack to cool. When cold, wrap in greaseproof paper and keep in an air-tight plastic container in a cold place until needed. The cake keeps well, in the fridge or the freezer, for 2–3 weeks.

Variation: add ½ tsp mixed spice to the mixture and sprinkle halved or slivered blanched almonds over the top of the cake before baking.

DUNDEE CAKE

One of the finest traditional British cakes, named after its original home in Scotland. The top of the cake is studded with circles of toasted almonds which contribute to the cake's lovely subtle flavour which is in marked contrast to the dark, heavy kind of fruit cake favoured at Christmas and for celebrations.

Oven: 160 °C / 325 °F / gas mark 3 ♦ Baking time: about 2 hours
Equipment: 18 cm / 7 in. tin – buttered and lined
Makes: 8–12-portion cake

175 g / 6 oz butter ♦ 175 g / 6 oz light muscovado or golden caster sugar
3 eggs ♦ 1 orange or lemon, finely grated zest
230 g / 8 oz plain flour ♦ 60 g / 2 oz ground almonds
1 tsp baking powder ♦ 1 tsp mixed spice
175 g / 6 oz sultanas ♦ 120 g / 4 oz seedless raisins
120 g / 4 oz currants ♦ 90 g / 3 oz glacé cherries, quartered
60 g / 2 oz candied orange peel, sliced or chopped
a little milk to mix ♦ 30–60 g / 1–2 oz split blanched almonds

Cream the butter with the sugar until light and fluffy. Beat in the eggs, one at a time, with the zest of orange. Sieve the the flour, almonds, baking powder and spice and fold into the mixture with the dried fruit, cherries and candied peel. The mixture should be stiff, but since flour varies in how much liquid it absorbs, if need be mix in a little milk if you find the mixture is really hard to stir. Spoon into the prepared cake tin and smooth level. Then, starting at the outside edge of the cake, arrange the split almonds – almost touching – in three concentric rings. Place a few almonds in the space left in the centre.

Bake in the preheated oven for 2 hours or until a wooden skewer comes out clean from the centre of the cake. If you find during baking that the almonds are darkening too much, place a double layer of brown paper – or a large envelope – over the cake, but not touching it, to protect the crust from the heat. Cool the cake in its tin for 45 minutes then turn out on to a wire rack.

CLYST WILLIAM BARTON CAKE

A fruit cake that I devised using the old method of rubbing the butter into the mixture; named after the thatched Devon farmhouse that was our family home for twenty years and which dates from Domesday Book. Clyst is Old English for the spring which feeds the well in one corner of the flag-stoned kitchen.

Oven: 160°C/325°F/gas mark 3 ♦ Baking time: 1½ hours
Equipment: 1 kg/2 lb loaf tin – buttered and base-lined
Makes: 12-portion cake

300 g/10 oz plain flour ♦ 175 g/6 oz demerara sugar
175 g/6 oz butter ♦ 400 g/14 oz mixed dried fruit
60 g/2 oz glacé cherries, quartered ♦ 1 tsp mixed spice
1 tsp baking powder ♦ 3 eggs ♦ 1 tbs black treacle

Measure the flour into a bowl and mix in the sugar. Add the butter in pieces and rub in with your fingertips until the mixture resembles breadcrumbs. Stir in the dried fruit, cherries, spice and baking powder. Beat the eggs with the treacle and mix in well. Spoon the mixture into the prepared cake tin and smooth level.

Bake in the preheated oven until cooked when a wooden skewer comes out clean from the centre of the cake. Cool in the tin for 15 minutes then transfer to a wire rack.

DEVON CIDER FRUIT CAKE

Dried fruit soaked in Devon cider for a few hours imparts an excellent flavour to this cake.

Oven: 180 °C / 350 °F / gas mark 4 ♦ Baking time: 60–70 minutes
Equipment: 20 cm / 8 in. tin – buttered and base-lined
Makes: 8–12-portion cake

265 g / 9 oz mixed dried fruit – seedless raisins, sultanas and currants
4 tbs sweet or dry cider ♦ 175 g / 6 oz butter
175 g / 6 oz light muscovado sugar ♦ 3 eggs
265 g / 9 oz self-raising flour ♦ 1 tsp mixed sweet spice

Measure the fruit into a bowl, pour over the cider and leave overnight or until the liquid has been absorbed by the fruit. If need be, this stage can be speeded up by warming the fruit and the cider in a pan over low heat, but cool the mixture before adding to the other ingredients.

Cream the butter with the sugar until pale and fluffy. Add the eggs, one at a time, beating each in well with a little flour to prevent the mixture from separating. Sift in the rest of the flour with the mixed spice, folding this into the mixture alternately with the cider-soaked fruit. Spoon into the prepared cake tin and smooth level.

Bake in the preheated oven until a wooden skewer comes out clean from the centre of the cake. Cool in the tin for 10 minutes then turn out on to a wire rack.

QUICK-MIX GLACÉ CHERRY AND ALMOND CAKE

An easy-to-make cake: measure the ingredients, mix with a wooden spoon, then bake. The liqueur or brandy is not essential to the recipe but does contribute a lovely flavour to the cake.

Oven: 180 °C / 350 °F / gas mark 4 ♦ Baking time: 50–60 minutes
Equipment: 20 cm / 8 in. spring-clip tin – buttered and base-lined
Makes: 12–16-portion cake

175 g / 6 oz butter, softened ♦ 175 g / 6 oz caster sugar
3 eggs ♦ 1–2 drops almond essence ♦ 175 g / 6 oz self-raising flour
120 g / 4 oz ground almonds ♦ 120 g / 4 oz flaked or slivered almonds
300 g / 10 oz glacé cherries, rinsed of syrup and dried
1 tbs caster sugar ♦ 2 tbs almond liqueur or cherry brandy (optional)

In a mixing bowl, stir together the butter, sugar, eggs, essence, flour and ground almonds. When well combined, beat for 1 minute. Cut half the cherries in two, then stir in all the cherries with the flaked almonds. Spoon the mixture into the prepared cake tin and smooth level, sprinkle the extra caster sugar over the top.

Bake the cake in the preheated oven until springy on top and a wooden skewer comes out clean from the centre. Cool in the tin for 10 minutes then trickle over the liqueur or brandy and leave for half an hour. Open the clip and remove the sides of the tin and leave the cake to cool. This cake improves if wrapped in plastic and stored in a cold place for 1–2 days before cutting.

RING FRUIT CAKE

From ancient times, the circle and the ring have been important symbols at times of festivity, possibly a reference to the significance of the sun and the moon during the growing season. The round garlands of greenery tied on to doors at Christmas are a relic of such early belief. So a fruit cake baked in a ring shape seems particularly apt for the festivities that fall close to the shortest day.

Instead of marzipan and royal icing as the cake's decoration, I prefer preserved fruits and nuts as a wintry reminder of summer. When giving the cake as a present, I tie a ribbon around it and finish with a bow or streamers.

Oven: 150 °C / 300 °F / gas mark 2, then 140 °C / 275 °F / gas mark 1
Baking time: 3½ – 4 hours
Equipment: 20–23 cm / 8–9 in. ring tin – buttered;
double layer of brown parcel paper
Makes: 16-portion cake

230 g / 8 oz butter ♦ 230 g / 8 oz light muscovado sugar ♦ 4 eggs
265 g / 9 oz plain flour ♦ 1 tsp mixed spice ♦ ½ tsp ground cinnamon
½ tsp grated nutmeg ♦ 350 g / 12 oz seedless raisins
175 g / 6 oz ready-to-eat dried apricots, sliced
175 g / 6 oz glacé pineapple, chopped ♦ 175 g / 6 oz glacé cherries, quartered
175 g / 6 oz pecan nuts or almonds, halved
4 tbs dark Jamaican rum

decoration:
2–3 tbs apricot jam, warmed and sieved
175 g / 6 oz mixed candied fruits: cherries, pineapple, plums, apricots, etc.
60 g / 2 oz blanched almonds, toasted ♦ 60 g / 2 oz pecan nuts, halved

Cream the butter with the sugar until light and fluffy. Add the eggs, one at a time, beating them in well. Add a little flour if the mixture begins to separate. Mix in the flour sieved with the spices, then stir in the fruit and nuts until well distributed. Turn the mixture into the prepared cake tin and smooth level. Tie a double layer of brown paper around the outside of the tin allowing it to project 8–10 cm / 3–4 in. above the rim.

Bake in the preheated oven for 1½ hours. Then lower the heat and bake for a further 1–2 hours or until a wooden skewer comes out clean from the deepest part of the cake. Cool in the tin, then turn out on to a wire rack. Use a fine wooden skewer to make several holes in the base of the cake and trickle in the rum. If you have time, wrap the cake in greaseproof paper and store in an air-tight container (not a tin) in a very cold place for 3–4 weeks for the flavour to mellow.

To decorate, brush some warmed apricot jam over the top of the cake to glaze it and arrange the fruit – cut into pieces, where need be – and nuts on it. Brush over with the rest of the glaze and leave in a warm dry place overnight for the glaze to dry.

PINEAPPLE FRUIT CAKE

The pineapple in this Australian recipe contributes the fresh flavour of the fruit and keeps the cake fairly moist, so this is not a keeping cake. Store the cake, wrapped in greaseproof paper, in the refrigerator for up to a week.

Oven: 160 °C / 325 °F / gas mark 3 ♦ Baking time: 2 hours
Equipment: 20 cm / 8 in. tin – buttered and base-lined
Makes: 10–12-portion cake

150 g / 5 oz butter ♦ 150 g / 5 oz light muscovado sugar
2 large eggs ♦ 230 g / 8 oz self-raising flour
½ tsp baking powder ♦ 400 g / 14 oz mixed dried fruit
90 g / 3 oz glacé cherries, quartered ♦ 90 g / 3 oz candied peel, chopped
230 g / 8 oz crushed or grated pineapple, fresh or tinned

Cream the butter with the sugar until light and fluffy. Add the eggs one at a time, beating them in well. Sift the flour with the baking powder and fold into the mixture alternately with the dried fruit, cherries and peel. Drain the pineapple in a sieve to remove surplus liquid, and fold the fruit into the mixture. Spoon the mixture into the prepared tin and smooth level.

Bake in the preheated oven for 2 hours or until the cake is shrinking slightly from the tin. Cool the cake in the tin for 30 minutes then transfer to a wire rack.

RAISIN, ALMOND AND WHISKY CAKE

Whisky goes particularly well in this cake though brandy or rum can replace it.

Oven: 180 °C / 350 °F / gas mark 4 ♦ *Baking time: 35–40 minutes*
Equipment: 20 cm / 8 in. tin – base-lined
Makes: 10-portion cake

90 ml / 3 fl oz whisky ♦ 300 g / 10 oz seedless raisins
120 g / 4 oz butter ♦ 120 g / 4 oz caster sugar ♦ 2 eggs
1–2 drops vanilla or bitter almond essence ♦ 230 g / 8 oz plain flour
60 g / 2 oz ground almonds ♦ ¼ tsp ground cinnamon
1 tsp baking powder
120 g / 4 oz flaked or slivered blanched almonds

Start by warming 60 ml / 2 fl oz of whisky with the raisins. Leave the mixture in a warm place for at least 30 minutes to allow the fruit to absorb the liquid. Mix the remaining whisky with 1 tablespoon of the caster sugar and set aside until the cake is cooked.

Cream the butter with the sugar until light and fluffy. Beat in the eggs and essence. Gently mix in the flour sieved with the ground almonds, cinnamon and baking powder and stir in the whisky-soaked raisins and flaked almonds. Turn the mixture into the prepared tin and smooth level.

Bake in the preheated oven for 40 minutes or until a wooden skewer comes out clean from the centre. Cool in the tin for 5 minutes then spoon over the reserved sweetened whisky and leave until almost cold before serving.

BOILED FRUIT CAKE

This economical method of making a fruit cake, where the dried fruit is first simmered with butter, sugar and water or wine, produces a well-flavoured, moist cake with rather less butter and fewer eggs than usual.

Oven: 160°C/325°F/gas mark 3 ♦ *Baking time: 1–1¼ hours*
Equipment: 18 cm/7 in. tin – lined
Makes: 8-portion cake

120 g/4 oz butter ♦ 120 g/4 oz demerara sugar
150 ml/5 fl oz water, white wine or sherry ♦ 90 g/3 oz dried apricots
90 g/3 oz stoned dates ♦ 90 g/3 oz seedless raisins
90 g/3 oz sultanas ♦ 90 g/3 oz currants
230 g/8 oz self-raising flour ♦ ½ tsp mixed spice
1 large egg ♦ 1–2 tbs sherry or orange juice

Measure the butter, sugar and water or wine into a large pan. Add the dried fruit and bring the mixture to the boil. Turn down the heat and simmer very gently for 20 minutes. Remove from the heat and cool the mixture until it thickens but is still soft – for speed place the pan in cold water to cool.

Add the flour sieved with the spice and mix in the egg and sherry or orange juice. Turn the mixture into the prepared tin and smooth level.

Bake in the preheated oven until the cake is cooked – when a thin wooden skewer comes out clean from the centre of the cake. Cool in the tin for 30 minutes then turn out on to a wire rack.

JONNY RUFF CAKE

In response to family demand, my mother used to bake this Canadian cake almost every week. She writes, 'The beauty of this recipe is that any kind of dried fruit can be added using the quick and easy rubbing-in method.'

Oven: 200 °C / 400 °F / gas mark 6, then 180 °C / 350 °C / Gas Mark 4
Baking time: 20 minutes at higher temperature, 40 minutes at lower one
Equipment: 18 cm / 7 in. square tin – buttered and base-lined
Makes: 16-portion cake

300 g / 10 oz self-raising flour ♦ 1 tsp baking powder
120 g / 4 oz granulated sugar ♦ 120 g / 4 oz butter
175 g / 6 oz mixed dried fruit
2 rounded tbs marmalade – orange or three-fruit
2 eggs ♦ 2–3 tbs milk

Sift the flour and baking powder into a mixing bowl and stir in the sugar and butter, cut in pieces. Use your fingertips to rub the butter into the dry ingredients until the mixture resembles breadcrumbs. Mix in the dried fruit, marmalade, eggs and sufficient milk to make a stiff mixture.

Spoon into the prepared cake tin and smooth level. Bake in the preheated oven until golden-brown and a wooden skewer comes out clean from the centre.

Remove from the oven and allow the cake to cool in the tin, then turn it out on to a wire rack and peel off the baking paper.

SPICED DATE LOAF

A lightly spiced fruit loaf positively crammed with dates, some are softened and the rest are chopped before adding to the mixture which gives a pleasing texture to the cake.

Oven: 180°C/350°F/gas mark 4 ♦ Baking time: 45–50 minutes
Equipment: 1 kg/2 lb loaf tin – buttered and base-lined
Makes: 10-portion cake

265 g/9 oz stoned dates ♦ 90 ml/3 fl oz boiling water
175 g/6 oz butter ♦ 175 g/6 oz dark muscovado sugar
3 eggs ♦ 265 g/9 oz plain flour
1 tsp baking powder ♦ ½ tsp grated nutmeg
½ tsp ground allspice or cloves

icing:
120 g/4 oz icing sugar ♦ 2 tbs hot water

Chop the dates and place two-thirdss of them in a pan or bowl and pour on the boiling water, leave to soften. In a mixing bowl, cream the butter and add the sifted sugar, beat together until fluffy. Mix in the softened dates and the eggs until well combined. Sift in the flour, baking powder, nutmeg and allspice and mix together, then stir in the remaining chopped dates. Spoon the mixture into the prepared tin and smooth level.

Bake in the preheated oven until a wooden skewer comes out clean from the centre and the cake is just starting to shrink from the tin. Cool in the tin for 5 minutes then turn the cake on to a wire rack.

When the cake is cool, make the icing by sifting the icing sugar into a bowl. Mix in just enough hot water to make a pouring consistency. Use the spoon to trail lines of icing back and forth across the cake in a random pattern. Set the cake aside until the icing is set.

ORANGE RAISIN LUNCH-BOX CAKE

Slightly adapted from the original *Cake Stall* version.

Oven: 180°C/350°F/gas mark 4 ♦ Baking time: 35–40 minutes
Equipment: 23 cm/9 in. square tin – buttered and base-lined
Makes: 16 portions

175 g/6 oz butter ♦ 175 g/6 oz golden caster sugar
1 orange or 2 tangerines, finely grated zest and juice
3 eggs ♦ 265 g/9 oz self-raising flour
¼ tsp ground cinnamon ♦ 350 g/12 oz seedless raisins
60 g/2 oz candied orange peel, chopped
1 rounded tbs demerara sugar

Cream the butter with the sugar and the orange zest until light and fluffy. Beat in the eggs one at a time. Mix in the flour sifted with the ground cinnamon and stir in the orange juice, raisins and candied peel. Spoon the mixture into the prepared tin and smooth level. Sprinkle the demerara sugar evenly over the top.

Bake in the preheated oven until golden-brown and a wooden skewer comes out clean from the centre. Cool the cake in the tin and, when cold, cut into 16 pieces.

WINE CUPBOARD FRUIT CAKE

Clearing out my kitchen cupboards led to this cake. Rarely was virtue so well rewarded – and aged dried fruit and spirituous bottle ends have never tasted so good.

Oven: 150 °C / 300 °F / gas mark 2, then 140 °C / 275 °F / gas mark 1
Baking time: 3¾–4 hours
Equipment: 20 cm / 8 in. square tin – buttered and lined
Makes: 16-portion cake

200 ml / 7 fl oz mixed spirits: brandy, rum, sherry, fruit liqueurs
900 g / 2 lb mixed dried fruit – the older the better: seedless raisins, sultanas, currants, chopped figs and dates, chopped candied peel, halved glacé or dried cherries
230 g / 8 oz unsalted butter ♦ 230 g / 8 oz dark muscovado sugar
4 eggs ♦ 350 g / 12 oz plain white flour
¼ tsp bicarbonate of soda ♦ ¼ tsp ground cinnamon
¼ tsp ground nutmeg ♦ 60 g / 2 oz ground almonds
60 g / 2 oz flaked almonds

Stir the brandy mixture into the dried fruit in a mixing bowl and leave in a warm place for 2–4 hours, stirring now and again, until the fruit has absorbed all the liquid.

Cream the butter with the sifted sugar until light and fluffy. Beat in the eggs, one at a time. Stir the flour sifted with the bicarbonate of soda and spices into the mixture. Mix in the ground and flaked almonds and the steeped fruit. Spoon into the prepared tin and smooth level.

Bake in the preheated oven for 2 hours at the higher temperature, lower the heat and bake for a further 1¾–2 hours, or until a wooden skewer comes out clean from the centre of the cake. Cool in the tin for 30 minutes then transfer to a wire rack.

TRADITIONAL STRAWBERRY SHORTCAKE

A famous North American cake, this is my mother's recipe, entitled 'Old-fashioned' in her 1929 copy of *Anyone Can Bake*. As a child my job was to pick and prepare the strawberries while she made the cake. Then I'd watch her pull apart the layers, cover one with the fruit, the other with thick cream and then sandwich them. Serve the cake straight away while warm.

Oven: 200°C/400°F/gas mark 6 ♦ Baking time: 25–30 minutes
Equipment: baking sheet – floured ♦ Makes: 8-portion cake

230 g / 8 oz self-raising flour ♦ 1 tsp baking powder ♦ 60 g / 2 oz sugar
60 g / 2 oz butter ♦ 1 egg ♦ 4 tbs milk or water
30 g / 1 oz butter, melted

filling:
1 kg / 2 lbs ripe strawberries ♦ 2–3 tbs caster sugar
300 ml / 10 fl oz double cream ♦ 1 tsp icing sugar

Sift the flour, baking powder and sugar into a mixing bowl. Add the butter, cut in pieces, and rub together with the fingertips until the mixture resembles breadcrumbs. Add the egg and the milk and stir together to make a soft dough.

Turn this on to a floured board and divide in half. Shape each piece into a ball and then gently flatten or use a rolling pin until each disc of dough is 1 cm / ½ in. thick. Place one piece of dough on the prepared baking sheet. Brush with the melted butter and place the other disc on top. Bake in the preheated oven until well-risen and golden brown.

To prepare the filling, wash and hull the strawberries. Slice thickly or if small, just halve them, into a bowl and stir in the sugar. Use a fork to crush some of the riper strawberries to make a syrup with the sugar. Whisk the cream until thick but still glossy.

Transfer the shortcake to a wooden board and use a palette knife to gently prise off the top half of the shortcake. Spoon the strawberries over the lower half, and spoon over the cream. Replace the other half of the cake on top. Dust the cake lightly with sieved icing sugar and serve.

GOOSEBERRY KUCHEN

When gooseberries are out of season, this recipe works equally well with blueberries, loganberries or quartered apricots, with the added advantage that these fruits can be added to the cake while still raw.

Oven: 220°C/425°F/gas mark 7, then 180°C/350°F/gas mark 4
Baking time: 45–50 minutes
Equipment: 20 cm/8 in. shallow cake or tart tin – buttered
Makes: 8–10-portion cake

cake base:
120 g/4 oz plain flour ♦ ¼ tsp baking powder ♦ 30 g/1 oz caster sugar
60 g/2 oz butter ♦ 1 egg yolk ♦ 1 tbs milk

fruit layer:
2 egg whites ♦ 90 g/3 oz caster sugar
60 g/2 oz ground almonds or hazelnuts ♦ ½ lemon, finely grated rind
350 g/12 oz cooked sweetened gooseberries ♦ ¼ tsp ground cinnamon
2 tbs caster sugar

Sift the flour, baking powder and sugar into a bowl, cut and rub in the butter and mix to a dough with the egg yolk blended with the milk. Roll out the dough to line the base and to reach about 2 cm/1 in. up the side of the cake tin.

Whisk the egg whites until stiff. Add half the sugar and whisk again, then fold in the rest of the sugar with the grated lemon rind and the ground nuts. Spread the meringue over the pastry base, drain the gooseberries of any juice and arrange the fruit on top. Mix the ground cinnamon with the extra sugar and sprinkle over the fruit.

Bake in the preheated oven for 15 minutes then lower the heat and bake until the pastry is cooked. Serve straight from the oven, just as it is or with a scoop of sorbet or ice-cream made from the same fruit.

FRESH CHERRY CAKE

An almond cake with the cherries baked on top. Sweet cherries that are only just ripe are fine for this cake – save the riper fruit for dessert. To remove the stones use a cherry / olive stoner or a small vegetable knife.

Oven: 180 °C / 350 °F / gas mark 4 ♦ *Baking time: 30 minutes*
Equipment: 20 cm / 8 in. spring-clip tin – buttered and base-lined
Makes: 8-portion cake

cake layer:
100 g / 3½ oz butter ♦ 100 g / 3½ oz caster sugar ♦ 2 eggs
a few drops of almond essence or orange flower water
100 g / 3½ oz self-raising flour ♦ 60 g / 2 oz ground almonds

fruit layer:
450 g / 1 lb fresh cherries, stones removed ♦ 2 tbs caster sugar

Cream the butter with the sugar until pale and fluffy. Add the eggs separately, beating them in well, stir in the essence and fold in the flour and ground almonds.

Spoon the mixture into the prepared cake tin and smooth level. Scatter the cherries over the top in a single layer and sprinkle the extra sugar over the fruit.

Bake in the preheated oven until a wooden skewer comes out clean from the centre. Cool in the tin for 3 minutes then open the clip and remove the side. Serve the cake hot or warm with thick cream or mascarpone.

FIG AND NECTARINE GALETTE WITH RASPBERRY COULIS

Ripe summer fruits embedded in a hot cake with a cool coulis. Equally good made with halved apricots and blueberries.

Oven: 180°C/350°F/gas mark 4 ♦ Baking time: 30–35 minutes
Equipment: 28 cm/11 in. tart tin – buttered
Makes: 8–10-portion cake

120 g/4 oz butter ♦ 120 g/4 oz caster sugar
2 eggs ♦ ½ tsp vanilla essence
175 g/6 oz self-raising flour
450 g/1 lb fresh figs, washed and halved
3–4 large nectarines, washed and sliced
60 g/2 oz demerara sugar

raspberry coulis:
175 g/6 oz raspberries ♦ 1 tbs icing sugar

Cream the butter with the sugar until light and fluffy. Mix in the eggs one at a time with the vanilla essence. Fold in the flour until well mixed. Spoon the mixture into the prepared tin and smooth level. Arrange the figs and the sliced nectarines in circles on the mixture. Sprinkle the demerara sugar over the top. Bake in the preheated oven until the cake is cooked and a wooden skewer comes out clean from the centre.

To make the coulis: purée the raspberries with the sugar either in a blender or processor or by pressing the fruit through a sieve. Pour the coulis into a small jug and serve with the hot cake.

WHITE PEACH AND HAZELNUT TART

White peaches and nectarines are more fragrant and more delectable than their yellow siblings. Unfortunately the yellow-fleshed fruit are the more robust travellers on the motorways from southern Europe to our chilly shores. Use whichever fresh peaches are available for this lovely summer tart.

Oven: 200 °C / 400 °F / gas mark 6 ♦ *Baking time: 25–35 minutes*
Equipment: 30 cm / 12 in. tart tin – buttered
Makes: 12-portion tart

230 g / 8 oz prepared rich shortcrust pastry or *pâte brisée*
2 tbs apricot jam ♦ 100 g / 3½ oz butter
100 g / 3½ oz caster sugar ♦ 1 egg
150 g / 5 oz ground hazelnuts ♦ 1 tbs potato flour
4 large ripe peaches, or more if smaller ♦ 1 tbs caster sugar

Roll out the pastry to line the tart tin and bake blind in the preheated oven for 12–15 minutes until just starting to change colour. It may be more convenient to bake the pastry case a few days ahead to freeze until needed.

Spread the jam over the base of the pastry case. Cream the butter with the sugar until light and fluffy. Beat in the egg and stir in the ground hazelnuts and potato flour. Spread the mixture over the jam in an even layer.

Wash the peaches (I leave the skins on white peaches since they are very thin and contribute to the appearance of the tart) and cut each fruit into 8 segments. Arrange in concentric circles on top of the nut mixture leaving a small gap between each slice. Sprinkle the extra caster sugar on top.

Bake in the preheated oven until the fruit is cooked and the hazelnut mixture has a thin crust. Serve the tart hot or warm.

QUATRE-QUARTS AUX FRAMBOISES ET AUX ABRICOTS

A classic French cake – *Quatre-Quarts* is known in Britain and the U.S. as Pound Cake – at its best served warm from the oven with a bowl of crème fraîche. Pitted, fresh black cherries or blueberries with diced ripe peaches work equally well as the filling.

Oven: 180°C/350°F/gas mark 4 ♦ *Baking time: 40–45 minutes*
Equipment: 23 cm/9 in. spring-clip tin – buttered and base-lined
Makes: 10-portion cake

4 eggs, in their shells
butter, caster sugar and flour, each to the same weight as the eggs
1 tsp orange flower water ♦ 230 g/8 oz fresh raspberries or blueberries
230 g/8 oz fresh apricots, sliced ♦ 1 tsp icing sugar

Weigh the eggs and note the amount. Measure out the butter, sugar and flour to the same weight. Warm a mixing bowl in the preheated oven and melt the butter in it. Stir in the eggs, the sugar and flour with the orange flower water and mix together well.

Spoon a generous half of the mixture into the prepared tin and scatter the raspberries and sliced apricots on top. Cover with the rest of the cake mixture and smooth level.

Bake the cake in the preheated oven until golden brown and just beginning to shrink from the tin. Cool in the tin for 2 minutes then unclip and remove the side of the tin and slide the cake on to a serving dish or wooden platter. Dust the top of the cake with icing sugar and serve straight away with the crème fraîche.

CYPRUS ORANGE CAKE

The eastern Mediterranean is renowned for its sweet pastries and aromatic cakes which are served during the afternoon to accompany small glasses of very hot mint tea.

Oven: 180°C/350F/gas mark 4 ♦ Baking time: 45 minutes
Equipment: 23 cm/9 in. spring-clip tin – buttered and base-lined
Makes: 8–10-portion cake

2 large sweet navel oranges, ideally wax-free and unsprayed
6 eggs, separated ♦ 120 g/4 oz caster sugar
120 g/4 oz ground almonds ♦ 60 g/2 oz fine white breadcrumbs
1 tsp baking powder ♦ 1 tbs flaked almonds

decoration;
1 tsp icing sugar

Wash the oranges carefully and cover with cold water in a small pan. Bring to the boil and cook for 15–20 minutes or until tender, when a thin wooden skewer penetrates the skin easily. Drain the fruit then quarter, still unpeeled, into a processor and chop until puréed.

Whisk the egg yolks with the sugar until light and foamy. Gradually fold in the orange mixture alternately with the ground almonds. Then fold in 45 g/1½ oz of the breadcrumbs mixed with the baking powder. Sprinkle the remaining breadcrumbs over the inside of the prepared cake tin. Whisk the egg whites until stiff, then fold into the mixture. Spoon into the prepared cake tin and sprinkle the flaked almonds over the top.

Bake in the preheated oven until the cake is springy in the centre and is just starting to shrink from the tin. Cool in the tin for 2 minutes then open the clip and lift off the side. Dust the top of the cake with sieved icing sugar and serve while still warm or when cold.

MARTHA'S BANANA AND CHOCOLATE CHIP CAKE

This simple banana cake with a light texture appeared in the original *Cake Stall* as Anna's Banana Cake; the recipe has now been enlivened with chocolate chips by my young cooking friend, Martha. An easy way to crush the chocolate is to break it into a plastic bag, seal the bag and gently hit it with a rolling pin or a heavy stone until the chocolate is broken into fragments.

Oven: 180 °C / 350 °F / gas mark 4 ◆ Baking time: 35–40 minutes
Equipment: 18 cm / 7 in. tin – buttered and base-lined ◆ Makes: 8-portion cake

90 g / 3 oz butter ◆ 90 g / 3 oz caster sugar
1 large ripe banana, peeled and mashed ◆ 2 tsp lemon juice or milk
1 large egg ◆ 100 g / 3½ oz self-raising flour
60 g / 2 oz plain dessert chocolate, crushed into small pieces

chocolate frosting:
150 g / 5 oz plain dessert chocolate ◆ 3 tbs crème fraîche or double cream
1 tsp icing sugar (optional)

Cream the butter with the sugar until light and fluffy. Beat in the mashed banana and the lemon juice or milk. Mix in the egg and fold in the flour. Finally, stir in the chocolate pieces. Spoon the mixture into the prepared tin and smooth level.

Bake in the preheated oven until the cake is starting to shrink slightly from the tin and a wooden skewer comes out clean from the centre. Cool the cake in its tin for 3 minutes then turn it out on to a wire rack. When the cake is almost cold, make the chocolate frosting.

Break the chocolate into pieces in a bowl and melt in a microwave oven or by placing the bowl over simmering water for 4–5 minutes. When the chocolate is liquid remove the bowl from the heat and carefully stir in the cream. Spoon the frosting over the cake, if need be use the back of the spoon or a palette knife to spread it evenly. Set aside for 1 hour until the frosting has set.

Just before serving you can dust the top of the cake with icing sugar if you wish. Spoon the icing sugar into a fine-meshed sieve, hold the sieve above the cake and tap the edge gently with the spoon until a light cloud of icing sugar drifts over the cake.

RHUBARB AND KUMQUAT CAKE WITH ROSY CREAM

An early springtime cake that takes advantage of the slim sticks of forced rhubarb that are in season at that time. Serve the cake hot with spoonfuls of the cool, pink rhubarb cream.

Oven: 180°C/350°F/gas mark 4 ♦ Baking time: 55–60 minutes
Equipment: 20 cm/8 in. spring-form tin – buttered and base-lined
Makes: 8–10-portion cake

450 g/1 lb pink-skinned forced rhubarb, as thick as your thumb
30 g/1 oz golden caster sugar ♦ 6–8 kumquats
4 tbs cold water ♦ 300 ml/10 fl oz double cream

cake:
120 g/4 oz butter ♦ 120 g/4 oz golden caster sugar ♦ 2 eggs
1 orange, grated zest and juice ♦ 175 g/6 oz self-raising flour
30 g/1 oz ground almonds ♦ 1 tbs demerara or golden caster sugar

Wash and trim the rhubarb and cut the sticks, diagonally, into pieces about 2 cm/1 in. long. Toss the rhubarb and sugar together in a bowl and set aside.

Wash and dry the kumquats, trim off the ends and cut each fruit into about 8 slices. Gently simmer the sliced kumquats with the water in a covered pan for 3–4 minutes. Turn off the heat but leave covered.

To make the cake, cream the butter with the sugar until light and fluffy. Beat in the eggs one at a time, then mix in the grated zest and juice of half the orange. Stir in the flour and ground almonds until well combined. Spoon the mixture into the prepared cake tin and smooth level. Arrange about two-thirds of the rhubarb on the top of the mixture and place the kumquat slices in the gaps. Sprinkle the extra sugar on top.

Bake in the preheated oven until risen and golden and the cake is starting to shrink from the tin. Unclip and remove the side of the cake tin and slide the cake on its base on to a serving plate. Serve the cake hot with the cool rhubarb cream.

To make the cream, spoon the rest of the rhubarb pieces into a pan and add the grated zest and juice of the remaining half orange. Bring gently to the boil and cook over low heat for a few minutes until soft. Turn off the heat and cover the pan to allow the rhubarb to finish cooking but retain its pretty pink colour. Then place the pan in cold water to cool. Mash the fruit and juice together with a fork until mushy.

Whisk the cream until stiff but still glossy. Gently fold the rhubarb into the cream until pink but still streaky. Spoon the cream into a bowl and chill until ready to serve with the hot cake.

PEAR AND POIRE WILLIAM CAKE

One of my favourite cakes. In mid-winter I use Conference pears, in late summer thin-skinned Williams are best; the pear slices spiral out from the centre of the cake like the spokes of a wheel. Serve the cake warm with full-cream plain yoghurt.

Oven: 180°C/350°F/gas mark 4 ♦ Baking time: 45–50 minutes
Equipment: 20 cm/8 in. spring-clip tin – buttered and base-lined
Makes: 8-portion cake

2 medium-size ripe Williams pears ♦ 3 tbs Poire William liqueur
100 g/3½ oz butter ♦ 100 g/3½ oz caster sugar
¼ lemon, finely grated zest ♦ 2 eggs ♦ 100 g/3½ oz ground almonds
60 g/2 oz self-raising flour ♦ 1 tsp icing sugar

Wash and dry the pears – Conference pears should be peeled, thin-skinned Williams pears do not need to be peeled – then quarter and core them. Cut each pear into 10–12 slices and place them in a single layer on a plate. Spoon the liqueur over them and set aside for 15 minutes.

Cream the butter with the sugar and lemon zest until light and fluffy. Beat in the eggs separately. Mix in the ground almonds and flour. Spoon the mixture into the prepared cake tin and smooth level. Arrange the pear slices on top, radiating out from the centre. Set aside the remaining liqueur in the dish.

Bake the cake in the preheated oven until the cake is cooked and a wooden skewer comes out clean from the centre. Cool in the tin for 5 minutes then unclip and remove the side of the tin, slide the cake on to a serving plate. Drizzle the reserved liqueur over the cake and dust lightly with sieved icing sugar. Serve the cake straight away while it's still warm.

PLUM AND BLACKBERRY CRUMBLE CAKE

Late summer brings a harvest of dark red plums and lustrous blackberries to the kitchen. A month or so earlier I make this cake with apricots and blueberries. Crushed amaretti biscuits and flaked almonds form the crumble – a satisfyingly crisp foil to the baked fruit. The cake is nicest served warm with crème fraîche or vanilla ice-cream.

Oven: 180°C/350°F/gas mark 4 ♦ *Baking time: 45–50 minutes*
Equipment: 23 cm/9 in. spring-clip tin – buttered and base-lined
Makes: 8–10-portion cake

175 g/6 oz butter ♦ 175 g/6 oz golden caster sugar ♦ 3 eggs
2 tsp orange flower water ♦ 175 g/6 oz self-raising flour

fruit layer:
450 g/1 lb plums, stoned and quartered ♦ 175 g/6 oz blackberries

almond crumble:
100 g/3½ oz amaretti biscuits ♦ 30 g/1 oz flaked almonds
30 g/1 oz demerara sugar ♦ 60 g/2 oz butter, melted

Blend the butter with the sugar and beat together until pale and fluffy. Mix in the eggs one at a time, beating them in well with the orange flower water. Fold in the sifted flour. Spoon the mixture into the prepared cake tin and smooth level. Arrange the fruit on top in a single layer.

Crumble the amaretti biscuits into a bowl and mix in the almonds and sugar. Pour on the melted butter and stir until combined. Sprinkle the crumble mixture over the fruit.

Bake in the preheated oven until a wooden skewer comes out clean from the centre of the cake. Cool in the tin for 5 minutes then unclip and remove the side of the cake tin. Slide the cake on to a flat plate or board and serve straight away.

DUTCH APPLE CAKE

A sweet batter base is covered with sliced dessert apples and spiced sugar – at its best served warm, recommended for a late breakfast or brunch in mid-winter.

Oven: 200 °C / 400 °F / gas mark 6 ♦ Baking time: 35–40 minutes
Equipment: 20 cm / 8 in. square or round tin – buttered
Makes: 15 pieces

cake layer:
30 g / 1 oz butter, softened ♦ 90 g / 3 oz pale muscovado sugar
½ lemon or orange, finely grated zest
1 egg mixed with milk to make 150 ml / 5 fl oz
175 g / 6 oz self-raising flour

apple layer:
30 g / 1 oz butter, melted
3–4 ripe medium Cox's Orange Pippin apples, peeled and thinly sliced
60 g / 2 oz pale muscovado sugar ♦ ½ tsp ground cinnamon
¼ tsp grated nutmeg

Cream the butter with the sugar and the zest of lemon until well mixed. Gradually stir in the egg and milk alternately with the sifted flour and beat together for 1 minute. Pour into the prepared cake tin. Brush with the melted butter and arrange the sliced apples in rows on top. Mix the sugar with the spices and sprinkle over the apples.

Bake in the preheated oven until a wooden skewer comes out clean. Cut into squares and serve or leave to cool in the tin.

AUTUMN FRUIT AND NUT UPSIDE-DOWN CAKE

Both American Upside-down Cake and French *Tarte Tatin* share the idea of baking fruit under a kind of edible duvet. When turned out, the fruit and its buttery juices are embedded in their delicious coverlet. Autumn fruits such as plums, damsons, raspberries, blackberries and pears work particularly well in this recipe but it can be made with whatever soft and stone fruits you have to hand – even those from the freezer. Serve the cake hot with crème fraîche or spoonfuls of vanilla ice-cream.

Oven: 180 °C / 350 °F / gas mark 4 ♦ Baking time; 40–50 minutes
Equipment: 20–23 cm / 8–9 in. square tin – buttered and lined
Makes: 9-portion cake

1 tbs butter ♦ 2 tbs pale muscovado sugar
450 g / 1 lb ripe fruit, stoned or sliced as necessary
12 pecan nut halves ♦ 175 g / 6 oz butter
175 g / 6 oz pale muscovado sugar ♦ 3 eggs
few drops vanilla essence ♦ 200 g / 7 oz self-raising flour
1–2 tbs milk

Melt the tablespoon of butter in a small pan. Remove from the heat and mix in the sugar, pour into the base of the prepared cake tin. Arrange the fruit in a single layer on top and tuck the nuts, flat side uppermost into any spaces.

Cream the butter with the sugar until light and fluffy. Beat in the eggs, separately, then the vanilla essence. Sift the flour and fold into the mixture adding the milk to make a soft dropping consistency. Spoon the mixture into the cake tin, taking care not to disturb the fruit and nuts and smooth level.

Bake in the preheated oven until the cake is cooked and springy to the touch. Cool in the tin for 5 minutes then carefully turn out on to a flat plate or board for serving straight away.

CHAPTER FIVE

Chocolate Cakes

THE CONTENTS OF THIS CHAPTER

On those tea-party days, pulling myself up the staircase step by step, reason and memory already cast off like outer garments, and myself no more now than the sport of the basest reflexes, I would arrive in the zone in which the scent of Mrs Swann greeted my nostrils. I felt that I could already behold the majesty of the chocolate cake, encircled by plates heaped with little cakes, and by tiny napkins of grey damask with figures on them, as required by convention but peculiar to the Swanns.

Marcel Proust, Within a Budding Grove, 1913

Almost everyone likes chocolate cakes; dark intense chocolate cakes, moist almond-rich ones, coffee-flavoured mocha ones, fudge-like brownies, sticky cup cakes, triple-chocolate marble cake, even an orange chocolate biscuit cake that a child can make. This book could, in fact, have been devoted solely to chocolate cakes.

Apart from the recipe, the most important factor is the quality of the chocolate itself. Bars with approximately 50–70 per cent cocoa solids are now widely available and which brand you use is a matter of taste, though I usually prefer the darkest kind that can be sweetened accordingly.

Converting solid chocolate to a liquid for adding to a cake mixture is done by melting it in a heat-proof bowl that can be scraped clean. If your oven is already hot, simply break the chocolate into pieces and place the bowl in the centre of the oven for a few minutes until the chocolate has liquified. Remove from the heat and allow the chocolate to cool slightly before adding to the other ingredients. Alternatively, place the bowl of chocolate over a pan of gently simmering water until melted or heat the chocolate in a microwave oven for 1–2 minutes. Resist the temptation to stir the chocolate while it is melting because this can cause it to thicken. As it cools, melted chocolate sets hard again. When necessary, hot melted chocolate can be thinned with a modest amount of butter, cream, water or liqueur. This should be done carefully with the minimum of mixing.

Some cakes call for crushed chocolate rather than melted. Depending on the hardness of a chocolate bar this can be done by grating – using a metal box grater, or with a sharp potato peeler. The easiest method is to chop the broken chocolate pieces in a food processor, though this will result in a mixture of fine chocolate dust and larger gravel-like pieces – this may be ideal for some recipes. A low-technology way is to tip broken pieces into a strong, clear plastic bag before sealing it. Then hammer the pieces with a rolling pin or a wooden mallet – this is often best done outside or on a solid stone floor – until you have the right size fragments. The final alternative is to use bought chocolate chips or 'pepites' instead.

Powdered cocoa replaces melted chocolate in some recipes, for instance a fat-free sponge cake or Swiss roll. Again, use the best cocoa powder you can find. I prefer the dark, organic kind and either add the cocoa to the mixture by pressing through a fine sieve to remove all lumps, or blend it with warm water until smooth before stirring into the cake. If you wish to make a chocolate version of any cake, cocoa powder can replace some of the flour in the recipe – though too much cocoa changes the balance of ingredients, making the baked cake rather dry, whereas melted chocolate contributes moistness to a cake mixture due to the fat it contains.

FAVOURITE CHOCOLATE SPONGE CAKE

Derived from one of the most popular recipes in the original *Cake Stall*, the sponge cake is sandwiched with whipped cream and topped with shiny chocolate frosting.

Oven: 180°C/350°F/gas mark 4 ♦ Baking time: 30–35 minutes
Equipment: two 20 cm/8 in. sponge sandwich tins – buttered and base-lined
Makes: 8-portion cake

60 g/2 oz cocoa ♦ 6 tbs hot water ♦ 175 g/6 oz butter
175 g/6 oz light or dark muscovado sugar, sieved
175 g/6 oz self-raising flour ♦ 1 tsp baking powder
pinch ground cinnamon ♦ 3 eggs

filling:
150 ml/5 fl oz double cream

frosting:
90 g/3 oz icing sugar ♦ 30 g/1 oz cocoa powder
60 g/2 oz pale muscovado sugar ♦ 60 g/2 oz butter ♦ 2 tbs water

In a mixing bowl, blend the cocoa with the hot water until smooth. Add the butter in pieces and all the remaining ingredients: sugar, flour, baking powder, cinnamon and eggs. Mix together for 2–3 minutes, ideally using a hand-held electric beater, until completely smooth.

Divide the mixture between the prepared cake tins and smooth level. Bake in the preheated oven until the middle of the cake is springy to the touch and just starting to shrink from the tin. Cool in the cake tins for 3 minutes then turn the cakes out on to a wire rack to cool.

The cream filling: is made by whisking the cream until thick but still glossy. If you wish to sweeten the cream stir in a teaspoon of caster sugar. Spoon the cream over one of the cakes and place the other on top.

To make the chocolate frosting: sift the icing sugar and cocoa into a bowl. Measure the muscovado sugar, butter and water into a small pan and stir over low heat until dissolved, then bring to the boil. Remove from the heat, cool for half a minute, then pour on to the sugar / cocoa mixture and beat until smooth. Pour the frosting over the cake allowing it to trickle down the sides. Leave the cake in a cool place for 2 hours to set.

If you wish to replace the frosting with melted chocolate, melt 100 g / 3½ oz chocolate and pour over the cake then set aside until dry.

CHOCOLATE ORANGE RING CAKE

This attractive ring cake depends on that great marriage of chocolate with orange. I prefer dark, smooth orange-flavoured chocolate for the frosting and cream – if you have the kind containing small chips of orange or almond it will need to be melted and sieved before use. This cake produces 12 neatly-cut portions, making it ideal for a party or for fund-raising.

Oven: 180°C/350°F/gas mark 4 ♦ Baking time: 25–30 minutes
Equipment: 24 cm/9½ in. ring tin – buttered
Makes: 12-portion cake

60 g / 2 oz cocoa powder ♦ 6 tbs hot water ♦ 1 sweet orange
175 g / 6 oz butter ♦ 175 g / 6 oz dark soft brown sugar ♦ 3 eggs
150 g / 5 oz self-raising flour
2 tbs Orange Curaçoa or orange-based liqueur (optional)
2 tsp caster sugar

frosting:
200 g / 7 oz dark smooth orange-flavoured chocolate
150 ml / 5 fl oz single cream

Measure the cocoa into a warm mixing bowl and blend with the water until smooth. Halve the orange, cut a thin slice from each half and set them aside for decorating the cake later. Squeeze the juice from the orange into a cup, and grate the zest into the mixing bowl. Add the butter and sugar and use an electric beater to blend the mixture together until light and fluffy. Beat in the eggs one at a time. Gradually mix in the sifted flour until well combined. Spoon the mixture into the prepared cake tin and smooth level.

Bake in the preheated oven until a wooden skewer comes out clean from the cake. Rest the cake in the tin for 2 minutes then turn out on to a wire rack.

When the cake is almost cold, place it back in the cake tin. Stir the orange liqueur and the sugar into the reserved orange juice. Spoon half the mixture over the cake and leave until absorbed. Then trickle over the rest of orange mixture and set aside for 1 hour.

To make the frosting: break the chocolate into pieces and melt with half the cream in a microwave or a warm oven. Stir gently until smooth, then use a palette knife to spread two-thirds in an even layer over the cake.

Stir the rest of the cream into the remaining chocolate and stand the bowl in a little cold water to cool the mixture. Use an electric beater to whisk the cream until pale and thick. Spoon the chocolate cream into a piping-bag and pipe 12 rosettes of cream on top of the cake; pipe the remaining cream around the base of the cake. Cut the reserved orange slices into 12 triangular segments and place each one on a rosette of cream. Chill the cake before serving.

CHOCOLATE GINGER CAKE

I include this cake in tribute to Monica Cunningham, who publicized the first *Cake Stall* by sending this recipe on a postcard to every cookery editor in Britain. My original recipe used ginger preserved in syrup, however crystallized ginger is widely available these days, particularly in health food shops. This cake improves in flavour after 24 hours.

Oven: 180°C/350°F/gas mark 4 ♦ *Baking time: 45–50 minutes*
Equipment: 20 cm/8 in. spring-clip tin – buttered and base-lined
Makes: 8-portion cake

120 g/4 oz crystallized ginger ♦ 30 g/1 oz cocoa powder
4 tbs hot water ♦ 175 g/6 oz butter
175 g/6 oz dark muscovado sugar ♦ 3 large eggs
150 g/5 oz self-raising flour ♦ generous pinch ground cinnamon

icing:
120 g/4 oz plain dessert chocolate ♦ 3 tbs single cream

Cut the ginger into thin slices, and reserve 1 tablespoon for decorating the cake. In a mixing bowl blend the cocoa with the water until smooth. Add the butter, cut in pieces, and the sieved sugar. Beat together until smooth and fluffy. Beat in the eggs one at a time. Fold in the flour sifted with the ground cinnamon then stir in the sliced ginger. Spoon the mixture into the prepared tin and smooth level.

Bake in the preheated oven until the cake is springy to the touch and a wooden skewer comes out clean from the centre. Remove the cake from the oven and leave in the tin for 5 minutes, then unclip and remove the side of the tin and leave the cake to cool.

Break the chocolate into pieces and melt with the cream in a bowl in a microwave oven or over simmering water. Stir until smooth and spread over the top of the cake. Decorate the cake with the reserved sliced ginger and leave in a cool place until set.

CHOCOLATE ROLL WITH HAZELNUT CREAM

A good cake for a party since the flavour improves if made a day ahead.

Oven: 200°C / 400°F / gas mark 6 ♦ *Baking time: 12–15 minutes*
Equipment: 32 x 23 cm / 13 x 9 in. Swiss roll tin – lined; teacloth
Makes: 12-portion cake

3 eggs ♦ 100 g / 3½ oz caster sugar ♦ 60 g / 2 oz self-raising flour
30 g / 1 oz cocoa powder ♦ 2 tsp caster sugar

filling:
60 g / 2 oz hazelnuts, toasted ♦ 300 ml / 10 fl oz double cream
1 tbs caster sugar ♦ 30 g / 1 oz plain dessert chocolate, grated

frosting:
90 g / 3 oz plain dessert chocolate ♦ 2 tbs double cream or butter

Whisk the eggs with the sugar with an electric beater until the whisk leaves a trail across the surface of the mixture. Gradually fold in the flour sifted with the cocoa, taking care not to lose too much air. Pour into the prepared cake tin.

Bake in the preheated oven until the cake is springy in the centre and it is starting to shrink from the tin. Spread the teacloth over a pastry board or work surface, sprinkle over the extra caster sugar and turn the cake on to it. Peel off the baking paper and trim off any crisp edges of the cake. Fold one narrow end of the cloth over the cake and carefully roll up so that the cloth takes the place of the filling. Place on a wire rack to cool.

To make the filling: slice a few of the hazelnuts and set aside for decorating the cake. Finely chop the remainder. Whisk the cream with the sugar until thick but still glossy. Gently fold in the chopped nuts and the grated chocolate. Unroll the cake and spread over the cream then carefully re-roll. Place on a sheet of baking paper or a serving plate.

To make the frosting: break the chocolate into pieces and melt with the cream or butter in a microwave or warm oven. Stir gently until smooth then spoon over the cake. Sprinkle the chopped hazelnuts on top and place the cake in the refrigerator until ready to serve.

CHOCOLATE ESPRESSO CAKE

A coffee-rich chocolate cake for mocha fans, filled with coffee cream and covered in melted chocolate and a handful of chocolate coffee beans.

Oven: 180 °C / 350 °F / gas mark 4 ♦ Baking time: 40–45 minutes
Equipment: 23 cm / 9 in. spring-clip tin – buttered and base-lined
Makes: 10–12-portion cake

60 g / 2 oz cocoa powder
300 ml / 10 fl oz hot strong black coffee, ideally espresso
175 g / 6 oz butter ♦ 175 g / 6 oz dark muscovado sugar
3 large eggs ♦ 175 g / 6 oz self-raising flour ♦ 1 tsp baking powder

filling:
300 ml / 10 fl oz double cream ♦ 1 tbs caster sugar

frosting:
100 g / 3½ oz plain dessert chocolate
30 g / 1 oz chocolate coffee beans

Blend the cocoa powder with half the hot coffee until smooth. Set aside the rest of the coffee to cool. Add the butter and sieved sugar and beat the mixture together using an electric hand-held mixer until smooth and light. Add the eggs, one at a time, beating each in well. Gradually stir in the flour sieved with the baking powder.

Spoon the mixture into the prepared tin and smooth level. Bake in the preheated oven until the cake is springy in the centre and a wooden skewer comes out clean from the middle. Remove from the oven and leave in the tin for 10 minutes. Unclip and remove the side of the tin and leave the cake on its metal base to cool.

To make the filling: whisk the cream until thick but still glossy. Gently stir in some of the reserved coffee, with the sugar to taste, to make the coffee cream. Grate a little of the frosting chocolate into the cream. Use a long sharp knife to cut the cake into two even layers. Lift the top layer to one side and spread the cream over the lower layer. Cover the with the top layer.

To make the frosting: break the remaining chocolate into a bowl and add the rest of the coffee. Melt the chocolate in a microwave or a warm oven – or over simmering water. Gently stir the melted chocolate with the coffee until smooth and then pour over the top of the cake. Arrange the coffee beans around the edge of the cake and set aside for one hour until the frosting has set.

FLORENCE WHITE'S 'REALLY DELICIOUS' CHOCOLATE CAKE

The recipe for this cake appeared in a yellowing newspaper-cutting that fell from a 1920s cookery book that I was given. The flavour combination of chocolate pieces with ground almonds in the sugar-crusted cake does indeed justify its name – this is a good keeping cake that I bake again and again.

Oven: 160 °C / 325 °F / gas mark 3
Baking time: 1½–2 hours
Equipment: 20 cm / 8 in. spring-clip tin – buttered and base-lined
Makes: 8–12-portion cake

230 g / 8 oz caster sugar ♦ 230 g / 8 oz butter
6 eggs, separated ♦ few drops of vanilla essence
230 g / 8 oz plain dessert chocolate, coarsely grated
90 g / 3 oz plain flour ♦ 120 g / 4 oz ground almonds

Measure 60 g / 2 oz of the caster sugar and set aside for the top of the cake. Cream the butter with the remaining caster sugar until light and fluffy. Gradually beat in the egg yolks and the vanilla essence. Stir in the grated chocolate with the flour and ground almonds. Whisk the egg whites until moderately stiff and fold into the mixture. Spoon into the prepared cake tin and smooth level. Dust the reserved caster sugar over the top of the cake in an even layer.

Bake in the preheated oven until a thin wooden skewer comes out clean from the centre of the cake. Cool in the tin for 5 minutes, then open the spring-clip and remove the side of the tin. Transfer the cake to a wire rack to cool.

TRIPLE CHOCOLATE MARBLE CAKE

Marble cakes are part of my childhood, I've added extra chocolate – plain, milk, and white – broken into pieces and pressed into the mixture just before baking. This is an excellent cake to make with children and is recommended, already cut into pieces, for taking to a charity cake stall.

Oven: 180°C/350°F/gas mark 4 ♦ Baking time: 55–60 minutes
Equipment: 20 cm/8 in. square tin – buttered and base-lined
Makes: 16-portion cake

230 g/8 oz butter ♦ 230 g/8 oz caster sugar
4 large eggs ♦ ½ tsp vanilla essence
265 g/9 oz self-raising flour ♦ 30 g/1 oz cocoa
good pinch of ground cinnamon ♦ 4 tbs hot water
100 g/3½ oz plain dessert chocolate ♦ 100 g/3½ oz milk chocolate
100 g/3½ oz white chocolate

Cream the butter with the sugar in a bowl until light and fluffy. Beat in the eggs one at a time. Mix in the vanilla essence and the flour.

Draw a line across the mixture to divide it roughly into two halves. Spoon one half of the mixture into the prepared cake tin, spacing out the spoonfuls. Blend the cocoa and cinnamon with the hot water and when smooth mix into the remaining cake mixture. Spoon into the cake tin filling in the gaps. Use the spoon to roughly smooth the mixture level.

Break all the chocolate into quite large pieces and push them into the mixture vertically, varying the flavours so that the white chocolate is in the dark mixture and so on. Leave some pieces of chocolate sticking up above the mixture so that they melt on top.

Bake the cake towards the bottom of a preheated oven until a wooden skewer comes out clean from the middle – the chocolate will be liquid but the cake mixture should be cooked. Leave to cool in the cake tin for 30 minutes then serve warm or at room temperature.

CHOCOLATE HEDGEHOG CAKE

For centuries the hedgehog has been a desirable shape for puddings and cakes. The 'spines' are usually split almonds or candied fruit coated with custard, glaze or icing. Children, in particular, enjoy this decorative effect.

Oven: 180°C/350°F/gas mark 4 ♦ Baking time: 45–55 minutes
Equipment: 1 kg/2 lb loaf tin – buttered and lined
Makes: 12–16-portion cake

120 g / 4 oz butter ♦ 120 g / 4 oz pale muscovado sugar
150 g / 5 oz plain dessert chocolate, melted ♦ 6 eggs, separated
120 g / 4 oz ground almonds ♦ 60 g / 2 oz fine white breadcrumbs
90 g / 3 oz plain flour

icing:
60 g / 2 oz blanched almonds, slivered
150 g / 5 oz plain dessert chocolate
30 g / 1 oz butter ♦ 2 currants or circles of liquorice

Cream the butter with the sugar until light and fluffy. Beat in the melted chocolate with the egg yolks. Mix the ground almonds and breadcrumbs with the sieved flour and fold into the mixture. Whisk the egg whites until stiff and fold into the mixture. Spoon the mixture into the prepared cake tin and smooth level.

Bake in the preheated oven until the cake is springy in the centre and a wooden skewer comes out clean. Cool in the tin for 2 minutes then turn on to a wire rack.

When the cake is cold, use a sharp or serrated knife to trim off the sharp angles to make it resemble the shape of a hedgehog. Press the slivered almonds in all over the body, but leave the nose and face free of spines.

To make the icing: break the chocolate into pieces in a bowl, add the butter and melt in a microwave oven or over simmering water. Gently stir to mix well then spoon over the cake until the 'spines' are completely coated. Press on the currants or liquorice to make the hedgehog's eyes. Set aside until the icing has set.

CHOCOLATE, ALMOND AND AMARETTO CAKE

An almond cake made with plain dark chocolate and no flour. It is satisfyingly rich and intense, the flavour enhanced further with Amaretto di Saronno, the Italian almond liqueur.

Oven: 180°C/350°F/gas mark 4 ♦ Baking time: 25–30 minutes
Equipment: 20 cm/8 in. spring-clip tin – buttered and base-lined
Makes: 8–10-portion cake

230 g/8 oz plain dessert chocolate, minimum 70% cocoa solids
4 tbs Amaretto di Saronno ♦ 6 medium eggs, separated
200 g/7 oz caster sugar ♦ 135 g/4½ oz ground almonds
30 g/1 oz flaked blanched almonds

chocolate frosting:
175 g/6 oz plain dessert chocolate ♦ 30 g/1 oz unsalted butter
2–3 tbs Amaretto di Saronno

Break the chocolate into pieces in a bowl. Add the Amaretto and gently melt the chocolate in a hot oven or by placing the bowl over a pan of simmering water until the chocolate has become liquid. Stir gently to incorporate the liqueur but do not overheat or over-stir the chocolate or it may thicken.

Whisk the yolks with half the sugar until light and foamy. Fold in the melted chocolate. Whisk the whites until stiff then fold in the remaining caster sugar and whisk again until thick. Gradually fold the meringue into the chocolate alternately with the ground almonds. Finally, stir in the flaked almonds.

Pour the mixture into the prepared cake tin and smooth level. Bake in the centre of the preheated oven until a wooden skewer comes out cleanly from the centre. Cool the cake in its tin on a wire rack, then unclip and remove the side of the tin. Leaving the cake on its baking paper, use a palette knife or a spatula to transfer the cake to a flat plate.

To make the frosting: break the chocolate into pieces in a bowl, add the butter and liqueur and gently heat the mixture in a hot oven or over simmering water until the chocolate is liquid. Stir gently to incorporate the ingredients and pour the melted chocolate over the cake, use a palette knife to spread it in an even layer. Leave the cake in a cool place for 1 hour to set. Serve the cake plain, or with crème fraîche or thick cream.

CHOCOLATE CRACKER CAKE

My version of the familiar refrigerator chocolate cake is crammed with dried and candied fruits and toasted nuts. These can be varied according to taste as long as you retain the same weight of added ingredients. For Christmas, I shape the cake to resemble a cracker with ribbons tied around each end. Alternatively the cake can be simply spooned into a cake tin. There is no baking involved in this cake so it is simple and safe for children to make.

Equipment: mixing bowl set over hot water for melting the chocolate – or this can be done in a low oven; ideally a refrigerator for chilling the mixture
Makes: a cylindrical 20-portion cake

200 g / 7 oz plain dessert chocolate ♦ 1 tbs rum or brandy
120 g / 4 oz butter ♦ 1 egg yolk
60 g / 2 oz of each of the following ready-to-eat dried fruits and nuts:
dried apricots, chopped ♦ dried figs, chopped or sliced
fresh dates or prunes, sliced ♦ glacé pineapple, sliced
glacé cherries, sliced ♦ candied orange peel, chopped
toasted hazelnuts, chopped ♦ toasted almonds, sliced
30 g / 1 oz glacé ginger, sliced or chopped
60 g / 2 oz grated chocolate or chocolate flakes

Break the chocolate into pieces and melt with the rum or brandy in a bowl over simmering water. Remove from the heat. In a mixing bowl cream the butter with the egg yolk until light and fluffy. Gradually beat in the slightly cooled chocolate. Mix in all the fruit and nuts until well combined.

Spoon the mixture on to a sheet of baking parchment and form into the shape of a sausage. Wrap in the paper and chill until almost firm. Reshape by rolling in the paper if necessary, and finally roll in the flaked chocolate until well coated. Chill until firm.

Wrap in fresh paper with pretty ribbons and set aside in a cold place until ready to eat. Serve in thin slices.

TOTAL CHOCOLATE DEVIL'S FOOD CAKE

I grew up with the all-chocolate version of this classic American cake. But I also include the snowy-white seven-minute frosting alternative which some people prefer.

Oven: 160°C/325°F/gas mark 3 ♦ Baking time: 35–40 minutes
Equipment: three 18 cm/7in sponge sandwich tins – buttered and base-lined
Makes: 8–12-portion cake

60 g/2 oz cocoa powder ♦ 4 tbs hot water
4 eggs ♦ 175 g/6 oz butter
175 g/6 oz dark muscovado sugar, sieved
175 g/6 oz self-raising flour ♦ 2 tsp baking powder
¼ tsp ground cinnamon

chocolate fudge frosting:
120 g/4 oz plain dessert chocolate ♦ 120 g/4 oz butter
½ tsp vanilla essence ♦ 350 g/12 oz icing sugar

seven-minute frosting:
350 g/12 oz caster sugar ♦ ¼ tsp cream of tartar
2 egg whites ♦ 4 tbs hot water

In a large warmed mixing bowl, blend the cocoa with the hot water until smooth. Add the eggs, butter, sugar, flour sifted with the baking powder and ground cinnamon. Mix together well then beat for 1–2 minutes. Divide the mixture between the prepared cake tins and smooth level. Bake in the preheated oven until the cakes are cooked, springy to the touch and just starting to shrink from the tin. Cool in the tins for 2 minutes then turn the cakes out on to a wire rack.

To prepare fudge frosting: note that if only the filling for the three cakes is required (because you are going to coat their outsides with the seven-minute frosting), it is necessary to halve the quantities given above. Melt the chocolate in a bowl – in a hot oven, microwave, or over simmering water. Stir in the butter, vanilla essence and sufficient sifted icing sugar to make a soft spreadable mixture. Sandwich the three layers of cakes with half the filling and spread the rest over the top and sides. Place the cake in cool place until the frosting has set.

To make the white seven-minute frosting: place a large mixing bowl over simmering water. Add the sugar, cream of tartar, egg whites and hot water and whisk vigorously – preferably with a hand-held electric beater – for 7 minutes. Remove the bowl from the heat and continue whisking until the frosting stands in soft peaks. With a palette knife spread the frosting evenly over the top and sides of the filled cake making a swirling pattern. Set aside in a warm place for 1–2 hours for the icing to set. Serve the same day.

DARK CHOCOLATE MOUSSE CAKE

The rich velvety chocolate mousse sits on a base of flour-free sponge cake. The flavour of the cake improves if chilled for 24 hours before serving.

Oven: 180°C/350°F/gas mark 4 ♦ *Baking time: 20–25 minutes*
Equipment: 20 cm/8 in. spring-clip tin – buttered and base-lined; a strip of baking parchment to line the side of the cake tin
Makes: 8–10-portion cake

sponge cake base:
4 egg yolks ♦ 90 g/3 oz caster sugar
60 g/2 oz dark chocolate, melted ♦ 30 g/1 oz ground almonds

chocolate mousse layer:
4 leaves gelatine ♦ 3 tbs strong black coffee
4 egg yolks ♦ 90 g/3 oz caster sugar
200 g/7 oz dark chocolate, melted ♦ 300 ml/10 fl oz double cream
1–2 tbs dark Jamaican rum ♦ 1 tbs cocoa powder

Whisk the egg yolks with the caster sugar until pale and foamy. Use a balloon whisk to stir in the melted chocolate and the ground almonds. Spoon the mixture into the prepared cake tin and smooth level.

Bake in the preheated oven until the cake is springy to the touch and a wooden skewer comes out clean from the centre. Remove from the oven and leave to cool in the cake tin. Line the vertical surface of the cake tin with a strip of baking paper.

Soften the gelatine with the black coffee in a small pan. Warm gently until dissolved and set aside. Whisk the egg yolks with the caster sugar until thick and foamy. Whisk the cream with the rum until thick but still glossy. Pour the gelatine into the egg yolk mixture in a fine trickle whisking all the time. Gradually fold in the melted chocolate and the cream until well combined. Taste, and add a little more rum if desired. Pour the mousse mixture into the cake tin and tap the tin hard once or twice until the mixture is level. Chill until set.

Just before serving sieve a fine layer of cocoa powder over the cake, unclip the cake tin and remove the side and its paper lining. Slide the cake on its paper layer on to a flat serving plate. Chill until ready to serve.

TYROLESE SCHOKOLADE TORTE

Adapted from a recipe in the charming Medici Society edition of David de Bethel's *Tyrolese Cookery Book*, this excellent flour-free chocolate hazelnut cake is best made a day ahead of serving.

Oven: 180°C/350°F/gas mark 4 ♦ *Baking time: 40–45 minutes*
Equipment: 23 cm/9 in. spring-clip or sloping sided cake tin
– buttered, base-lined and dusted with caster sugar
Makes: 12-portion cake

5 eggs, separated ♦ 150 g/5 oz pale muscovado sugar
150 g/5 oz unskinned hazelnuts, fairly finely ground
150 g/5 oz plain dessert chocolate, finely chopped
¼ tsp ground cinnamon
4 cloves, ground to a powder in pestle and mortar

icing:
3 tbs warmed sieved apricot jam ♦ 175 g/6 oz plain dessert chocolate
6 tbs double cream

Whisk the egg yolks with the sugar until light and foamy. Fold in the ground hazelnuts, chopped chocolate and spices. Whisk the egg whites until fairly stiff and fold into the mixture using a balloon whisk or a large metal spoon. Turn the mixture into the prepared cake tin and smooth level.

Bake in the preheated oven until the cake is springy in the centre and a wooden skewer comes out clean. Cool in the tin for 2 minutes then turn out on to a wire rack and leave until cold.

To make the icing: break the chocolate into pieces in a bowl, add the cream and melt in a microwave or over simmering water until smooth. Brush the sieved jam over the cake and spoon the chocolate over the top and sides of the cake. Leave the cake in a cold place for 2 hours until the icing has set.

CHOCOLATE VELVET CAKE WITH CHERRY COMPOTE

A French chocolate cake with a soft, velvety texture due to the cream in the recipe – which I've adapted for double cream rather than crème fraîche. Serve this rich cake while still warm, on its own or with vanilla ice-cream. It is also excellent partnered with cherries poached in red wine.

Oven: 180°C/350°F/gas mark 4 ♦ *Baking time: 40 minutes*
Equipment: 23 cm/9 in. spring-clip tin – buttered and base-lined
Makes: 12-portion cake

400 g/14 oz plain dessert chocolate e.g. Green and Black's *Maya Gold*
300 ml/10 fl oz double cream ♦ 6 eggs
200 g/7 oz dark soft brown sugar
30 g/1 oz cornflour ♦ 1 tsp icing sugar

cherry compote:
300 ml/10 fl oz red wine such as Côtes du Rhône
120 g/4 oz light soft brown sugar ♦ cinnamon stick, thumb-length
450 g/1 lb fresh cherries ♦ ½ tsp arrowroot or potato flour

Break the chocolate into pieces and melt in a bowl in a microwave or a warm oven. Remove from the heat and add the cream, stirring gently until incorporated.

Use an electric beater to whisk the eggs with the sugar for 2 minutes until light and frothy, then beat in the sieved cornflour. Gently pour the chocolate into the egg mixture, stirring with a balloon whisk until well combined. Pour the mixture into the prepared cake tin.

Bake in the preheated oven until *just* baked, when a wooden skewer comes out clean from the centre. Cool the cake in the cake tin for 10 minutes then transfer to a flat serving plate and dust lightly with sieved icing sugar before serving.

To make the cherry compote: measure the wine into a wide pan, add the sugar and cinnamon stick and bring to the boil, stirring now and again until the sugar is dissolved. Lower the heat and simmer until the quantity is reduced by one third.

Meanwhile wash and drain the cherries and remove the stones. Add to the pan and bring back to the boil, lower the heat and cook gently for 5–10 minutes until tender. Blend the arrowroot or potato flour with a tablespoonful of cold water and add to the pan, stir until thickened then remove from the heat and pour the compote into a serving dish.

GUDRUN'S NORWEGIAN CHOCOLATE RAISIN CAKE

Unusual for the combination of chocolate, spices and dried fruit, this cake has a lovely flavour. The handwritten recipe arrived from Norway via a friend who asked me to try it.

Oven: 180 °C/350 °F/gas mark 4 ◆ Baking time: 50–60 minutes
Equipment: 20 cm/8 in. square tin – buttered and base-lined
Makes: 16-portion cake

175 g/6 oz butter ◆ 175 g/6 oz golden caster sugar
3 eggs ◆ 200 g/7 oz plain flour
1 tsp baking powder
¼ tsp ground allspice or cinnamon ◆ ¼ tsp ground mace or nutmeg
4 tbs milk ◆ 200 g/7 oz ground hazelnuts
160 g/5½ oz seedless raisins
160 g/5½ oz candied orange peel, diced
160 g/5½ oz plain dessert chocolate, crushed or coarsely grated
1 tsp icing sugar

Cream the butter with the sugar until pale. Beat in the eggs one at a time. Stir in the flour sifted with the baking powder and spices, then add the milk. Mix in the ground hazelnuts, raisins, orange peel and chocolate until well combined. Spoon the mixture into the prepared cake tin and smooth level.

Bake in the preheated oven until the cake is just shrinking from the sides of the tin. Cool in the tin for 5 minutes then turn out on to a wire rack to cool. Dust with sieved icing sugar before serving.

CHOCOLATE RUM TRUFFLE CAKE

Two layers of chocolate almond cake sandwiched with a truffle filling and decorated with twelve chocolate rum truffles. Ideal for a special tea-time or for serving with coffee at the end of a meal.

Oven: 180 °C / 350 °F / gas mark 4 ♦ *Baking time: 25–30 minutes*
Equipment: two 20 cm / 8 in. sponge sandwich tins – buttered and base-lined
Makes: 12-portion cake

200 g / 7 oz plain dessert chocolate
120 g / 4 oz dark muscovado sugar
120 g / 4 oz butter ♦ 3 eggs
90 g / 3 oz self-raising flour ♦ 60 g / 2 oz ground almonds

frosting and filling:
200 g / 7 oz plain dessert chocolate ♦ 200 ml / 7 fl oz single cream
2 tbs dark rum ♦ 2 tbs dark cocoa powder

Break the chocolate into pieces in a mixing bowl and melt in a microwave or a warm oven. Sift the sugar into the bowl and add the butter. Use an electric beater to mix the ingredients together until light and fluffy. Mix in the eggs, one at a time, and stir in the sifted flour, then the ground almonds. Divide the mixture between the prepared cake tins and smooth level.

Bake in the preheated oven until a wooden skewer comes out clean from the centre of each cake. Cool in the tin for 2 minutes then turn the cakes on to a wire rack and remove the lining paper. Leave the cakes upside down to cool.

To make the frosting and filling: break the chocolate into pieces and melt with the cream in a mixing bowl. Stir gently until well combined then mix in the rum. Scoop 4 tablespoons of the mixture on to a saucer and set aside.

Allow the mixture to cool slightly then use an electric beater to mix for 4–5 minutes until the chocolate cream is lighter and thicker – take care not to over-beat. Use about three-quarters of the cream to sandwich the two layers and cover the side of the cake. Chill the the rest of the chocolate cream until firm.

[148]

To make the chocolate truffles: take a rounded teaspoonful of the chocolate cream and gently shape into a truffle-size ball with your hands, then roll it in the cocoa powder and set aside. Repeat with the rest of the mixture to make 12 truffles. Warm the saucer of chocolate until liquid and spread over the top of the cake. Arrange the truffles around the edge of the cake and set aside in a cold place until ready to serve.

RUM, BANANA AND CHOCOLATE CAKE

A wholemeal flour chocolate cake enlivened with rum and bananas.

Oven: 180°C/350°F/gas mark 4 ♦ Baking time: 40 minutes
Equipment: 23 cm/9 in. square tin – buttered and base-lined
Makes: 16–25 pieces

2 large bananas ♦ 2 tbs dark Jamaican rum
300 g/10 oz plain dessert chocolate ♦ 175 g/6 oz unsalted butter
120 g/4 oz dark muscovado sugar ♦ 3 eggs
200 g/7 oz self-raising wholemeal flour
¼ tsp ground cinnamon

Peel the bananas and slice them into a bowl. Add the rum and stir to coat the fruit. Break 200 g/7 oz of the chocolate into pieces in a bowl and melt in a microwave oven or over simmering water. Chop the remaining 90 g/3 oz of chocolate into small pieces.

Cream the butter with the sieved sugar until light and fluffy. Gradually beat in the eggs, the melted chocolate, the flour and cinnamon. Finally fold in the bananas and the chopped chocolate. Turn the mixture into the prepared cake tin and smooth level.

Bake in a preheated oven until the cake is springy in the centre. Cool in the tin, then transfer to a wooden board or a flat plate to cut into fingers or squares. If you wish to serve the cake warm, accompany with crème fraîche or clotted cream.

CHILDREN'S CHOCOLATE CAKE

Although perfectly fine for adults to prepare, this cake is ideal for children to make because it's chilled rather than baked. Dark plain dessert chocolate works well, though two bars of intense orange chocolate with one bar of whole hazelnut chocolate produces an excellent flavour.

Equipment: 20 cm / 8 in. diameter, spring-clip cake tin – buttered and base-lined; plus large mixing bowl, wooden spoons, and one or more children
Makes: 12–16-portion cake

300 g / 10 oz plain dessert chocolate ♦ 100 g / 3½ oz butter
200 g / 7 oz plain digestive biscuits ♦ 120 g / 4 oz glacé cherries, halved
120 g / 4 oz candied orange and lemon peel, diced
120 g / 4 oz seedless raisins
120 g / 4 oz mixed nuts – pecans, almonds, hazelnuts, halved
1 tsp icing sugar

Break the chocolate into pieces and tip into a heat-proof mixing bowl. Melt the chocolate in a microwave oven or over simmering water. Remove from the heat and cool slightly before adding the butter in pieces. Stir gently to mix.

Break each biscuit into three or four pieces and add to the chocolate with all the other ingredients: glacé cherries, candied peel, raisins and nuts. Stir until the ingredients are well distributed. Spoon the mixture into the prepared cake tin and smooth level.

Place in a refrigerator for 2 hours or overnight until firm. Wrap a hot, dry cloth around the tin for a few minutes, then open the clip and lift off the curved side.

Transfer the cake – leaving it on the base of the tin, if you wish – to a flat serving plate or board. Spoon the icing sugar into a small sieve and tap it gently with the spoon as you move it across the top of the cake to give a snowy dusting. Use a long, sharp knife to cut the cake into portions.

CHOCOLATE CUP CAKES

Because my brothers and I were brought up with home-made cakes, bought ones inevitably acquired an irresistible appeal. Occasionally an aunt arrived with some shop cakes in a square white box tied with paper ribbon, and at tea-time the delicacies were demolished with gusto. We all loved the chocolate cup cakes in silver paper cases – especially nibbling off the rime of icing on the edge. I've always found them a sure-fire winner on a fund-raising cake stall.

Oven: 180°C/350°F/gas mark 4 ♦ Baking time: 25 minutes
Equipment: patty tins lined with fluted foil or paper cake cases
Makes: 18 cakes

3 tbs cocoa powder ♦ 2 tbs hot water ♦ 120 g / 4 oz butter
120 g / 4 oz light muscovado or caster sugar ♦ 2 eggs
120 g / 4 oz self-raising flour ♦ ½ tsp baking powder

icing:
120 g / 4 oz plain dessert chocolate, melted
54 Smarties or chocolate drops (optional)

In a mixing bowl, blend the cocoa with the hot water until smooth. Add the remaining ingredients and beat together for 1 minute. Place a rounded dessertspoonful of mixture in each paper case.

Bake in the preheated oven for 25 minutes until the cakes are risen and firm to the touch. Cool the cakes in the baking tin.

Break the chocolate into pieces in a bowl and melt in a microwave oven or over simmering water. Spoon chocolate over the top of each cake. Decorate with Smarties or chocolate drops and leave until the chocolate has set.

CHOCOLATE HONEY FUDGE SQUARES

Squares of dark chocolate cake topped with honey fudge frosting and choco-late chips – a natural partner for espresso coffee.

Oven: 180°C/350°F/gas mark 4 ♦ *Baking time: 25–30 minutes*
Equipment: 20 cm/8 in. square tin – buttered and base-lined
Makes: 16 squares

30 g/1 oz cocoa powder ♦ 4 tbs hot water
120 g/4 oz dark muscovado sugar ♦ 120 g/4 oz butter
2 eggs ♦ 120 g/4 oz self-raising flour

frosting:
120 g/4 oz pale muscovado sugar ♦ 60 g/2 oz butter
2 tbs honey ♦ 1 tbs milk ♦ 30 g/1 oz chocolate chips

Blend the cocoa with the hot water in a mixing bowl. Sieve the sugar into the bowl and add the butter, eggs and flour. Use an electric beater to mix for 1–2 minutes until smooth. Spoon the mixture into the prepared cake tin and smooth level.

Bake in the preheated oven until springy in the centre and just starting to shrink from the tin. Cool in the tin.

To make the frosting: sift the sugar into a small pan and add the butter, honey and milk. Stir over low heat until the mixture is smooth. Bring the frosting to the boil and allow to bubble steadily for 1 minute. Remove from the heat and stand the pan in cold water for 2 minutes, stirring all the time. Spoon the frosting over the cake and sprinkle the chocolate chips on top. Set aside until the frosting has set then cut into 16 squares.

CHOCOLATE NUT SLICES

Pastry layers enclose the buttery, chocolate nut filling.

Oven: 200°C/400°F/gas mark 6 ♦ Baking time: 35 minutes
Equipment: Swiss roll tin about 30 x 20 cm/12 x 8in – buttered
Makes: 18 squares

pastry:
400 g/14 oz plain flour ♦ 200 g/7 oz butter ♦ 6 tbs cold water

filling:
100 g/3½ oz butter ♦ 100 g/3½ oz light muscovado sugar
1 tbs plain flour ♦ 4 tbs cocoa powder ♦ pinch of ground cinnamon
120 g/4 oz mixed unsalted nuts, coarsely chopped

sugar crust:
1 tbs milk ♦ 1 tbs caster sugar

Sift the flour into a bowl and rub in the butter until the mixture resembles breadcrumbs. Add the water and mix to a soft dough. Wrap the pastry in plastic and chill in the fridge while preparing the filling.

In a pan, gently melt the butter with the sugar, flour, cocoa powder and cinnamon, then stir in the chopped nuts. When thick and well combined, remove from the heat and cool the mixture by standing the pan in cold water.

Divide the pastry in half, and roll out one piece to line the base and sides of the prepared tin. Spread the filling over the pastry. Roll out the other half to cover the filling, pressing the edges together. Brush the milk over the pastry and sprinkle with the sugar, then prick all over with a fork.

Bake in the preheated oven until the pastry is golden brown. Cool in the tin for 5 minutes, then cut into squares or triangles. Remove from the tin when completely cool.

CANADIAN BROWNIES

Another of my mother's well-tested recipes – in her sixty years of baking she produced thousands of these brownies, which are crumbly rather than gooey.

Oven: 180°C/350°F/gas mark 4 ♦ Baking time: 25–30 minutes
Equipment: 18 cm/7 in. square shallow tin – well buttered
Makes: 16 pieces

60 g/2 oz plain dessert chocolate ♦ 60 g/2 oz butter
1 egg ♦ 120 g/4 oz light muscovado sugar
¼ tsp vanilla essence ♦ 90 g/3 oz plain flour
60 g/2 oz pecans or walnuts, sliced or roughly chopped
30 g/1 oz glacé cherries, sliced

Break the chocolate into pieces and melt with the butter in a small bowl in a microwave oven or over simmering water. Remove from the heat and allow to cool slightly. In a mixing bowl, whisk the egg with the sugar and vanilla essence until frothy. Stir in the melted chocolate and butter and fold in the sifted flour with nuts and cherries. Pour the mixture into the prepared cake tin.

Bake in the preheated oven until a knife blade comes out clean from the centre. Cool in the tin for 15 minutes then cut into 16 squares. Remove and serve the brownies while still warm or leave to cool in the tin.

CHAPTER SIX

Spice Cakes and Nut Cakes

THE CONTENTS OF THIS CHAPTER

1. Devonshire Honey Spice Cake
2. Truly Ginger Cake
3. Frosted Carrot Cake
4. Poppy Seed Cake filled with Lemon Curd
5. Grasmere Gingerbread
6. Spiced Seville Marmalade Cake
7. Caraway Seed Loaf
8. Apricot, Pine Nut and Cardamom Cake
9. Iced Gingerbread
10. Pumpkin, Rice and Maple Syrup Cake
11. χ Hot Cinnamon and Pecan Nut Cake
12. Angelica and Almond Cake
13. χ French Coffee Walnut Cake
14. Coconut and Cranberry Loaf
15. Honey, Pistachio and Yoghurt Cake
16. French Almond Cake
17. English Almond Cake
18. Hazelnut Cake with Port Wine Cream
19. Orange, Polenta and Almond Cake
20. Walnut Layer Cake with White Frosting
21. Pine Nut, Honey and Lemon Cake
22. Macadamia Nut Coffee Cake

He swallowed the tiny portion of almond cake which a maid had put in front of him and filled his pipe.

Georges Simenon, *Maigret Stonewalled,* 1931 (the first food enjoyed by the Chief Inspector in the earliest Maigret novel)

Could it be the chilly, damp climate of Britain that accounts for our fondness for spice? Sweet-tasting, warm-scented cinnamon, fragrant flecks of freshly-grated nutmeg or the heady, comforting flavour of cloves added to the mixing bowl that all transform the flavour of a cake to make it beguiling.

Our love affair with spices is long established, and gives many of our traditional cakes their particular character. The spiced and gilded gingerbread of medieval times was so highly valued it was awarded as a prize in jousting tournaments. In the past, when spices were costly, their use in cooking was an indicator of wealth; now, almost all spices are easily affordable. Saffron is the exception, remaining the world's most expensive due to the labour involved in collecting the flower stamens of *Crocus sativa.*

Spices are an essential ingredient in much of Britain's best-loved baking – from Easter biscuits to rich fruit cakes. Most fragrant when freshly ground, spices can be bought ready-ground for immediate use or whole for grinding at home in a mortar or electric coffee mill. Two exceptions are cinnamon bark and dried ginger root – both notoriously difficult to grind at home – so for use in baking I buy these ready-ground by the professionals.

As a way of imparting the allure of spices to the simplest of recipes, I recommend topping a plain cake with a spice-flecked crust and serving it warm on a winter day. In summer, this streusel mixture can be sprinkled over a fresh fruit cake full of cherries or apples. To make a *Streusel* crust, melt in a bowl or a pan 2 tablespoons of butter and remove from the heat, stir in 3 tablespoons light brown sugar, 1 tablespoon plain flour, 1 teaspoon ground cinnamon and half a teaspoon of ground allspice. Stir together until the mixture resembles breadcrumbs, then scatter over the cake or over an open fruit tart.

'Nuts,' wrote Alan Davidson, author of *The Oxford Companion to Food,* 'are festive, mysterious, symbolic, and supremely versatile.' Like spices, nuts were once an expensive ingredient only used in the cooking of the court. These days, a wide range – from brazils to pecans, pistachios to macadamia nuts – are easily available, with the best choice often to be found in health food stores.

For the best flavour and food value, nuts should be fresh. If they are left too long at room temperature, they can become rancid due to their high fat content. Use either freshly bought nuts, or store them in a freezer to maintain their flavour and prevent any deterioration.

Nuts in various forms, ground, slivered, chopped or whole – either blanched or toasted – contribute not just taste but also a rich moistness to a cake due to their oils. Almonds and hazelnuts are essential to the character of certain cakes from France and Austria, imparting their unique flavour and texture. When used in their ground form, they may partly or wholly replace the flour in a mixture. Moreover, the transformation in flavour that develops when blanched nuts such as almonds and hazelnuts are grilled or toasted is a quality that can be used to considerable advantage in cake-making.

Flour-free cakes may be of interest to coeliac sufferers. But since some people are dangerously allergic to nuts in any form, it is essential when serving or selling any cake to state clearly the nature of the ingredients.

DEVONSHIRE HONEY SPICE CAKE

In his student days my son used to make this cake for friends' birthdays. It is indeed very simple to prepare and can be mixed in a saucepan. A fellow bee-keeper gave me the recipe years ago. The Continental spice mixture I've added makes the cake reminiscent of French *pain d'épices*. However, the cake is still good even without the spices, or the icing.

Oven: 180°C / 350°F / gas mark 4 ♦ *Baking time: 45 minutes*
Equipment: 18–20 cm / 7–8 in. tin – buttered and base-lined
Makes: 8-portion cake

150 g / 5 oz butter ♦ 90 g / 3 oz light muscovado sugar
175 g / 6 oz honey ♦ 1 tbs water
2 eggs ♦ 200 g / 7 oz self-raising flour
½ tsp mixed sweet spices, ideally a French, Dutch or German blend

icing:
120 g / 4 oz icing sugar ♦ 1 tbs clear honey ♦ 1 tbs water

In a medium-size saucepan, gently heat the butter, sugar and honey with the water until the butter has melted. Immediately remove from the heat and beat in the eggs and the flour sifted with the spice. Pour the mixture into the prepared cake tin.

Bake in the preheated oven until the cake is just starting to shrink from the tin. Cool the cake in the tin and ice while still warm. Or turn the cake on to a wire rack and leave until cold.

To make the icing: sift the icing sugar into a bowl. Stir in the honey and water and mix until smooth. Trickle the icing over the cake in a trellis pattern.

TRULY GINGER CAKE

For ginger devotees, a rich, dark cake that includes the candied, fresh and ground forms of this versatile plant.

Oven: 160°C/325°F/gas mark 3 ♦ *Baking time: 60 minutes*
Equipment: 20 cm/8 in. square tin – buttered and base-lined
Makes: 16–24-portion cake

150 g/5 oz butter ♦ 150 g/5 oz dark muscovado sugar
265 g/9 oz black treacle ♦ 2 eggs
265 g/9 oz self-raising flour ♦ 1 tsp baking powder
2–3 tsp ground ginger, as preferred ♦ ½ tsp ground cinnamon
a knob of fresh ginger, walnut-size, peeled and grated
150 g/5 oz candied ginger, chopped
150 g/5 oz ready-to eat prunes or candied orange peel, chopped

Cream the butter with the sifted sugar until light, then mix in the treacle and beat in the eggs one at a time. Stir in the flour sifted with the baking powder, ground ginger and cinnamon, and mix in the fresh ginger, candied ginger and prunes or candied peel. When well combined, spoon the mixture into the prepared cake tin and smooth level.

Bake in the preheated oven until the cake is starting to shrink from the tin and a wooden skewer comes out clean from the centre. Cool the cake in the tin for 10 minutes then turn out on to a wire rack. Serve the cake warm or cold, cut into portions.

FROSTED CARROT CAKE

In the days when sugar was an expensive ingredient, cooks looked for alternatives to sweeten their baking. Parsnips and potatoes, pumpkin and marrow all found their way into cakes. Perhaps because it is the most successful, the longest survivor seems to be the carrot cake. My version has a light texture and delicately spiced flavour and is topped with the customary cream cheese frosting.

Oven: 180°C/350°F/gas mark 4 ♦ *Baking time: about 60 minutes*
Equipment: 23 cm/9 in. square tin – buttered and base-lined
Makes: 25 squares

150 g/5 oz butter ♦ 200 g/7 oz light muscovado sugar
175 g/6 oz carrots, peeled and finely grated
½ orange, finely grated zest ♦ 2 eggs
200 g/7 oz self-raising white flour
2 tsp baking powder ♦ 1 tsp ground cinnamon
½ tsp ground coriander ♦ ½ tsp grated nutmeg
½ tsp salt ♦ 120 g/4 oz seedless raisins
60 g/2 oz walnuts, chopped ♦ 3 tbs milk

frosting:
45 g/1½ oz cream cheese ♦ 175 g/6 oz icing sugar
1–2 drops vanilla essence or ¼ tsp finely grated zest of lemon

Melt the butter in a mixing bowl and beat in the sugar, carrots, orange zest and eggs. Fold in the flour sieved with the baking powder, spices and salt. Add the raisins, walnuts and milk and mix until well combined. Turn the mixture into the prepared cake tin and smooth level.

Bake in the preheated oven until the cake is springy in the middle and a wooden skewer comes out clean from the centre. Cool in the tin for 5 minutes then turn out on to a wire rack.

To make the frosting: beat the cream cheese until smooth, then gradually blend in the sifted icing sugar for a spreadable frosting. Add vanilla essence to taste. Spread over the cake and make a pattern of swirls with the knife. Set aside for 1–2 hours until the frosting has set, then cut the cake into squares.

POPPY SEED CAKE FILLED WITH LEMON CURD

Poppy seeds are rarely utilized in home-baking these days. Yet they contribute an unusual and delicate flavour which goes well with fresh lemon curd.

Oven: 350°F/180°C/Gas Mark 4 ♦ Baking time: 25 minutes
Equipment: two 23 cm/9 in. sponge sandwich tins – buttered and lined
Makes: 12-portion cake

120 g/4 oz blue poppy seeds ♦ 200 ml/7 fl oz milk
175 g/6 oz butter, softened ♦ 230 g/8 oz caster sugar
230 g/8 oz plain flour ♦ 2 tsp baking powder
½ tsp vanilla essence ♦ 4 egg whites ♦ 1 tsp icing sugar

lemon curd:
1 lemon ♦ 4 egg yolks ♦ ¼ tsp cornflour
60 g/2 oz caster sugar ♦ 60 g/2 oz unsalted butter

Stir the poppy seeds into the milk in a pan over moderate heat for 5 minutes, then set aside in a warm place, stirring now and then, until all the milk has been absorbed by the seeds.

Cream the butter with the sugar until light and fluffy. Sift the flour with the baking powder and gradually add to the butter mixture alternately with the poppy seed mixture and the vanilla essence. Whisk the egg whites until stiff and gently fold into the mixture using a balloon whisk. Divide the mixture between the prepared cake tins and smooth level.

Bake in the preheated oven until the cakes are springy to the touch and just shrinking away from the tins. Cool for 1 minute then transfer to a wire rack.

To make the lemon curd: use a wooden spoon or whisk to mix the strained juice of the lemon with the egg yolks, cornflour and sugar in the ceramic top of a double-boiler or in a bowl set over simmering water. Cook, stirring, for 10–15 minutes or until the mixture thickens. Remove from the heat and gradually beat in the butter, adding it in small pieces. Place the bowl in cold water to cool the curd, then sandwich the cake layers with it and sift the icing sugar over the top.

GRASMERE GINGERBREAD

A traditional recipe from the Lake District for a gingerbread whose crumbly texture is akin to Scottish shortbread.

Oven: 160 °C / 325 °F / gas mark 3 ♦ Baking time: 30 minutes
Equipment: 25 x 15 cm / 10 x 6 in. shallow tin – well-buttered
Makes: 16 pieces

120 g / 4 oz plain flour ♦ 120 g / 4 oz light muscovado sugar
¼ tsp baking powder ♦ 1 tsp ground ginger
60 g / 2 oz preserved ginger, chopped
120 g / 4 oz fine or medium oatmeal
½ lemon, finely grated zest ♦ ½ orange, finely grated zest
120 g / 4 oz butter, melted

Sift the flour, sugar, baking powder and ground ginger into a mixing bowl. Stir in the chopped ginger, oatmeal and grated citrus zest. Pour in the melted butter and quickly mix with a knife until slightly bound together but still crumbly. Turn the mixture into the prepared cake tin, smooth level with the back of a spoon then gently press down into the tin.

Bake in the preheated oven until golden. Remove from the oven and cut the gingerbread into 16 fingers. Leave to cool in the tin, then gently remove with a palette knife.

SPICED SEVILLE MARMALADE CAKE

A combination of orange, honey and spices gives this cake an attractive flavour.

Oven: 180°C/350°F/gas mark 4 ♦ Baking time: 60 minutes
Equipment: 20 cm/8 in. tin – buttered and base-lined
Makes: 8–10-portion cake

175 g/6 oz butter ♦ 175 g/6 oz honey
2 eggs ♦ 5 tbs Seville orange marmalade
175 g/6 oz self-raising wholemeal flour
175 g/6 oz self-raising white flour
½ tsp grated nutmeg ♦ ½ tsp ground cinnamon
¼ tsp ground cloves or allspice
3 tbs milk ♦ 2 tbs demerara sugar for top of cake

Cream the butter with the honey. Beat in the eggs, separately. Mix in the marmalade and the wholemeal flour. Sift the white flour with the spices and stir into the cake with the milk. Spoon the mixture into the prepared cake tin and smooth level. Sprinkle the demerara sugar over the top.

Bake in the preheated oven until the cake is cooked and just shrinking from the tin. Cool in the tin for 5 minutes then turn out on to a wire rack.

CARAWAY SEED LOAF

In *The Trumpet Major*, Thomas Hardy describes a seed-cake as 'so richly compounded that it opened to the knife like a freckled buttercup'. Seed cake dates back for centuries, notably in Scotland. Though not often baked these days, this cake with that pervading aniseed taste imparted by the seeds has a definite following.

Oven: 180 °C/350 °F/gas mark 4 ♦ Baking time: 50–60 minutes
Equipment: 1 kg/2 lb loaf tin – buttered and base-lined
Makes: 10–12-portion cake

175 g/6 oz butter ♦ 175 g/6 oz caster sugar
3 eggs ♦ 2–3 tsp caraway seeds, according to taste
200 g/7 oz plain flour ♦ 1 tsp baking powder
30 g/1 oz ground almonds ♦ 1 tbs milk

Cream the butter with the sugar until light and fluffy. Beat in the eggs one at a time then mix in the caraway seeds. Sift the flour with the baking powder and fold into the mixture with the ground almonds and the milk. Spoon the mixture into the prepared tin and smooth level.

Bake in the preheated oven until the cake is springy in the centre and a wooden skewer comes out clean. Cool in the tin for 3 minutes then turn out on to a wire rack.

APRICOT, PINE NUT AND CARDAMOM LOAF

The tiny black seeds of cardamom enclosed in their pale green pods carry a haunting scent of eucalyptus, a natural ally for apricots and pine nuts. But if you prefer a different spice, such as freshly grated nutmeg or ground mace, simply substitute it for the cardamom in the recipe. A long narrow loaf tin works well for this cake since it yields more slices.

Oven: 180°C/350°F/gas mark 4 ♦ Baking time: 60 minutes
Equipment: 26 x 12 cm/10 x 4½ in. loaf tin, capacity 1.5 l/2¾ pt
– buttered and base-lined
Makes: 12–16-portion cake

400 g/14 oz ready-to-eat dried apricots ♦ ½ orange, grated zest and juice
175 g/6 oz pale muscovado sugar ♦ 175 g/6 oz butter
3 eggs ♦ 6 cardamom pods, seeds finely crushed
175 g/6 oz self-raising flour ♦ 60 g/2 oz ground almonds
90 g/3 oz pine nuts

Use scissors to snip 60 g/2 oz of the apricots into small pieces straight into the bowl of a processor. Cut each of the remaining apricots into 4 slices. These should be left to steep in a bowl with the orange zest and juice. Measure 60 g/2 oz of the sugar into the processor, then operate it for 1–2 minutes until the fruit is finely chopped. Tip the contents into a mixing bowl, add the remaining sugar and the butter and beat together until pale and fluffy. Then you should beat in the eggs one at a time, before adding the crushed cardamom seeds. Fold the sieved flour and the ground almonds into the mixture alternately with the apricots steeped in orange juice. Finally, mix in the pine nuts. Spoon into the prepared tin and smooth level.

Bake in the preheated oven until the top of the loaf is springy and a wooden skewer comes out clean from the centre. Cool in the tin for 4 minutes then turn out on to a wire rack.

ICED GINGERBREAD

A light, well-flavoured gingerbread cake enhanced by the cinnamon icing.

Oven: 150°C/300°F/gas mark 2 ♦ Baking time: 1¼ hours
Equipment: 23 cm/9 in. square tin – buttered and lined
Makes: 25 squares

230 g/8 oz plain flour ♦ 1 tsp bicarbonate of soda
60 g/2 oz dark muscovado sugar ♦ 2 tsp mixed spice
3 tsp ground ginger ♦ 120 g/4 oz butter
175 g/6 oz black treacle ♦ 60 g/2 oz golden syrup
150 ml/5 fl oz milk ♦ 2 eggs

icing:
230 g/8 oz icing sugar ♦ ¼ tsp ground cinnamon
½ orange or lemon ♦ 1–2 tsp hot water
60 g/2 oz preserved or candied ginger

Sift the flour, bicarbonate of soda, sugar and spices into a mixing bowl. In a saucepan melt the butter with the treacle and syrup over low heat. Remove from the heat and stand the pan in a bowl of cold water to cool. Stir in the milk and the beaten eggs. Pour on to the dry ingredients and stir well until the mixture is smooth. Pour into the prepared cake tin.

Bake in the preheated oven until a wooden skewer comes out clean from the centre of the cake – during the baking ensure that the oven door is not opened during the first half of baking time or the cake could sink in the middle. Cool in the tin for 10 minutes then turn out on to a wire rack.

To make the icing: sift the icing sugar and cinnamon into a bowl and mix in the strained orange or lemon juice and just enough hot water to make a pouring consistency. Pour the icing over the top of the cake and decorate with pieces of preserved ginger. Leave the cake in a warm place for 1 hour for the icing to set. Serve cut into squares.

PUMPKIN, RICE AND MAPLE SYRUP CAKE

An autumn brunch cake, flavourful and fragrant with freshly grated nutmeg. If served as a pudding, accompany the warm cake with scoops of maple syrup or honey ice-cream.

Oven: 160°C/325°F/gas mark 3 ♦ Baking time: 1¼ – 1½ hours
Equipment: 18 cm/7 in. square tin, ideally with detachable base
– buttered and base-lined
Makes: 16-portion cake

450 g/1 lb pumpkin flesh, seeded and peeled ♦ 2 tbs water
175 g/6 oz long-grain white rice, dry weight (or 1 teacupful);
or 350 g/12 oz plain boiled rice
3 eggs, separated ♦ 1 egg white
120 g/4 oz caster sugar ♦ 120 g/4 oz butter
120 g/4 oz ground almonds ♦ 120 g/4 oz candied peel, chopped
¼ tsp freshly grated nutmeg ♦ ⅛ tsp ground allspice
3 tbs maple syrup

Chop the pumpkin and place in a saucepan with the water. Cover and bring to the boil, turn down the heat and cook for 20–30 minutes until the pumpkin is tender. Line a colander with 2 layers of kitchen paper and tip in the contents of the saucepan. Leave for 5 minutes until the surplus liquid has drained away. Return the pumpkin to the pan and use a potato masher to crush the pumpkin to a purée, then set aside to cool.

Meanwhile wash the rice under running water, drain well and place in a pan with an equal quantity of cold water. Bring to the boil and stir. Cover the pan and cook on moderate heat for 18–20 minutes until tender, when all the water should have been absorbed by the rice. Cool the boiled rice.

Whisk the egg whites until stiff, then whisk in half the sugar. In a separate mixing bowl, beat the butter with the remaining sugar until light and fluffy. Mix in the egg yolks, almonds, pumpkin purée, rice and candied peel with the spices. Gradually fold in the egg white. Pour the mixture into the prepared cake tin and smooth level.

Bake in the preheated oven until a wooden skewer comes out clean from the centre and the cake is just starting to shrink from the tin. Cool the cake in the tin for 5 minutes then brush the maple syrup over the top. Leave for 20 minutes then transfer the cake to a flat serving plate or board and cut into slices or squares. Serve the cake warm.

HOT CINNAMON AND PECAN NUT CAKE

A batter-based cake with a streusel top, at its best served straight from the oven accompanied by a bowl of thick, cool cream.

Oven: 180 °C / 350 °F / gas mark 4 ♦ Baking time: 30–35 minutes
Equipment: 18 cm / 7 in. square tin – buttered and base-lined
Makes: 16 squares

350 g / 12 oz plain white flour ♦ 175 g / 6 oz caster sugar
2 tsp baking powder ♦ ½ tsp finely grated lemon zest
1 egg ♦ 175 ml / 6 fl oz milk
60 ml / 2 fl oz sunflower oil

streusel layer:
90 g / 3 oz butter, melted ♦ 100 g / 3½ oz dark muscovado sugar
½ tsp ground cinnamon ♦ 60 g / 2 oz pecan nut halves

Sieve the flour, sugar and baking powder into a bowl. Mix together the lemon zest, egg, milk and oil, pour on to the dry ingredients and beat together until smooth. Pour into the prepared cake tin. Pour the melted butter on top and sprinkle over the sugar sifted with the cinnamon. Distribute the nuts over the mixture, slightly pressing them into the streusel layer.

Bake in the preheated oven until a wooden skewer comes out clean from the centre of the cake. Cool in the tin for 5 minutes then cut into squares and serve plain or with cream.

ANGELICA AND ALMOND CAKE

The candied stalks of the herb angelica, used as an ingredient rather than as a decoration, are largely neglected these days. This lovely aromatic cake with its macaroon crust exploits angelica's distinctive flavour.

Oven: 180 °C / 350 °F / gas mark 4 ♦ Baking time: 50–60 minutes
Equipment: 20 cm / 8 in. spring-clip tin – buttered and base-lined
Makes: 8–12-portion cake

120 g / 4 oz butter, softened ♦ 120 g / 4 oz caster sugar
3 eggs ♦ 1 drop of bitter almond essence
150 g / 5 oz self-raising flour
60 g / 2 oz ground almonds
120 g / 4 oz candied angelica, chopped
60 g / 2 oz candied orange peel, chopped

macaroon layer:
90 g / 3 oz caster sugar ♦ 90 g / 3 oz ground almonds
30 g / 1 oz blanched slivered almonds

Cream the butter with the sugar until light and fluffy. Gradually beat in 2 eggs and the yolk of the third – reserve the remaining egg white in a bowl. Mix in the flour and the ground almonds and fold in the angelica and orange peel.

Spoon the mixture into the prepared cake tin and spread level. Whisk the reserved egg white until stiff, then fold in the sugar and the ground almonds. Spread over the cake mixture and sprinkle the slivered almonds on top.

Bake in the preheated oven until the cake is cooked, when a wooden skewer comes out clean from the centre. Halfway through the baking, place a sheet of paper (a large brown envelope works well) over the cake to prevent the almonds from browning too much.

Cool the cake in the tin for 3 minutes then unclip and remove the side of the tin and transfer the cake, still on its base, to a serving plate or a wire rack. Serve warm or cool.

FRENCH COFFEE WALNUT CAKE

The new season's walnuts from Grenoble arrive in early autumn when their flavour is still mild and sweet. This is the coffee walnut cake that I bake in France.

Oven: 180°C/350°F/gas mark 4 ♦ Baking time: 45–50 minutes
Equipment: 20 cm/8 in. spring-clip tin – buttered and base-lined
Makes: 10–12-portion cake

175 g/6 oz butter ♦ 175 g/6 oz light soft brown sugar
3 eggs ♦ 200 g/7 oz self-raising flour
90 g/3 oz walnuts, coarsely chopped
2 tbs strong black coffee ♦ ¼ tsp vanilla essence

coffee butter cream:
90 g/3 oz butter ♦ 90 g/3 oz caster sugar
90 ml/3 fl oz strong black coffee, tepid ♦ 10–12 walnut halves

Cream the butter with the sugar until light and fluffy. Beat in the eggs, one at a time. Fold in the sifted flour alternately with the walnuts, coffee, and vanilla essence until well mixed. Spoon the mixture into the prepared cake tin and smooth level.

Bake in the preheated oven until golden brown and just starting to shrink from the tin. Cool in the tin for 5 minutes, then unclip and remove the side of the cake tin and transfer the cake to a wire rack to cool.

To make the coffee butter cream: blend the butter with the sugar using a hand-held electric mixer until light and fluffy. Gradually beat in the coffee, a tablespoon at a time. The finished butter cream should be completely smooth and have a good coffee flavour.

Spread the butter cream over the sides and top of the cake. Use the blade of a knife to make a swirled design. Arrange the walnut halves around the edge of the cake and set aside in a cold place – ideally overnight – before serving.

COCONUT AND CRANBERRY LOAF

The refreshingly sharp flavour of dried cranberries complements the sweetness of desiccated coconut. Allow this cake to cool completely before cutting into slices with a serrated knife.

Oven: 180°C/350°F/gas mark 4 ♦ Baking time: 55–60 minutes
Equipment: 1 kg/2 lb loaf tin – buttered and base-lined
Makes: 10-portion cake

120 g/4 oz butter ♦ 120 g/4 oz caster sugar
2 eggs ♦ 2 tbs milk
150 g/5 oz self-raising flour
60 g/2 oz grated dried coconut ♦ 60 g/2 oz shaved dried coconut
90 g/3 oz dried cranberries

Set aside for the top of the cake 1 tablespoon each of the sugar, shaved coconut and cranberries.

Cream the butter with the rest of the sugar until light and creamy. Beat in the eggs one at a time, then the milk. Stir in the flour, both kinds of coconut and the cranberries. Spoon the mixture into the prepared cake tin and smooth level. Sprinkle the reserved coconut, cranberries and then the sugar over the top of the cake.

Bake in the preheated oven until the cake is shrinking from the sides of the tin and a wooden skewer comes out clean from the centre. Cool the cake in the tin for 5 minutes then turn out on to a wire rack.

HONEY, PISTACHIO AND YOGHURT CAKE

The flavour of this cake develops nicely if made a day ahead of serving.

Oven: 180 °C / 350 °F / gas mark 4 ♦ Baking time: 40 minutes
Equipment: 20 cm / 8 in. spring-clip tin – buttered and base-lined
Makes: 8–10-portion cake

60 g / 2 oz butter ♦ 100 g / 3½ oz clear honey
3 eggs, separated ♦ 100 g / 3½ oz light soft brown sugar
150 ml / 5 fl oz natural yoghurt
175 g / 6 oz plain flour ♦ 1 tsp bicarbonate of soda
90 g / 3 oz shelled unsalted pistachio nuts, halved

icing:
100 g / 3½ oz icing sugar ♦ 1 tbs honey
¼ tsp vanilla essence ♦ 2–3 tsp hot water

Cream the butter and honey together. Beat in the egg yolks, sugar and yoghurt. Mix in the flour sifted with the bicarbonate of soda. Reserve 1 tablespoon of pistachio nuts for decoration, and stir the remainder into the mixture. Whisk the egg whites until stiff and fold in carefully. Spoon the mixture into the prepared tin and smooth level. Bake in the preheated oven until the cake is just shrinking from the tin. Cool for 5 minutes then carefully remove the sides of the tin.

To make the icing: while the cake is still warm, sift the icing sugar into a bowl and stir in the honey, vanilla essence and just enough hot water to make a pouring consistency. Mix the icing until smooth, then spoon over the cake and let it run down the sides. Chop the reserved pistachios and sprinkle over the top. Set the cake aside until the icing is set.

FRENCH ALMOND CAKE

A perfect almond cake – just almonds, eggs and sugar. *Tout simple.* Very good served warm accompanied by fresh raspberries and crème fraîche.

Oven: 180 °C / 350 °F / gas mark 4 ♦ *Baking time: 25–30 minutes*
Equipment: 20 cm / 8 in. spring-clip tin – buttered and base-lined
Makes: 8–10-portion cake

5 eggs, separated ♦ 200 g / 7 oz caster sugar
200 g / 7 oz ground almonds ♦ 1 tsp icing sugar (optional)

Beat the egg yolks with the sugar until light and foamy. Gradually mix in the ground almonds. In a separate bowl, whisk the egg whites until stiff. Gently fold into the almond mixture, taking care not lose too much air. Turn the mixture into the prepared cake tin and smooth level.

Bake in the preheated oven until the cake is springy in the centre. Cool in the tin for 10 minutes. Then carefully run a knife blade around the cake to loosen it, open the clip to release the sides of tin and slide the cake, on its baking paper, on to a wire rack to cool. Dust the top of the cake with sieved icing sugar if desired.

ENGLISH ALMOND CAKE

A light almond cake with a delicate flavour of sweet butter and ground almonds. Like many cakes, this one is most delectable when served warm.

Oven: 180 °C / 350 °F / gas mark 4 ♦ *Baking time: 30–35 minutes*
Equipment: 23 cm / 9 in. spring-clip tin – buttered and base-lined
Makes: 8-portion cake

120 g / 4 oz butter ♦ 90 g / 3 oz caster sugar ♦ 2 large eggs
1 drop vanilla essence ♦ 1–2 drops bitter almond essence
60 g / 2 oz unbleached self-raising flour ♦ 60 g / 2 oz ground almonds
30 g / 1 oz flaked almonds ♦ 30 g / 1 oz caster sugar

Cream the butter with the caster sugar until light and fluffy. Beat in the eggs separately with the vanilla and almond essences. Fold in the sieved flour and the ground almonds. Spoon into the prepared cake tin and smooth level. Mix the flaked almonds with the extra caster sugar and sprinkle evenly over the mixture.

Bake in the preheated oven until the cake is cooked and just beginning to shrink from the tin. Cool in the tin for 10 minutes then release the sides and slide the cake on its paper on to a wire rack.

HAZELNUT CAKE WITH PORT WINE CREAM

A single-layer nut cake topped with wine cream, suitable for serving at a buffet party.

Oven: 160 °C / 325 °F / gas mark 3 ♦ *Baking time: 30 minutes*
Equipment: 23 cm / 9 in. spring-clip tin – buttered and base-lined
Makes: 12-portion cake

100 g / 3½ oz hazelnuts, shelled but in their brown skins
60 g / 2 oz day-old white bread including crust ♦ 60 g / 2 oz cornflour
4 egg whites ♦ 230 g / 8 oz caster sugar

port wine cream:
160 g / 5½ oz butter ♦ 160 g / 5½ oz caster sugar
2 tbs very hot water ♦ 4–5 tbs tawny port
60 g / 2 oz plain dessert chocolate

Place the hazelnuts and the bread, cut into small pieces, in a processor and grind together until fine. Add the cornflour and process briefly to mix. Whisk the egg whites until stiff. Gradually whisk in half the sugar then whisk in the remainder. Fold in the hazelnut mixture. Spoon into the prepared cake tin, heaping the mixture slightly in the centre.

Bake in the preheated oven until a wooden skewer comes out clean from the centre of the cake. Allow to cool in the tin.

To prepare the wine cream: using a hand-held electric beater, blend the butter with the sugar until light and creamy. Gradually beat in the hot water and then the tawny port until you are happy with the flavour and the cream is completely smooth.

Transfer the cake to a flat serving dish and spread the cream over the top of the cake. Using a sharp potato peeler or a box grater, shave or grate the chocolate over the cream. Set aside for 1–2 hours before serving.

ORANGE, POLENTA AND ALMOND CAKE

A wheat-free cake made with maize flour or polenta and ground almonds; served with warm orange sauce and plain natural yoghurt.

Oven: 180 °C / 350 °F / gas mark 4 ♦ *Baking time: 45–50 minutes*
Equipment: 20 cm / 8 in. tin – buttered and base-lined
Makes: 8–10-portion cake

175 g / 6 oz butter ♦ 175 g / 6 oz golden caster sugar
1 orange, grated zest and juice ♦ 1 lemon, grated zest and juice
3 eggs ♦ 150 g / 5 oz fine maize / polenta flour
1 tsp baking powder
120 g / 4 oz ground almonds ♦ 30 g / 1 oz flaked almonds
100 g / 3½ oz candied orange and lemon peel, diced

orange sauce:
2 large oranges ♦ ½ tsp arrowroot ♦ sugar to taste
plain natural yoghurt for serving

Cream the butter with the sugar and grated orange and lemon zest until light and fluffy. Mix in the eggs beaten with the strained orange and lemon juice, and stir in the polenta, baking powder, the ground and flaked almonds, and candied peel. Spoon the mixture into the prepared baking tin and smooth level.

Bake in the preheated oven until a wooden skewer comes out clean from the centre. Allow the cake to cool slightly in the tin then turn on to a serving plate.

To make the sauce: squeeze the juice from the oranges, pour a little into a small pan and mix in the grated zest from half an orange and the arrowroot. Stir in the rest of the orange juice and cook over moderate heat, stirring all the time until the sauce has thickened. Sweeten to taste and pour into a small jug and keep warm. Serve the cake with the sauce poured over each portion and a spoonful of yoghurt.

WALNUT LAYER CAKE WITH WHITE FROSTING

I include this cake for old time's sake and in tribute to Helen Peacocke, long-established cookery writer for the *Oxford Times*. Some readers may share childhood memories of the tall walnut cake smothered with absurdly sweet white frosting which was served at Fuller's pink and white tea-shops – I fondly remember the Oxford one in Cornmarket – until they sadly disappeared. Of course, if you're too young to have visited Fuller's, you may prefer to sandwich the layers of walnut cake with coffee-flavoured whipped cream or mascarpone cheese instead.

Oven: 180°C/350°F/gas mark 4 ♦ Baking time: 25 minutes
Equipment: three 18 cm/7 in. sponge sandwich tins – buttered and base-lined
Makes: 8–10-portion cake

4 eggs ♦ 120 g/4 oz caster sugar ♦ 120 g/4 oz plain flour
1 tsp baking powder ♦ 150 g/5 oz walnuts, finely chopped but not ground
60 g/2 oz butter, melted ♦ ¼ tsp vanilla essence

frosting:
2 egg whites ♦ 350 g/12 oz caster sugar ♦ ¼ tsp cream of tartar
4 tbs hot water ♦ ¼ tsp vanilla essence ♦ 8 walnut halves

Whisk the eggs with the sugar using an electric mixer, or in a mixing bowl over hot water, until the beater leaves a trail across the surface of the mixture. Fold in the flour sieved with the baking powder alternately with the walnuts, butter and vanilla essence, taking care to retain as much air in the mixture as possible. Divide the mixture between the prepared cake tins and smooth level.

Bake in the preheated oven until the cakes are just starting to shrink. Cool in the tins for 2 minutes then turn on to a wire rack.

To make the frosting: whisk the egg whites with the sugar, cream of tartar and hot water in a large mixing bowl set over a pan of simmering water. This usually takes about 7 minutes, hence in North America the icing is known as seven-minute frosting. The frosting is ready when the meringue is really

SPICE CAKES AND NUT CAKES

thick and stands up in peaks. Remove the bowl from the heat, stand it on a damp cloth and continue whisking until the mixture is cool. Whisk in the vanilla essence. Sandwich the cakes with the frosting and use a palette knife to spread the remainder over the top and sides of the cake making a pattern of big swirls. Decorate the top with the walnut halves and set aside in a warm place for 1–2 hours for the frosting to set.

PINE NUT, HONEY AND LEMON CAKE

Dark amber-coloured honey from Greece imparts its unique resinous flavour to this nut cake.

Oven: 180 °C / 350 °F / gas mark 4 ♦ Baking time: 40–45 minutes
Equipment: 18–20 cm / 7–8 in. spring-clip tin – buttered and base-lined
Makes: 8-portion cake

120 g / 4 oz butter ♦ 60 g / 2 oz golden caster sugar
60 g / 2 oz Greek honey ♦ 1 lemon, finely grated zest
2 eggs ♦ 120 g / 4 oz self-raising flour
60 g / 2 oz ground almonds ♦ 75 g / 2½ oz pine nuts

Beat the butter with the sugar and honey until light and smooth. Gradually mix in the lemon zest and the eggs. Stir in the flour and ground almonds. Reserve 1 tablespoon of pine nuts and stir the rest into the mixture.

Spoon the mixture into the prepared tin, smooth level and scatter the reserved pine nuts over the top.

Bake in the preheated oven until golden brown and a wooden skewer comes out clean from the centre. Cool in the tin for 5 minutes then open the clip and remove the side of the tin to allow the cake to cool.

MACADAMIA NUT COFFEE CAKE

A single-layer coffee-flavoured cake covered with crunchy macadamia nuts. Pecan nut halves can be used instead, if you wish. Cut this cake into squares for serving.

Oven: 180 °C / 350 °F / gas mark 4 ♦ *Baking time: 30–35 minutes*
Equipment: 28 x 18 x 4 cm / 11 x 7 x 1½ in. shallow tin
– buttered and base-lined
Makes: 21 squares

2 tbs ground coffee ♦ 6 tbs milk ♦ 150 g / 5 oz butter
150 g / 5 oz light soft brown sugar ♦ 3 eggs
230 g / 8 oz self-raising flour ♦ 30 g / 1 oz ground almonds
150 g / 5 oz macadamia nuts ♦ 1 tsp icing sugar

Infuse the coffee in the milk in a small pan over low heat and bring almost to the boil. Remove the pan from the heat, stir and leave for 5 minutes then strain through a fine sieve into a cup.

Measure the butter into a mixing bowl and sift the sugar on top. Take a tablespoon of the sugar and keep aside. Cream the butter with the rest of the sugar until light and fluffy. Separate one egg and reserve the white in a small mixing bowl. Beat in the remaining yolk and the other two eggs to the butter and sugar, adding a little flour to prevent the mixture from separating. Then fold in the remaining flour with the strained coffee milk. Spoon the mixture into the prepared cake tin and spread level. Whisk the egg white until stiff then whisk in the reserved sugar. Fold the ground almonds into this meringue and spread over the cake mixture. Scatter the macadamia nuts in a single layer on top.

Bake the cake in the preheated oven until golden brown and just starting to shrink from the tin. Cool in the tin for 30 minutes then dust with sieved icing sugar. Cut the cake into squares in the tin and serve warm or at room temperature.

CHAPTER SEVEN

Small Cakes and Pastries

THE CONTENTS OF THIS CHAPTER

The little cakes were delicious. The tea, one of Madame's few self-indulgences, was of the finest in all Europe, or even China.

M.F. K. Fisher, *Sister Age,* 1983

From madeleines to éclairs, meringues to curd tarts, small individual cakes have great charm. Arrayed on cake-stands at the Ritz and Claridges, where afternoon tea is still taken seriously, these are the miniature versions of grander confections. Such delightful morsels rarely fail to enchant; the best exhibit a degree of finesse and precision. As an example of baking expertise, small cakes resemble the perfectly executed doll's-house-size chairs or cupboards once made by apprentice cabinet makers.

Cup cakes – single-portion cakes baked in a paper-lined patty or bun tin, and which in Britain were once known as fairy cakes – have become immensely popular. Easy to make and highly profitable to sell, cup cakes naturally appeal to children, and even adults have been known to buy a single cup cake to enjoy as a secret indulgence. A good one has a balanced proportion of cake to decoration, yet some produced commercially are so sparing with the cake and overloaded with frosting that they are just an excuse to eat sugar.

The flavour of a small cake should be quite distinctive, each dainty mouthful a pleasure to savour. If you enjoy decorating cakes, then making a small cake look irresistible – almost an edible jewel – is a happy challenge.

And if you wish to explore doll-size cakes even further, try making more diminutive versions of small cakes and pastries for serving on a pretty plate as *petits fours* at the end of a meal.

One of the merits of small cakes is that most of them freeze perfectly, but reach room temperature in less time than it takes to bake another batch. Moreover, if you keep several kinds in separate containers in the freezer, a plate of assorted marvels can be assembled quite quickly.

Individual sweet pastry cases can be baked and stored in the freezer until needed. By the time you've filled each of them with cream and fresh fruit, the pastry will have defrosted nicely. And trays of plain cup cakes also freeze well; they can be iced or covered with frosting just before serving.

A particular small favourite of my childhood that I remember with affection and almost Proustian clarity was known as a 'Kunzle' cake, after the name of the company who produced them. These were the only cakes my mother was prepared to buy – everything else was home-made. Their defining characteristic was the chocolate case containing sponge cake overlaid with rich butter cream. 'Reconstitution of the past is a delicate pleasure of which one should not be deprived,' wrote Pierre de Pressac. Nostalgia has led me to create my own version of the little 'Kunzle' cake of long ago; I have called them Chocolate Dreams.

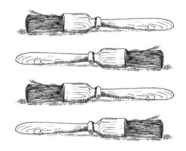

MADELEINES

It is possible that the legendary little cakes baked by Françoise and offered the young Marcel Proust by his aunt Léonie at Combray were made to this recipe from the popular nineteenth-century cookery book, *La Cuisinière de la campagne et de la ville* by Louis-Eustache Audot. It's an appealing notion because this version is both simple and delightful. Serve the madeleines freshly baked – with lime tea, of course.

Oven: 180°C/350°F/gas mark 4 ◆ Baking time: 15 minutes
Equipment: madeleine tin with shell-shaped moulds, preferably non-stick
– brushed with clarified butter
Makes: 24 cakes

60 g / 2 oz butter ◆ 150 g / 5 oz caster sugar
½ lemon, finely grated zest ◆ 3 eggs, separated ◆ 1 tsp orange flower water
120 g / 4 oz plain fine white cake flour, preferably French
1 tbs clarified butter, melted for brushing cake tins

Cream the butter in a warmed bowl and gradually beat in the sugar with the lemon zest. Beat in the egg yolks with the orange flower water. Whisk the egg whites until stiff and fold into the mixture alternately with the sieved flour.

Brush the shaped moulds of the cake tin with clarified butter. Place a rounded teaspoon of the mixture in each and smooth fairly level.

Bake in the preheated oven until golden and the little cakes are just starting to shrink from the tin. Cool in the tin for 1 minute, then transfer to a wire rack. Wash the tin with hot water only, dry and brush with more clarified butter and make the second batch of cakes with the remaining mixture.

LIME CURD TARTS

When, in the eighteenth century, the Royal Navy replaced the daily issue of lemons – given to sailors to prevent scurvy – with cheaper limes, English sailors were dubbed 'Limeys', a nickname which survived until fairly recently. These tarts have an attractive fresh citrus flavour.

Oven: 200 °C / 400 °F / gas mark 6, then 180 °C / 350 °F / gas mark 4
Baking time: 10–12 minutes
Equipment: 7.5 cm / 3 in. fluted pastry cutter; patty tins, buttered
Makes: 18 tarts

pastry:
175 g / 6 oz plain flour ♦ 30 g / 1 oz caster sugar .
90 g / 3 oz butter, softened ♦ 1 egg yolk

lime curd filling:
2 limes ♦ 2 large eggs
90 g / 3 oz caster sugar ♦ 60 g / 2 oz butter, softened or melted

Sieve the flour and sugar into a shallow mixing bowl or on to a cold work surface. Add the butter and egg yolk and use the fingertips to mix the ingredients together. Slide small handfuls of the mixture sideways until the dough easily forms a ball. Wrap the pastry in plastic and chill for 15 minutes. On a lightly floured board, roll out the pastry thinly and use the cutter to make 18 circles to line the prepared patty tins. Prick the bases and chill for 15 minutes while you prepare the filling.

Bake the pastry cases blind in the preheated oven for 6–7 minutes until the pastry is set and is starting to change colour at the edge. Remove from the oven and lower the heat as above.

Wash and dry the limes. Finely grate the zest into a bowl and add the strained juice. Beat in the eggs, sugar and butter. Spoon the filling into the pastry cases and bake for 5–6 minutes until the filling is set. Cool slightly, then carefully transfer the tarts from the patty tins to a wire rack.

QUEEN CAKES

Light, dainty cakes, traditionally scented with mace and studded with currants. The earliest recipe that I've found appears in a manuscript cookery book inscribed by 'Radolphus Ayres Cook Oxford 1721'. This manuscript was published in facsimile by the Bodleian Library in 2006.

Oven: 180°C/350°F/gas mark 4 ◆ Baking time: 15–20 minutes
Equipment: patty tins – buttered or lined with paper cases
Makes: about 18 cakes

120 g / 4 oz butter ◆ 120 g / 4 oz caster sugar ◆ 2 eggs
½ lemon or small orange, finely grated zest
175 g / 6 oz self-raising flour ◆ generous pinch ground mace
120 g / 4 oz currants ◆ milk to mix ◆ 1 tbs granulated sugar

Cream the butter and sugar until light and fluffy. Beat in the eggs one at a time with the grated lemon zest, adding a little flour if need be to prevent the mixture from separating. Fold in half the sifted flour, then the remainder with the ground mace and currants, adding a little milk to make a fairly soft consistency. Spoon dessertspoonfuls of the mixture into the prepared patty tins or paper cases. Sprinkle a little granulated sugar over the top of each.

Bake in the preheated oven until well risen with a golden crust. Cool in the tin for 2 minutes then transfer the cakes to a wire rack to cool.

JAPONAIS CAKES

This version of these delightful little cakes is far easier to make at home than those perfectly shaped ones produced by a professional pâtisserie. Shelled but still brown-skinned hazelnuts are now available ready-ground though, of course, the flavour is more intense if you grind your own in a processor as you need them.

Oven: 160°C/325°F/gas mark 3 ♦ Baking time: 25–30 minutes
Equipment: baking sheets, lined ♦ Makes: 12 cakes

2 egg whites ♦ 120 g / 4 oz caster sugar
1 tbs cornflour ♦ 60 g / 2 oz ground hazelnuts

butter icing:
90 g / 3 oz butter ♦ 120 g / 4 oz icing sugar
coffee essence to flavour ♦ 60 g / 2 oz melted chocolate (optional)

Whisk the egg whites until stiff. Sprinkle half the sugar over the meringue and whisk in. Sift the rest of the sugar with the cornflour and fold into the mixture with the ground hazelnuts until well combined. Use a dessertspoon to place spoonfuls, well spaced, on the prepared baking sheets, allowing 12 on each.

Bake in the preheated oven until just changing colour at the edges. Cool on the baking sheet for 5 minutes then use a palette knife to carefully transfer the cakes to a wire rack.

To make the butter icing: sift the icing sugar into a bowl, add the butter and cream together until smooth. Flavour to taste with coffee essence, adding a few drops at a time. Sandwich the cakes with the butter icing. Melted chocolate can be trickled over the top of each cake, if desired. Serve the cakes within an hour or so, before the meringue softens – otherwise freeze the cakes in an air-tight container until required.

BUTTER TARTS

One of my mother's Canadian specialities – crisp, spicy, and very good – and a family favourite for many years.

Oven: 190 °C /375 °F/gas mark 5 ♦ *Baking time: 20 minutes*
Equipment: 7.5 cm /3 in. fluted pastry cutter; patty tins – buttered
Makes: 15 tarts

shortcrust pastry:
175 g/ 6 oz plain flour ♦ 100 g / 3½ oz butter
2–3 tbs cold milk or water

filling:
60 g /2 oz butter ♦ 60 g /2 oz dark muscovado sugar
1 egg ♦ ½ tsp ground cinnamon
½ tsp mixed ground spice ♦ 90 g /3 oz currants

Sieve the flour into a mixing bowl. Rub in the butter and mix to a dough with the milk. Wrap and chill the dough while making the filling. Cream the butter and sifted sugar. Beat in the egg, cinnamon, mixed spice and currants.

On a lightly floured board, roll out the pastry until 3 mm /⅛ in. thick, cut out rounds of pastry and line the prepared patty tins. Place a heaped teaspoon of filling into each pastry case.

Bake in the preheated oven until the pastry is just changing colour. Cool the tarts in their patty tin for a few minutes then serve warm.

FLORENTINES

Almonds, cherries, angelica and chocolate are bound together with a layer of caramel – small, crisp and totally irresistible.

Oven: 180°C/350°F/gas mark 4 ♦ Baking time: 10–15 minutes
Equipment: non-stick baking sheet, buttered
Makes: 18 biscuits

45 g / 1½ oz butter ♦ 60 g / 2 oz caster sugar ♦ 15 g / ½ oz flour
1 tbs double cream ♦ 1 tsp lemon juice
60 g / 2 oz candied orange peel, chopped
60 g / 2 oz natural glacé cherries, sliced ♦ 30 g / 1 oz sultanas
15 g / ½ oz candied angelica, diced
60 g / 2 oz blanched almonds, slivered
175 g / 6 oz plain dessert chocolate

Melt the butter with the sugar in a pan over medium heat. Remove from the hob and beat in the sieved flour, cream and lemon juice. Stir in the orange peel, cherries, sultanas, angelica and almonds. Place rounded teaspoons of the mixture on the prepared baking sheet, allowing room for the biscuits to spread.

Bake in the preheated oven until golden brown, taking care not to over-cook or the flavour will be spoiled. Cool the biscuits on the baking sheet, then carefully transfer to a wire rack.

Break the chocolate into pieces and melt in a bowl in a microwave oven or over simmering water. Spread a thin layer of chocolate on the flat underside of each biscuit. When half-set, drag the prongs of a fork across the chocolate in a zig-zag pattern to give a combed effect. Leave the biscuits on a wire rack until set. If not for serving straight away, store the biscuits in an air-tight container to keep them crisp.

MARZIPAN TARTLETS FILLED WITH
SUMMER FRUITS AND FLOWERS

Making tartlet cases with home-made marzipan is a French practice dating at least from the great chef La Varenne's book *The French Cook* of 1651. Not only do they taste good but they are possibly less troublesome for some people than tackling pastry. Fill the baked cases with thick cream and top with summer fruits such as raspberries, blueberries and small edible flowers or petals.

Oven: 180°C/350°F/gas mark 4 ♦ Baking time: 12–15 minutes
Equipment: 6.5 cm/2½ in. fluted pastry cutter; two 12-cup patty tins – buttered
Makes: 24 tartlets

175 g/6 oz ground almonds ♦ 90 g/3 oz caster sugar
90 g/3 oz icing sugar ♦ 1 egg, beaten
1–2 tsp brandy or lemon juice ♦ 1–2 drops of bitter almond essence
1 tsp cornflour

filling:
300 ml/10 fl oz crème fraîche or whipped cream
350 g/12 oz raspberries or wild strawberries ♦ 150 g/5 oz blueberries
small edible flowers such as anchusa, forget-me-not, heart's-ease pansies,
petals of geranium or cottage pinks
1 tsp icing sugar

Measure the ground almonds and caster sugar into a bowl and add the sieved icing sugar. Mix in the egg, brandy and almond essence until the mixture forms a soft dough that can be shaped into a ball. Sprinkle some cornflour on to a work surface and roll out half the dough until 3 mm/⅛ in. thick. Use the pastry cutter to cut out 12 circles and place them in the prepared patty tins, pressing them gently into place. Prick the base of each two or three times with a fork. Repeat with the remaining marzipan.

Bake the cases in the preheated oven until just changing colour at the edges. Leave to cool in the tins, then use the blade of a small knife to gently transfer them to a wire rack or a serving plate.

Place a rounded teaspoon of cream into each case and arrange a selection of fruit and flowers on top. Dust lightly with icing sugar and serve within 2 hours.

ÉCLAIRS

Few people are not tempted by these delectable creations, light and puffy, filled with cream, and glossy with coffee and chocolate icing. Once you've mastered choux pastry, larger cakes beckon such as the Gâteau Paris-Brest on p. 252.

Oven: 220°C / 425°F / gas mark 7 ♦ Baking time: 25–30 minutes
Equipment: piping-bag fitted with 1 cm / ½ in. plain nozzle;
1 or 2 non-stick baking sheets
Makes: 12 éclairs

90 g / 3 oz plain flour ♦ pinch of salt ♦ 150 ml / 5 fl oz hot water
60 g / 2 oz butter ♦ 2 eggs, lightly beaten

cream filling:
300 ml / 10 fl oz whipping cream ♦ 1 tbs vanilla sugar

coffee icing:
90 g / 3 oz icing sugar ♦ 2–3 tsp strong black coffee

chocolate icing:
90 g / 3 oz strong plain chocolate ♦ 2 tbs cream

Sift the flour and salt on to a sheet of paper. Measure the water into a pan, add the butter in pieces and when melted bring the mixture to the boil. Remove from the heat and tip in the flour and salt, then beat the mixture with a wooden spoon over moderate heat for a few minutes until the paste forms a ball and leaves the sides of the pan. Remove from the heat. Gradually add the eggs, beating in each addition. Continue to beat the mixture for 1 minute until smooth and glossy.

Spoon the mixture into a piping-bag fitted with a plain 1 cm / ½ in. nozzle. For éclairs, pipe the mixture on to the prepared baking sheets to form 12 neat strips measuring 7.5 cm / 3 in. long – make sure they are well spaced to allow for expansion in the oven. Alternatively, to make cream puffs, place 12 or more rounded spoonfuls on the baking sheet.

Bake in the preheated oven until the pastry is puffed up and golden brown. Remove from the oven and immediately make a short cut on one side of each pastry to allow the steam to escape, then transfer the éclairs to a wire rack to cool.

For the cream filling: whisk the cream until stiff but still glossy and stir in the sugar. Spoon or pipe the cream into each éclair through the small side opening.

To make the coffee icing: sift the icing sugar into a bowl and mix in just enough coffee to make a smooth pouring consistency. Spread the coffee icing over half the filled éclairs and leave on a wire rack until set.

To make the chocolate frosting: break the chocolate into pieces and melt with the cream in a bowl in a microwave oven or set over simmering water. Stir until smooth then spoon over the remaining éclairs and set aside to cool. Serve the éclairs within 2 hours while the pastry is still crisp.

BUTTERFLY CAKES

Pretty little cup cakes that rarely fail to charm: children in particular like them. My 3 year-old grandson bent over the plate, carefully inspected the cakes, then asked, 'How did you catch them?' Butterfly cakes can be made in a variety of flavours: coffee, vanilla, almond, lemon, or – as in this recipe – tangerine.

Oven: 180°C/350°F/gas mark 4 ♦ *Baking time: 25 minutes*
Equipment: patty tins – lined with paper cases ♦ *Makes: 15–18 cakes*

120 g / 4 oz butter ♦ 120 g / 4 oz caster sugar
1 tangerine, finely grated zest and juice
2 eggs ♦ 150 g / 5 oz self-raising flour

tangerine cream:
60 g / 2 oz butter ♦ 60 g / 2 oz caster sugar ♦ 2 tsp icing sugar

Cream the butter with the sugar and grated tangerine zest until light and fluffy. Beat in the eggs one at a time. Set aside 3 tablespoons of the tangerine juice and add the rest to the mixture. Fold in the sifted flour until well combined.

Place a rounded dessertspoonful of the mixture in each paper case in the patty tins. Bake in the preheated oven until risen and golden brown. Cool the cakes on a wire rack.

To make the tangerine cream: use a hand-held electric beater to blend the butter with the sugar until light and fluffy. Gradually beat in the reserved tangerine juice, a teaspoon at a time. The cream should now be completely smooth and have a good flavour of the fruit.

Use a small serrated knife to remove a shallow disc measuring 3–4 cm / 1½ in. diameter from the top of each cake. Place a rounded teaspoon of cream in each cake. Turn over the disc of cake and cut in half. Place the two halves on top of the tangerine cream to represent butterfly wings. Place the icing sugar in a small sieve and dust a little over each cake. Set aside until ready to serve.

RICHMOND MAIDS OF HONOUR

Two traditional tales are associated with these small cheesecakes. One claims that they were the favourite cakes of Elizabeth I who sent her ladies-in-waiting out of the palace to collect them from a baker in Richmond. The other says that the tarts were so popular with Anne Boleyn when she was maid-of-honour to Catherine of Aragon that Henry VIII named the cakes after her. Whatever the truth of it, the cakes are a delight.

Oven: 200°C/400°F/gas mark 6 ♦ Baking time: 20–25 minutes
Equipment: 7.5 cm/3 in. fluted pastry cutter; patty tins – buttered
Makes 18 tarts

200 g/7 oz prepared puff pastry or rich shortcrust pastry
a little flour for rolling out the pastry

filling:
175 g/6 oz curd cheese ♦ 150 ml/5 fl oz clotted cream
3 egg yolks ♦ ½ lemon, finely grated zest
pinch of ground cinnamon ♦ pinch of ground nutmeg
90 g/3 oz currants ♦ 30 g/1 oz caster sugar
3 tbs brandy ♦ 15 g/½ oz flaked or slivered almonds

On a floured surface roll out the pastry until very thin. Use the pastry cutter to make 18 circles, to line the prepared patty tins. Slide each patty tin tray into the fridge to chill the pastry while you prepare the filling.

Mix together the curd cheese with the cream and egg yolks. Stir in the zest of lemon, spices, currants, sugar and brandy. Spoon the filling into the pastry cases and sprinkle the flaked almonds on top.

Bake the tarts in a preheated oven until well-risen and golden-brown. Cool in the tins for 5 minutes then transfer to a wire rack rack to cool.

MERINGUES

Meringues are, of course, totally frivolous. Little more than a puff of sugar, yet they have a dedicated following. If, though, you vary the kind of sugar added, the meringue acquires a quite different taste – light muscovado, for instance, gives an enticing caramel flavour. Or if you fold in chopped or ground nuts – hazelnuts, almonds or pecans – the meringue gains a softer consistency and a more interesting texture. The same mixture is used for small individual meringues – served clasped together with a generous dollop of cream – or for making flat discs, as in Gâteau Madeleine (p. 244) where they are sandwiched with rich chocolate cream. Alternatively, the meringue mixture can be spooned or piped into a nest or basket shape for filling with fruit and whipped cream.

Oven: 100°C/200°F/gas mark 1 ♦ Baking time: 2–3 hours
Equipment: non-stick baking sheet – lined
Makes: about 30 small single meringues

2 egg whites ♦ 120 g / 4 oz caster or light muscovado sugar

Use a hand-held or electric whisk to beat the egg whites until they are firm and frothy and do not slide across the bowl when you tilt it. Gradually whisk in half the sugar, a spoonful or so at a time. Fold in the remaining sugar. Once you have added the first half, take care not to whisk the mixture too long, otherwise sugar syrup can leak out of the meringues while they bake. Place heaped teaspoonfuls of the mixture on the prepared baking sheet allowing room to spread.

Bake in the preheated oven for 2 hours. Turn off the oven and leave the meringues for at least another hour. Cool on the baking sheet then transfer to an air-tight container until needed.

Variations
Coffee Meringues – whisk 2 tsp of coffee essence into the prepared meringue mixture.

Rose Petal Meringues – whisk 2 tsp of rose-water and 1–2 drops of cochineal or pink food colouring into the prepared meringue to produce a shell pink shade.

Orange or Lemon Meringues – fold the finely grated zest of an orange or lemon into the prepared mixture.

Almond Meringues – fold 30 g / 1 oz finely chopped or slivered blanched almonds into the prepared meringue.

Hazelnut Meringues – fold 30–60 g / 1–2 oz ground or finely chopped hazelnuts into the prepared meringue.

Pecan or Walnut Meringues – fold 60 g / 2 oz finely chopped pecans or walnuts into the prepared meringue.

COCONUT PYRAMIDS

Miniature rocky mountains of coconut and sugar that have devoted fans.

Oven: 180 °C / 350 °F / gas mark 4 ◆ Baking time: 20–25 minutes
Equipment: baking sheet – lined with baking paper or rice paper (optional)
Makes: about 24 cakes

4 egg whites ◆ 150 g / 5 oz caster sugar
150 g / 5 oz granulated sugar
230 g / 8 oz unsweetened desiccated coconut
30 g / 1 oz cornflour

Whisk the egg whites until stiff. Gradually add the caster sugar, whisking it in each time. Mix the granulated sugar with the coconut and cornflour and carefully fold into the meringue. Spoon the mixture into small pyramid-shaped heaps on the prepared baking sheet, allowing room for them to spread a little.

Bake in the preheated oven until golden-brown. Cool on the baking sheet for 5 minutes then use a palette knife to remove to a wire rack or, if using rice paper, leave it in contact with each cake and cut or tear around each one.

CHOCOLATE DREAMS

As a child I sometimes day-dreamed about the little shaped cakes known as Showboats produced by the Kunzle enterprise. Encased in chocolate, filled with sponge cake and decorated with flavoured cream, these were the only cakes my mother would consider buying, This is my home-made version, not as handsome as the originals, yet offering a memorable echo of their flavour.

Oven: 200 °C / 400 °F / gas mark 6 ♦ Baking time: 12–15 minutes
Equipment: 32 x 20 cm / 13 x 8 in. baking tray – lined;
5 cm / 2 in. fluted pastry cutter; 2 patty tins; 2 sheets cling-film
Makes: 18 cakes

sponge cake:
2 eggs ♦ 60 g / 2 oz light soft brown sugar
30 g / 1 oz self-raising flour ♦ 30 g / 1 oz cocoa powder
3–4 tbs rum or brandy (optional)

chocolate cases:
200 g / 7 oz plain dessert chocolate, 50% cocoa solids

chocolate cream:
120 g / 4 oz plain chocolate ♦ 150 ml / 5 fl oz single cream

decoration:
60 g / 2 oz plain chocolate, grated

Whisk the eggs with the sugar until light and foamy and the whisk leaves a trail across the surface of the mixture. Sift the flour with the cocoa and replace in the sieve. Sift a layer of the flour mixture over the whisked eggs and gently fold in with a balloon whisk. Repeat until all the flour and cocoa has been incorporated. Pour the cake mixture into the prepared cake tin and smooth level.

Bake in the preheated oven until the surface of the cake is springy to the touch. Cool in the tin for 2 minutes then lift out the baking paper with the cake attached and place on a pastry board. When the cake has cooled, use the pastry cutter to cut out 18 circles.

To make the chocolate cases: place a sheet of cling-film over each patty tin and press gently into the separate depressions to line the cake cups. Break the chocolate into pieces and melt in a heat-proof bowl in a microwave oven or over simmering water. Place a rounded teaspoon of melted chocolate in each cake cup and use a small knife to spread it up the sides in an even layer. Chill the patty tins in the refrigerator until the chocolate cases are almost set then gently press a circle of sponge cake into each chocolate case. Sprinkle the cakes with the rum or brandy and chill until cold.

To make the chocolate cream: break the chocolate into pieces in a heat-proof bowl and melt in the microwave oven or over simmering water. Remove from the heat and add the cream. Stir gently until combined. Use an electric beater to whisk the cream until light and glossy and a little paler. Do not over-beat or the cream may separate. Either pipe – using a piping-bag fitted with a star nozzle – or spread the cream over the cakes then sprinkle over the grated chocolate. Chill the cakes until ready to serve, then carefully pull the cling-film out of each cup of the patty tin and lift off each cake for arranging on a serving plate.

LEMON DROPS

Small cakes described as drops have virtually disappeared from English baking. This recipe from the 1920s is for pleasing little discs of cake joined together by fresh, buttery lemon curd.

Oven: 200°C/400°F/gas mark 6 ♦ Baking time: 15–20 minutes
Equipment: baking sheet – lined or buttered
Makes: 10 sandwiched cakes

175 g / 6 oz self-raising flour ♦ 60 g / 2 oz caster sugar
90 g / 3 oz butter ♦ 1 large egg ♦ ½ lemon, finely grated zest and juice
30 g / 1 oz granulated sugar

lemon curd:
1 large or 2 small lemons, finely grated zest and juice
1 large egg or 3 egg yolks ♦ ¼ tsp cornflour
60 g / 2 oz caster sugar ♦ 60 g / 2 oz butter

Sift the flour and sugar into a bowl and rub in the butter until the mixture resembles breadcrumbs. Add the egg beaten with the grated rind and juice of half a lemon and mix to a soft dough. Divide the mixture into twenty pieces and roll each into a ball. Toss each one in granulated sugar and flatten slightly on to the prepared baking sheet.

Bake in the preheated oven until light golden-brown. Transfer to a wire rack to cool.

To make the lemon curd: wash and dry the lemon(s), finely grate the zest of quarter of a lemon into a small bowl. Add the strained juice of the lemon(s), the egg (or yolks), the cornflour and the sugar. Place the bowl over a pan of simmering water and using a non-metal implement such as a small wooden spoon, or a beech twig or bent cane whisk, stir the mixture continuously for 8–10 minutes or until it has cooked and thickened. Remove the bowl from the heat, and arrest the cooking by standing the bowl in cold water for a few minutes. Gradually beat in the butter in small pieces. Leave until completely cold then sandwich the lemon drops.

CUSTARD TARTS

The filling for this classic recipe of the English kitchen is inspired by Hannah Glasse's baked custard in *The Art of Cookery made Plain and Easy* (1747). The custard is a simple but lovely blend of eggs and cream flecked with nutmeg and cinnamon and scented with rose-petal and orange flower water.

Oven: 200 °C / 400 °F / gas mark 6 then reduce to 180 °C / 350 °F / gas mark 4
Baking time: 25–30 minutes
Equipment: 7.5 cm / 3 in. pastry cutter;
deep patty or small muffin tins – buttered
Makes: about 12 tarts

120 g / 4 oz plain flour ♦ 30 g / 1 oz caster sugar
60 g / 2 oz butter, softened ♦ 1 egg yolk

custard:
300 ml / 10 fl oz single cream ♦ 30 g / 1 oz caster sugar
2 large eggs, beaten ♦ pinch of freshly grated nutmeg
pinch of ground cinnamon ♦ pinch of ground mace
rose-water and orange flower water

Sieve the flour and sugar into a bowl. Add the butter and egg yolk and work together with the fingertips to make a soft dough. Chill the dough and the prepared patty tins in a fridge for 15 minutes. On a lightly floured board, roll out the pastry thinly and cut out circles with the cutter. Line the prepared patty tins and prick the base of each tart with a fork to let out the air while baking. Place the patty tins back in the fridge for 15 minutes until well chilled.

Bake the pastry cases in the preheated oven at the higher temperature for 10–12 minutes until the pastry is golden. Remove from the oven and reduce the heat to the lower temperature.

To make the custard: whisk the cream with the sugar and the eggs and strain into a jug. Stir in the spices and add the flower waters to taste. Carefully pour or spoon the custard into the pastry cases and replace in the oven for 15–20 minutes until the custard is just set. Cool the tarts in the patty tins then carefully transfer to a wire rack. Serve while still warm or almost cool.

PALMIERS

Crisp, heart-shaped palmiers are, for me, a lasting reminder of Paris. I prefer these pastries quite plain to nibble with an espresso. But for an English tea-time palmiers sandwiched with thick cream are popular. While nothing beats home-made puff pastry, the ready-made all-butter kind is a great time-saver.

Oven: 230 °F 450 °F / gas mark 8 ♦ *Baking time: 15–20 minutes*
Equipment: baking sheet – lined
Makes: 20 palmiers

375 g / 13 oz prepared puff pastry ♦ 45 g / 1½ oz caster sugar

cream filling:
150 ml / 5 fl oz whipped cream ♦ 1 tbs vanilla sugar

Sprinkle a pastry board or working surface with caster sugar. Roll out the puff pastry to make an oblong of 32 x 18 cm / 13 x 7 in., brush very lightly with cold water and sprinkle with caster sugar. With the long side facing you, fold the two short sides to the centre. Press down gently with the rolling pin. Brush lightly with water and sprinkle with more caster sugar. Fold the sides into the centre to give four layers of pastry. Brush lightly with water and sprinkle with sugar and fold the halves of pastry together to make eight layers of pastry, then press gently together.

Use a sharp knife to cut the folded pastry into 20 slices. Brush both sides of each slice with water and place on the prepared baking sheet leaving plenty of room for expansion. Sprinkle the rest of the caster sugar over the pastries and chill the loaded baking sheet in the refrigerator for 15 minutes.

Bake in the preheated oven until golden brown. Leave to cool for 3 minutes then use a palette knife to remove to a wire rack to cool. If sandwiching the palmiers, sweeten the whipped cream with the sugar and, just before serving, spoon on to half the biscuits and cover with the rest.

ALMOND MACAROONS

The name of these crisp small cakes comes from the same root as *macaroni*, meaning dolt or buffoon. Clearly related to Italian amaretti, this French version has a more delicate flavour.

Oven: 180°C/350°F/gas mark 4 ♦ *Baking time: 15–17 minutes*
Equipment: baking sheet – lined
Makes: 24 macaroons

2 egg whites ♦ 175 g / 6 oz caster sugar
120 g / 4 oz ground almonds ♦ 30 g / 1 oz ground rice
a drop or two of bitter almond essence
24 split blanched almonds

Whisk the egg whites until stiff. Gently stir in half the sugar and whisk briefly. Then stir in the rest of the sugar with the ground almonds, ground rice and the almond essence. The mixture will be quite stiff. Place rounded teaspoons of the mixture on the prepared baking sheet, allowing for expansion during baking. Press a split almond in the centre of each cake.

Bake in the preheated oven until just turning golden at the edges. Cool on the baking sheet for 5 minutes before lifting the cakes on to a wire rack.

WALNUT AND LEMON SQUARES

Only after baking this excellent and unusual recipe for some years did I discover that my thanks should go to the well-respected cookery writer, Katie Stewart, who first published it.

Oven: 180 °C/350°F/gas mark 4 ♦ Baking time: 45 minutes
Equipment: 23 cm/9 in. square shallow baking tin – buttered
Makes: 16 squares

175 g/6 oz self-raising flour ♦ 175 g/6 oz granulated sugar
120 g/4 oz rolled oats ♦ 60 g/2 oz walnuts, chopped
175 g/6 oz butter, softened ♦ 2 large eggs
½ lemon, finely grated zest and juice

glacé icing:
150 g/5 oz icing sugar ♦ ½ lemon, finely grated zest and juice
drop or two of lemon food colouring (optional)

Sift the flour into a mixing bowl. Stir in the sugar, oats and walnuts. Add the butter in pieces and use a knife to cut it into the mixture. Beat the eggs with the zest and lemon juice and stir into the mixture for 1 minute. Spoon the mixture into the prepared cake tin and smooth level.

Bake in the preheated oven until cooked. Remove from the oven and leave the cake in the tin.

To make the icing: while the cake is still warm, sift the icing sugar into a bowl and stir in just enough lemon juice to make a smooth pouring consistency. Add a drop of yellow food colouring if you wish to make a pale shade. Pour the icing over the cake while it is still warm and sprinkle over the finely grated lemon zest. Leave to cool, then cut into squares before removing from the tin.

QUEEN OF HEARTS TARTS

I devised these almond-pastry tarts years ago for an Alice in Wonderland children's party but a friend who holds bridge parties now serves them.

Oven: 200°C/400°F/gas mark 6 ♦ Baking time: 12–15 minutes
Equipment: large and small heart-shaped pastry cutters; baking sheet – lined
Makes: 12–15 tarts

150 g / 5 oz plain white flour ♦ 90 g / 3 oz ground almonds
30 g / 1 oz icing sugar ♦ 120 g / 4 oz butter, softened
1 egg yolk mixed with 1 drop of almond essence
1–2 tsp milk ♦ raspberry jam

Sieve the flour, ground almonds and icing sugar into a mixing bowl. Add the butter and egg yolk with almond essence and mix together with the fingertips to make a soft dough. Shape into a ball, wrap in plastic and chill for 20 minutes.

On a lightly floured board, roll out the dough thinly. Use a heart-shaped cookie cutter to cut out 30 shapes. Place half the shapes on a prepared baking sheet, spoon jam into the centre of each and brush around the jam with milk. Use the smaller cutter to remove the centre from the remaining shapes and place evenly on top of the jam hearts, pressing down to seal the join.

Bake the tarts in the preheated oven until the pastry is golden and crisp. Transfer to a wire rack to cool.

DATE AND ORANGE OAT SQUARES

I grew up with these nutritious oat squares. My only change to my mother's recipe is the addition of orange zest and juice to the date filling.

Oven: 180 °C/350°F/gas mark 4 ♦ Baking time: 25–30 minutes
Equipment: 28 x 18 cm/11 x 7 in. shallow tin – buttered
Makes: 15 squares

date and orange filling:
230 g/8 oz stoned dried dates ♦ finely grated zest and juice of 1 large orange
♦ 1 tsp cornflour ♦ 1 tbs milk ♦ 1 tbs demerara sugar

oat crust:
230 g/8 oz rolled oats ♦ 120 g/4 oz self-raising flour
120 g/4 oz light muscovado sugar ♦ 120 g/4 oz butter ♦ 1 large egg

Prepare the filling first. Roughly chop the dates and soften with the orange juice in a pan over moderate heat until the mixture can be mashed to a purée. Remove from the heat and mix in the orange zest and the cornflour. Set aside to cool while you make the oat crust.

Measure the oats, flour and sugar into a mixing bowl. Add the butter in pieces and rub into the mixture with your fingertips. Mix to a dough with the beaten egg.

On a floured board roll out half the dough to fit the base of the tin. Spread the date purée in an even layer over the crust. Roll out the remaining dough and place on top of the date layer, lightly pressing the edges together. Brush milk over the top and sprinkle with demerara sugar. Prick all over with a fork.

Bake in the centre of the preheated oven until the crust is golden brown. Cool in the tin for 2 minutes then mark into squares. Cut through completely when cold and remove the squares from the tin.

Variation
Apricot and Orange Oat Squares – replace the dates in the above recipe with chopped ready-to-eat dried apricots, if necessary adding a little water when making the purée.

CONGRESS TARTS

Small iced tarts filled with almond mixture – from my mother's notebook.

Oven: 190 °C / 375 °F / gas mark 5 ♦ *Baking time: 20 minutes*
Equipment: 7.5 cm / 3 in. fluted pastry cutter; patty tins – buttered
Makes: 12 tarts

pastry:
175 g / 6 oz plain flour ♦ 90 g / 3 oz butter ♦ 2 tbs milk or water

filling:
30 g / 1 oz butter ♦ 90 g / 3 oz caster sugar ♦ 1 egg
drop of almond essence ♦ 45 g / 1½ oz ground rice
45 g / 1½ oz ground almonds ♦ 1–2 tbs raspberry or strawberry jam

glacé icing:
60 g / 2 oz icing sugar ♦ 1 tbs hot water
few strips of angelica for decoration

Sieve the flour into a bowl and rub in the butter until the mixture resembles breadcrumbs. Mix to a soft dough with the milk or water. Form the dough into a ball and rest it under the upturned bowl while you prepare the filling.

To make the filling, cream the butter with the sugar and beat in the egg and almond essence until smooth. Fold in the ground rice and almonds.

Roll out the pastry until 3 mm / ⅛ in. thick, and cut out 12 rounds to line the prepared patty tins. Place a coffee-spoonful of jam in the base of each and and cover with a heaped teaspoonful of the almond mixture.

Bake in the preheated oven until the filling is risen and golden brown. Cool in the tin for 3 minutes then transfer to a wire rack.

To make the glacé icing: blend the sieved icing sugar with just enough hot water to make a pouring consistency, and spoon over the top of each tart. Decorate with a sliver of angelica and leave in a warm kitchen until set.

MINCE PIES

At home, I make mince pies only in December, but I discovered on the cake stall that they are popular all winter. For Christmas, I cut out a star shape from the pastry lids before covering the mincemeat and baking. Not only does this look attractive but it's then easy to add a touch of festive spirit to the hot mince pies by trickling rum or brandy into them just before serving. For speed, a high-quality bought mincemeat can be used, though the home-made kind is naturally rather more delicious and distinctive.

Oven: 200°C/400°F/gas mark 6 ♦ Baking time: 20 minutes
Equipment: 7.5 cm/3 in. and 6.5 cm/2½ in. fluted pastry cutters;
patty tins – buttered
Makes: 12 pies

230 g/8 oz plain flour ♦ 30 g/1 oz icing sugar ♦ 135 g/4½ oz butter
½ lemon or orange, finely grated zest ♦ 4 tbs milk

filling:
230 g/8 oz mincemeat ♦ a little extra milk ♦ 1–2 tbs granulated sugar

Sift the flour and sugar into a bowl, cut and rub in the butter with the grated citrus zest until the mixture resembles breadcrumbs. Mix to a soft dough with the milk and shape it into a ball. If you have time, rest the pastry under an upturned bowl or chill it, wrapped, in the fridge for 30 minutes. This allows the gluten to be released from the flour making the dough easier to handle.

On a floured board, roll out just over half the pastry to 3mm/⅛ in. thickness. With the larger pastry cutter, cut out 12 discs of pastry and line the patty tins. Place one well-rounded dessertspoon of mincemeat in each pastry case.

Roll out the rest of the pastry and use the smaller cutter to cut out another 12 discs for lids. Brush milk over the underside of each lid and place over the mincemeat, making sure it's central. Press down gently at the edge to join the two pastry layers. Brush milk over the top of each pie and sprinkle with sugar.

Bake in the preheated oven until the pastry is golden brown. Cool the pies in their tins for 10 minutes then transfer to a plate for serving straight away or on to a wire rack to cool.

APRICOT AND PECAN MINCEMEAT

One of the advantages of these two excellent mincemeats which include butter in place of suet is that they can be used for filling pies straight away or can be stored in a cold place for up to 3 months.

Makes about 1.5 kg / 3 lb 8 oz mincemeat

500 g / 1 lb 2 oz traditionally dried apricots
265 g / 9 oz mixed dried fruit – raisins, sultanas, currants
200 g / 7 oz diced mixed peel
2 tangerines or 1 orange, grated zest and juice
150 ml / 5 fl oz rum, whisky or brandy
150 g / 5 oz dark soft brown sugar
½ tsp ground cinnamon ♦ ½ tsp ground cloves
¼ tsp freshly grated nutmeg ♦ 120 g / 4 oz butter, melted
120 g / 4 oz ground almonds
120 g / 4 oz shelled pecans, roughly chopped

Use kitchen scissors to snip each apricot into about 10 pieces. In a large bowl mix together the apricots, dried fruit and mixed peel with the zest and juice of the tangerines and the rum or whisky. Leave in warm place for at least 2 hours for the liquid to be absorbed.

Stir in the sugar, cinnamon, cloves and nutmeg with the butter, almonds and pecans. Mix for 4 minutes until well combined, then spoon the mincemeat into hot, dry jars, packing the mixture down well. Cover the jars with tight-fitting screw tops, label and store in a cold place until needed.

LEMON AND WALNUT MINCEMEAT

Makes 2 kg / 4 lb 6 oz

2 large lemons ♦ 2 large dessert apples such as Cox's Orange
230 g / 8 oz seedless raisins ♦ 230 g / 8 oz sultanas
230 g / 8 oz currants ♦ 230 g / 8 oz candied peel, chopped
230 g / 8 oz walnut pieces, chopped ♦ 230 g / 8 oz soft dark brown sugar
230 g / 8 oz melted butter or grated suet
1 tsp ground cinnamon ♦ ½ tsp ground cloves
¼ small nutmeg, grated
150 ml / 5 fl oz marsala wine or medium sherry

Wash and dry the lemons and slice thinly, discarding the pips. Arrange the slices in a single layer on a heatproof plate and cook in a microwave oven for 4–6 minutes until mushy. Alternatively, cook the lemon slices with 2 tablespoons of water in a lidded pan over low heat until soft. While the lemon slices are cooling, peel and quarter the apples, remove the cores and slice thickly. Place the apples, lemon slices, raisins and sultanas in a processor and chop together until quite small but not to a purée. Scoop the mixture into bowl and add all the remaining ingredients. Stir well until combined. Taste to check the flavour, adjusting the spices accordingly.

Use straight away or spoon into hot dry jars, seal tightly and store in a cool, dry place for 3–4 weeks. I usually keep spare jars of this mincemeat in the refrigerator until needed.

CHAPTER EIGHT

Biscuits and Cookies

THE CONTENTS OF THIS CHAPTER

It is a pleasant contrast to have biscuits as well as cakes on the tea-table and a tin of home-made biscuits is always useful ... a stand-by for unexpected visitors or for days when there just isn't enough time to make a cake.

George and Cecilia Scurfield, *Home-made Cakes and Biscuits,* 1963

Cakes are convivial. To my mind, the pleasure they bring is intended for sharing, whereas a delicate almond tuile, a crisp brandy snap or a square of chewy flapjack is often best enjoyed in solitude, in a comfortable chair with tea or coffee, when the biscuit's flavour and texture can be properly appreciated.

What is the difference between a biscuit and a cookie? I'm sometimes asked. Neither word is originally English – biscuit is clearly French, meaning twice cooked, yet until the the eighteenth century we spelled it bisket, while cookie is a more recent introduction, derived from the Dutch word *koekje* which became cookie in North America. Biscuits are usually thinner and smaller with a definite shape, and a cookie is often larger with a more chewy consistency. But the distinction can easily blur – there are crisp cookies and chewy biscuits.

Though it's easy enough to mix the dough, roll it out and shape, or arrange spoonfuls on the tray, once you've slid the baking sheets into the oven total vigilance is necessary. 'Timing in cooking is essential,' says the talented chef Angela Hartnett.

While cakes may give you a little leeway on timing, baking a biscuit is particularly exacting. There is a stage when a shortbread biscuit reaches a peak of perfection and its flavour and texture cannot be improved. But a little too long in the oven and the sugar caramelizes, the biscuit darkens, the flavour becomes intense rather than subtle – and that precious moment is lost for ever. In baking, the eye is as important as the hand and the palate. But take heart, practice does make perfect and you will soon discover that a flawless shortbread biscuit is truly a triumph of home baking.

A convenient aspect of making your own biscuits and cookies is that – given the chance – they store well. Baked and cooled then sealed in plastic box or bag, they will maintain their flavour in the freezer for weeks, or in a refrigerator for a fortnight. When stored at room temperature, however, their oven-fresh buttery taste can deteriorate.

I find home-made biscuits and cookies – arranged on a plate or in a pretty box – make especially welcome gifts to those who are elderly or who live alone and who might not feel up to baking. And when presented in this way, biscuits and cookies fly off a fund-raising stall in no time at all.

SHORTBREAD BISCUITS

Simple and good – the queen of home-made biscuits.

Oven: 160°C/325°F/gas mark 3 ♦ Baking time: 15–17 minutes
Equipment: 6 cm/2½ in. fluted pastry cutter; baking sheet – buttered
Makes: about 20 biscuits

120 g/4 oz butter ♦ 60 g/2 oz caster sugar
175 g/6 oz plain flour ♦ 1 tbs caster sugar for the end

In a warmed mixing bowl, beat the butter until soft. Add the sugar and cream together. Gradually add the sieved flour and continue beating until the mixture binds together in a lump. On a floured board, roll out the dough until 5 mm/¼ in. thick. Use the pastry cutter to cut out rounds of dough. Place on the prepared baking sheet and prick each biscuit a couple of times with a fork.

Bake in the preheated oven until just changing colour at the edges. Do not overcook or the subtle buttery flavour will be lost. Cool on the baking sheet for 3 minutes then transfer to a wire rack and sprinkle with the extra caster sugar.

Variations
Orange Shortbread Biscuits – add ½ tsp finely grated zest of orange and/or 30 g/1 oz finely shredded candied orange peel to the sieved flour.
Lemon Shortbread Biscuits – add ½ tsp finely grated zest of lemon and/or 30 g/1 oz finely shredded candied lemon or citron peel to the sieved flour.
Ginger Shortbread Biscuits – add 45 g/1½ oz finely chopped preserved or candied ginger to the sieved flour.
Cherry Shortbread Biscuits – add 45 g/1½ oz chopped dried cherries to the sieved flour – glacé cherries can be used instead but they are rather sweet.
Rosemary Shortbread Biscuits – add ½ tsp finely chopped fresh young rosemary leaves to the butter.
Lavender Shortbread Biscuits – add ½ tsp finely chopped fresh lavender flowers or young leaves to the butter.

WHOLEMEAL SHORTBREAD

A tiptop shortbread with a satisfying texture and nutty flavour.

Oven: 160°C/325°F/gas mark 3 ♦ *Baking time: 20–25 minutes*
Equipment: baking sheet – buttered
Makes: about 24 pieces

230 g / 8 oz butter
60 g / 2 oz caster sugar
60 g / 2 oz dark muscovado sugar
350 g / 12 oz stone-ground plain wholemeal flour

Soften the butter in a warmed bowl, add the caster sugar and the sieved muscovado sugar and beat together until well combined. Gradually beat in the flour until the dough forms a lump. On a floured board roll out the dough until 1 cm / ½ in. thick. With a sharp knife cut strips about 5 cm / 2 in. wide and then across at 2 cm / ¾ in. intervals to make oblong biscuits. Alternatively, cut into triangles. Place on the prepared baking sheet.

Bake in the preheated oven until the edges are just changing colour. Cool on the baking sheet for 3 minutes then transfer to a wire rack to cool.

DIGESTIVE BISCUITS

Home-made digestive biscuits are a treat – they can be left plain or dipped in chocolate.

Oven: 180°C/350°F/gas mark 4 ♦ Baking time: 15–20 minutes
Equipment: 6.5 cm/2½ in. plain or fluted pastry cutter; baking sheet – buttered
Makes: about 20 biscuits

230 g/8 oz wholemeal flour ♦ 30 g/1 oz dark muscovado sugar
¼ tsp bicarbonate of soda ♦ 90 g/3 oz butter
1 egg yolk or half a beaten egg ♦ 3 tbs milk
120 g/4 oz plain dessert chocolate, melted (optional)

Measure the flour into a mixing bowl. Stir in the sieved sugar and bicarbonate of soda and add the butter in pieces, then rub in with your fingertips until absorbed. Mix the egg with the milk and stir into the dry ingredients to make a soft dough. Turn out on to a lightly floured work surface and roll out thinly until about 3 mm/⅛ in. thick. Use the pastry cutter to cut out the biscuits, then place them on the prepared baking sheet.

Bake the biscuits in the preheated oven until turning light brown at the edges. Transfer the biscuits to a wire rack to cool.

Chocolate Digestives: dip one side, or part, of each biscuit into the melted chocolate, or simply trickle spoonfuls of chocolate in fine lines over the top of each biscuit. Leave in a cold place until the chocolate is set.

EASTER BISCUITS

These spiced biscuits are traditionally baked for Easter Sunday tea-time. However, they are enjoyable all year round.

Oven: 180 °C / 350 °F / gas mark 4 ♦ Baking time: 15 minutes
Equipment: 7.5 cm / 3 in. fluted pastry cutter; baking sheet – lined or buttered
Makes: about 20 biscuits

120 g / 4 oz butter ♦ 120 g / 4 oz caster sugar
1 small egg ♦ 230 g / 8 oz plain flour
1 tsp ground mixed spice ♦ 60 g / 2 oz currants
a little beaten egg white for glazing biscuits
1 tbs golden or white granulated sugar for decoration

Cream the butter with the sugar then beat in the egg. Gradually work in the flour sieved with the spice, and then the currants. Knead lightly with the fingertips to make a soft dough and shape into a ball On a lightly-floured board, roll out the dough to just under 5 mm / ¼ in. thick. Cut out the biscuits with the cutter. Place the biscuits on the prepared baking sheet, brush lightly with beaten egg white and sprinkle over a little granulated sugar.

Bake in the preheated oven until the biscuits are pale gold. Cool on the baking sheet for a few minutes then transfer to a wire rack.

PECAN AND CRANBERRY COOKIES

I devised these cookies to be crisp yet chewy with a rich buttery taste.

Oven: 160 °C / 325 °F / gas mark 3 ◆ *Baking time: 15–18 minutes*
Equipment: baking sheets – lightly buttered
Makes: 18 large cookies

1 tbs golden syrup ◆ 100 g / 3½ oz light muscovado sugar
100 g / 3½ oz butter ◆ 100 g / 3½ oz flour
100 g / 3½ oz rolled oats
100 g / 3½ oz dried cranberries
100 g / 3½ oz pecan nuts, halved

Measure the syrup into a heavy-based saucepan and add the sugar and butter. Stir together over low heat until the butter has melted. Remove from the heat and cool slightly before mixing in the other ingredients: flour, oats, cranberries and pecans.

Place rounded tablespoons of the mixture on the prepared baking sheet leaving room for the cookies to spread. Use your fingers to shape each one into a circle. There should be about 3 pecan halves on each cookie.

Bake in the preheated oven until the edge of the cookie is starting to change colour. Cool the cookies on the baking tray, then use a palette knife to transfer them to a wire rack.

ALMOND TUILES

These light, crisp biscuits, curved like Provençal tiles, can be served on their own or to accompany delicate summer desserts such as syllabub and chilled creams.

Oven: 190°C/375°F/gas mark 5 ♦ *Baking time: 7–8 minutes*
Equipment: baking sheet – lined or buttered;
wooden rolling pin for shaping the biscuits
Makes: about 30 biscuits

60 g / 2 oz butter
2 egg whites ♦ 120 g / 4 oz caster sugar
60 g / 2 oz plain flour
60 g / 2 oz flaked almonds

Melt the butter in a pan and set aside in a warm place. Whisk the egg whites until foamy but not dry. Add half the sugar and whisk again, repeat with the rest of the sugar. Fold in the sieved flour and the melted butter with the almonds. Place teaspoonfuls of the mixture on the prepared baking sheet, allowing plenty of room for the biscuits to spread. Make the biscuits in batches unless you have several rolling pins for shaping them.

Bake in the preheated oven until golden. Use a palette knife to remove each biscuit and immediately place on the rolling pin so that it bends to its curve. Remove the biscuits as soon as they have cooled and store in an air-tight container.

BUTTERSCOTCH BISCUITS

When I ran my cake stall, this was the first recipe requested by a customer. Quite soon, on market mornings, I was too busy selling cakes to scribble out cake details. So I wrote *Cake Stall* instead, with my customers at Tiverton Pannier Market mainly in mind. This recipe came from a small 1920s cookery book but I can't remember which one! These biscuits can be tricky to make, though the flavour is worth the effort.

Oven: 180 °C / 350 °F / gas mark 4 ♦ Baking time: 8–10 minutes
Equipment: 6.5 cm / 2½ in. plain pastry cutter; baking sheet – lined or buttered
Makes: about 24 biscuits

175 g / 6 oz self-raising flour ♦ 60 g / 2 oz butter
175 g / 6 oz golden syrup ♦ ½ tsp vanilla essence
½ tsp bicarbonate of soda ♦ 24 walnut halves or split almonds

Sieve the flour into a mixing bowl. Melt the butter with the syrup in a saucepan over moderate heat. Remove from the hob and beat in the vanilla and bicarbonate of soda. Pour on to the flour and mix until smooth. Set aside until cold or chill in the fridge.

Put the mixture – or half at a time – on to a lightly floured pastry board or work surface and roll out very thinly, 3 mm / ⅛ in. thick. Cut out the biscuits with the cutter. Transfer to the prepared baking sheet and place a walnut or almond in the centre of each.

Bake in the preheated oven until just changing colour. Cool the biscuits on the baking sheet for 2 minutes then use a palette knife to transfer them to a wire rack. The biscuits become crisp as they cool.

HAZELNUT MACAROONS

Wheat-free hazelnut biscuits sandwiched with coffee cream.

Oven: 160°C/325°F/gas mark 3 ♦ *Baking time: 25–30 minutes*
Equipment: baking sheet – lined
Makes: 18 sandwiched biscuits

120 g / 4 oz hazelnuts, toasted
30 g / 1 oz almonds, blanched
30 g / 1 oz cornflour
2 egg whites
175 g / 6 oz caster sugar

coffee butter cream:
60 g / 2 oz butter ♦ 60 g / 2 oz caster sugar
1–2 tbs hot strong black coffee ♦ 1 tsp icing sugar

Chop the hazelnuts with the almonds and cornflour in a processor until fine. Whisk the egg whites until stiff, then whisk in half the sugar. Gently fold in the rest of the sugar with the nut and cornflour mixture. Place rounded teaspoons of the mixture, well spaced, on the prepared baking sheet.

Bake in the preheated oven until just changing colour at the edges. Cool for 4 minutes then transfer the macaroons to a wire rack to cool.

To make the butter cream: use an electric beater to blend the butter with the caster sugar until pale and fluffy. Gradually beat in the hot coffee – half a teaspoon at a time – until the sugar is dissolved and the cream is completely smooth. Sandwich the biscuits with the filling and dust them lightly with sifted icing sugar.

COFFEE MARYSES

Diminutive, buttery biscuits shaped with a piping-bag – or with a spoon if you prefer – that go well with ice-creams and sorbets.

Oven: 190 °C / 375°F / gas mark 5 ♦ Baking time: 9–12 minutes
Equipment: piping-bag with 5 mm / ¼ in. star nozzle;
baking sheet – lined or buttered and lightly floured
Makes: about 30 biscuits

120 g / 4 oz butter
30 g / 1 oz icing sugar
drop of vanilla essence
1–2 tsp coffee essence
120 g / 4 oz plain flour
a little extra icing sugar

Soften the butter in a mixing bowl, blend in the sieved icing sugar with the vanilla and coffee essences. Gradually work in the sieved flour. Spoon the mixture into a piping-bag fitted with a star nozzle. Pipe rosettes on to the prepared baking sheet, allowing a little room for the biscuits to spread.

Bake in the preheated oven until just changing colour. Cool on the baking sheet for 2 minutes then transfer the biscuits to a wire rack to cool.

ANZACS

I include this recipe for coconut and rolled oats biscuits from *Cake Stall* in memory of a kind Australian reader, Eileen Lewis, who for many years wrote to me with recipes and presents after the book appeared there.

Oven: 160°C/325°F/gas mark 3 ♦ Baking time: 15–20 minutes
Equipment: baking sheet- lined or buttered
Makes: about 30 biscuits

120 g / 4 oz plain flour ♦ 120 g / 4 oz rolled oats
120 g / 4 oz unsweetened desiccated coconut
120 g / 4 oz light muscovado sugar
½ tsp baking powder ♦ 120 g / 4 oz butter
2 tbs golden syrup ♦ 2 tbs water

Stir all the dry ingredients – flour, oats, coconut, sugar and baking powder – together in a mixing bowl. In a saucepan, gently heat the butter with the syrup and water until melted. Pour into the mixing bowl and stir well. Roll teaspoons of the mixture into small balls, flatten them and place on the prepared baking sheet.

Bake in the preheated oven until golden-brown. Cool on the baking sheet for 2 minutes then transfer the biscuits to a wire rack.

LEMON AND RAISIN REFRIGERATOR COOKIES

The idea of storing ready-to-bake cookie dough in the refrigerator came, I believe, from North America. Wrapped in plastic, the dough keeps well on a shelf in the fridge for up to a week while, at the same time, the lemon flavour develops.

Oven: 180 °C / 350 °F / gas mark 4 ◆ Baking time: 15 minutes
Equipment: baking sheet – lined or buttered
Makes: about 36 cookies

175 g / 6 oz butter
90 g / 3 oz light muscovado sugar
90 g / 3 oz caster sugar
1 small lemon, finely grated zest
1 large egg
300 g / 10 oz plain flour
1 tsp baking powder
60 g / 2 oz seedless raisins

Cream the butter with both kinds of sugar and the zest of lemon. Beat in the egg and stir in the flour sifted with the baking powder, then stir in the raisins. Mix well to form a soft dough. Divide and form into two rolls about 5 cm / 2 in. across. Wrap in plastic and chill in the fridge for at least 2 hours before using.

When ready to bake the cookies, dip a sharp cook's knife in hot water and dry on a cloth, then cut thin slices from the roll using a gentle sawing action. Place the slices on the prepared baking sheet allowing space for them to spread a little.

Bake in the preheated oven until changing colour at the edges. Transfer to a wire rack to cool.

Variation: replace the zest of lemon with the zest of a tangerine or a small sweet orange.

FRUIT AND NUT FLAPJACK

Plain flapjack – just butter, oats, syrup and sugar – has a definite appeal, but my enriched fruit, nut and seed version appears rather more popular.

Oven: 180°C/350°F/gas mark 4 ♦ Baking time: 25–30 minutes
Equipment: large saucepan; 30 x 23 cms/12 x 9 in. shallow tin
– lined or buttered
Makes: 24 squares

175 g/6 oz demerara sugar ♦ 2 rounded tbs golden syrup
230 g/8 oz butter ♦ 350 g/12 oz rolled oats
120 g/4 oz seedless raisins ♦ 120 g/4 oz dried apricots, thinly sliced
60 g/2 oz ground almonds ♦ 60 g/2 oz hazelnuts, chopped or sliced
30 g/1 oz sunflower seeds ♦ 30 g/1 oz sesame seeds
15 g/½ oz hemp seed ♦ 15 g/½ oz linseed

Measure the sugar, syrup and butter into a saucepan and heat gently until the butter has melted then remove from the heat. Spoon 60 g/2 oz of the rolled oats into a food processor and grind for about 1 minute until the powder resembles fine oatmeal.

Add the ground oats and the rolled oats to the saucepan. Stir well then add the remaining ingredients and mix together until evenly coated with butter. Turn the mixture into the baking tin and spread evenly. Use the back of the spoon to smooth the top of the mixture, slightly compressing it.

Bake in the preheated oven until golden brown. Remove from the oven and leave to cool for 2 minutes. Use a sharp knife to mark the flapjack into 24 pieces and set aside until cold. Then cut through into pieces and carefully remove from the tin.

CHOCOLATE CRUNCH COOKIES

A crisp chocolate cookie popular with children. The recipe came from a good friend who helped on the cake stall and later launched her own old-fashioned tea-shop.

Oven: 160 °C / 325 °F / gas mark 3 ◆ *Baking time: 15 minutes*
Equipment: baking sheet – lined or buttered
Makes: about 24 cookies

175 g / 6 oz butter ◆ 120 g / 4 oz light muscovado sugar
few drops of vanilla essence ◆ 230 g / 8 oz self-raising flour
30 g / 1 oz cocoa powder ◆ 60 g / 2 oz crushed cornflakes

icing:
120 g / 4 oz plain dessert chocolate, melted ◆ 1 tbs flaked almonds

Cream the butter with the sugar and vanilla essence. Gradually work in the flour sieved with the cocoa powder until well combined. Stir in the cornflakes. Shape a teaspoon of the mixture into a ball. Place on the prepared baking sheet and gently flatten the cookie but allow room for expansion. Repeat with the rest of the mixture.

Bake in the preheated oven until just firm. Cool on the baking sheet then transfer to a wire rack. Spoon some melted chocolate into the centre of each cookie and sprinkle with a few flaked almonds. Leave until the chocolate has set.

PARLIAMENT CAKES OR PARLIES

Said to have been named after members of parliament, these intensely-flavoured ginger biscuits were once sold on street stalls in Edinburgh. They are best made with freshly bought ground ginger instead of the tired old stuff at the back of the cupboard.

Oven: 160°C/325°F/gas mark 3 ♦ *Baking time: 15–20 minutes*
Equipment: baking sheet – buttered or lined
Makes: 20 biscuits

120 g / 4 oz butter
120 g / 4 oz dark muscovado sugar
120 g / 4 oz black treacle
230 g / 8 oz plain flour
1–2 tsp ground ginger

Cream the butter with the sieved sugar and treacle until light. Gradually work in the flour sieved with the ground ginger to make a stiff dough. Drop teaspoons of the mixture on to the prepared baking sheet leaving room for the biscuits to spread.

Bake in the preheated oven for 15–20 minutes. Transfer the biscuits to a wire rack to cool.

GINGERBREAD PEOPLE

Home-made gingerbread men are part of childhood. They feature principally in Scandinavian cooking, where they are even more richly spiced. In her book *Lark Rise to Candleford*, Flora Thompson remembers gingerbread men on sale in her Oxfordshire village during the nineteenth century.

Oven: 200°C/400°F/gas mark 6 ♦ Baking time: 15 minutes
Equipment: gingerbread people cutter; baking sheet – lined or buttered
Makes: 12 biscuits

230 g / 8 oz self-raising flour
90 g / 3 oz dark muscovado sugar
2 tsp ground ginger ♦ 1 tsp ground mixed spice
120 g / 4 oz butter ♦ 3–4 tbs milk
currants for eyes and buttons
white icing for piping (optional)

Sieve the flour, sugar, ginger and mixed spice into a mixing bowl. Rub in the butter until the mixture resembles breadcrumbs. Mix to a dough with the milk. On a lightly floured board, roll out the dough until 5 mm / ¼ in. thick.

Use the cutters of a gingerbread man and woman to make as many biscuits as possible. Re-roll the trimmings and repeat. Place the biscuits on the prepared baking sheet and press the currants into them for eyes and buttons.

Bake in the preheated oven until just changing colour. Cool on the baking sheet for 2 minutes then use a palette knife to transfer to a wire rack to cool completely. Decorate the biscuits with piped icing if wished.

SMILERS, WHIRLIGIGS AND CHEQUER-BOARDS

Cookies from the birthday parties my mother gave. Strictly for children – cookies shaped like faces, spinning pin-wheels, and chessboards. Once you've discovered how well the two mixtures combine during cooking, you'll be able to make up your own designs – as animals with spots, cars and houses with chocolate doors and windows, and so on.

Oven: 180°C/350°F/gas mark 4 ♦ Baking time: 12 minutes
Equipment: 6 cm/2¼ in. plain pastry cutter;
small crescent-shaped pastry cutter; baking sheet – lined or buttered
Makes: 16 biscuits

vanilla mixture:
120 g/4 oz butter ♦ 60 g/2 oz caster sugar
150 g/5 oz plain flour
few drops of vanilla essence

chocolate mixture:
120 g/4 oz butter ♦ 60 g/2 oz caster sugar
135 g/4½ oz plain flour
3 tbs cocoa powder

For each mixture, cream the butter and sugar until fluffy and gradually work in the other ingredients until a soft dough is formed. Knead well with the fingers. On a lightly floured pastry board, roll out the vanilla mixture until 5 mm/¼ in. thick. Use the pastry cutter to cut out as many biscuits as you can. Place these on the prepared baking sheet.

Now roll out the chocolate mixture in just the same way. Use the crescent-shaped cutter for making the mouth, and thimble-sized circles – cut round a bottle top – for eyes, a triangle for a nose. Cut out these shapes (and any others that take your fancy) and gently position them on the vanilla rounds to make faces. The mouths can be made to curve up or down – for the cake stall, I used to make most of them 'smilers', and a few with down-turned mouths as 'miseries'. Repeat the biscuits with chocolate faces and vanilla features.

Whirligig Cookies

Prepare the vanilla and chocolate mixtures to the dough stage as above. On a lightly floured board roll out the chocolate mixture to a rectangular shape and 5 mm / ¼ in. thickness. Roll out the vanilla dough on another board in the same way. Lower the vanilla dough on to the chocolate one – it's sometimes easier to do this if you leave the dough on the second board then lower it upside down on to the first one. Run a palette knife against the board to free the dough and very gently press the two doughs together with the rolling pin. Starting at the long side, roll up the two doughs as for a Swiss roll.

Wrap the dough in plastic and chill in the fridge for at least 60 minutes. Then cut 5 mm / ¼ in. slices and place on the prepared baking sheet.

Chequer-board Cookies

Prepared the vanilla and chocolate mixtures to the dough stage as above. On a lightly floured board pat each dough into the shape of a brick. For both doughs, make two lengthways cuts on two of the long sides – as if cutting potato chips – to produce 9 long rectangular strips. Now reassemble the brick-shaped dough by exchanging every other strip for the alternate flavour, so that at each end of the brick you have a chess-board effect. Gently press the dough from each side to make the pieces stick to each other.

Wrap the dough in plastic and chill in the fridge for at least 30 minutes until firm to prevent distortion when slicing. Then cut 5 mm / ¼ in. slices from the dough and place on the prepared baking sheet.

Bake the cookies in the preheated oven until the vanilla part is pale gold. Leave on the baking sheet for 2 minutes then use a palette knife to transfer the biscuits to a wire rack.

BRANDY SNAPS

Originally from Yorkshire, these attractive biscuits are now produced all over Britain, particularly for Christmas. Despite their name, the biscuits contain little brandy but they do have a buttery, ginger flavour. The biscuits are very good just as they are, or filled with whipped cream and diced preserved ginger just before serving and while still crisp. Plain brandy snaps, baskets and tuiles can be stored in an airtight plastic box in the freezer.

Oven: 160°C/325°F/gas mark 3 ♦ Baking time: 8 minutes
Equipment: baking sheet – lined or buttered; wide palette knife;
six 15 cm/6 in. lengths of 1 cm/½ in. dowel,
or wooden spoons with the same size handles
Makes: about 30 biscuits

120 g/4 oz butter
120 g/4 oz demerara sugar
120 g/4 oz golden syrup
120 g/4 oz plain flour
1 tsp ground ginger
1 tsp lemon juice
1 tsp brandy

In a medium-sized saucepan, gently heat the butter, sugar and syrup until the butter has melted and the sugar has completely dissolved. Remove from the heat and cool slightly. Mix the sieved flour and ginger into the pan, add the lemon juice and brandy and stir until smooth. Drop well-spaced teaspoons of the mixture on to the prepared baking sheet – the biscuits spread a lot during baking.

Bake in the preheated oven until the biscuits are golden brown. Cool on the baking sheet for 30 seconds then carefully lift a biscuit with the palette knife and, while still soft, wrap – but not too tightly – around a length of dowel or the handle of a wooden spoon. Place on a wire rack until cooled then slip the biscuit from the piece of dowel so that it can be used again. Make the biscuits in batches.

Brandy Snap Baskets

These are for serving sorbets and ice-creams. A variation on the traditional rolled version can be made with the hot, pliable brandy snap by gently pressing the biscuit either over the outside of or inside a small, smooth dish or bowl. Leave for a few minutes until set into the shape, then carefully remove and store in an air-tight container until required. Fill each basket with a scoop or two of sorbet or ice-cream just before serving so that the biscuit container remains crisp.

Brandy Snap Tuiles

These delicate lacy biscuits are easier to make than the curled version. Follow the recipe and just before placing the baking sheets in the oven sprinkle some grated plain chocolate or a few chopped nuts – almonds or hazelnuts – in the centre of each spoonful of mixture. While the biscuits bake, place all available rolling pins (or use jam jars on their sides and wedged into place on a crumpled drying cloth) on your work surface. Gently remove a biscuit from the baking sheet and place over the rolling pin, curving it round to resemble the shape of a Roman roof tile. Leave for 5 minutes then transfer to a cooling rack. Keep in an air-tight bag or plastic box until ready to serve.

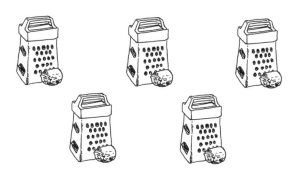

CHOCOLATE PADDINGTON BEARS

Paddington Bear cookie cutters can sometimes be found in kitchenware shops. But, if need be, trace the shape from a Paddington book to make a cardboard template. The chocolate icing incorporates the famous bear's favourite food – marmalade.

Oven: 200°C/400°F/gas mark 6 ♦ Baking time: 10–12 minutes
Equipment: Paddington Bear cutter or template;
baking sheet – lined or buttered
Makes: 8–10 biscuits

2 tbs cocoa ♦ 2 tbs hot water
90 g/3 oz butter ♦ 150 g/5 oz light muscovado sugar
1 egg ♦ 175 g/6 oz plain flour

icing:
150 g/5 oz plain dessert chocolate ♦ 2 tbs orange jelly marmalade
60 g/2 oz icing sugar ♦ 1–2 tsp hot water

Blend the cocoa with the hot water in a bowl then add the butter, in pieces, and the sugar. Beat together until smooth. Mix in the egg and the flour until you have a stiff dough that can be shaped into a ball.

Roll out the dough on a floured board until 5 mm/¼ in. thick. Cut out the biscuits and place them, well spaced, on the prepared baking sheet.

Bake the biscuits in the preheated oven until the edges are just changing colour. Cool on the baking sheet, then transfer the biscuits to a wire rack.

To make the icing: break the chocolate into pieces in a heatproof bowl and melt in a microwave oven or over simmering water. Stir in the marmalade and spoon the chocolate over the hat and boots of each biscuit bear – sometimes I cover the paws too. Mix the icing sugar with just enough hot water to make a thin piping mixture. Spoon into a forcing bag fitted with a fine line nozzle and pipe a decoration to outline the clothes and face of each bear. Leave in a cool place for 1–2 hours for the icing to set.

CINNAMON STARS

Star-shaped biscuits are usually reserved for Christmas, if you make a small hole in each one before baking, they can be tied on to the tree with ribbon.

Oven: 160°C/325°F/gas mark 3 ♦ *Baking time: 15–20 minutes*
Equipment: star-shaped pastry cutter; baking sheet – buttered
Makes: about 24 biscuits

3 egg whites ♦ 175 g / 6 oz icing sugar
230 g / 8 oz ground almonds ♦ 2–3 tsp ground cinnamon
1 tsp grated zest of lemon
a little extra caster sugar

Whisk the egg whites with the sieved icing sugar in a mixing bowl set over simmering water until the mixture is thick and foamy. Remove from the heat and set aside 3 tablespoons of the meringue until later. Sieve a tablespoon of the ground almonds with the cinnamon into the mixture and fold in the rest with the lemon zest. Stand the bowl in cold water for about 30 minutes until the mixture is cool.

Carefully roll out the mixture on a surface lightly dusted with caster sugar until 5 mm / ¼ in. thick. Use a star cutter to cut out the biscuits. Place on the prepared baking sheet and spread or brush the reserved meringue over the top of each biscuit.

Bake in the preheated oven until just set. Cool on the baking sheet, then transfer the biscuits to a wire rack.

CHRISTMAS COOKIES

With ribbon ties, these pretty cookies can be used to decorate the festive tree or Christmas garlands. Note that after a couple of days the cookies begin to soften, so serve or give them away in good time while still fresh and crisp. There's now a wide variety of Christmas cookie cutters available in the shops, otherwise make your own shapes using cardboard templates – a bell, a tree, and a star. Keep the cookies plain, or decorate with piped white icing and silver and gold dragees.

Oven: 180°C/350°F/gas mark 4 ♦ *Baking time: 10–12 minutes*
Equipment: Christmas cookie cutters; baking sheet – lined or buttered
Makes: about 20 cookies

120 g/4 oz butter ♦ 120 g/4 oz caster sugar
4 tbs golden syrup ♦ 265 g/9 oz plain flour
1 tsp ground ginger ♦ ½ tsp bicarbonate of soda

icing:
120 g/4 oz icing sugar ♦ hot water

Cream the butter and sugar until light and fluffy. Add the syrup and beat well. Gradually mix in the flour sieved with the ginger and bicarbonate of soda until you have a soft dough. On a floured board, roll out the dough to 5 mm/¼ in. thickness. Cut out the cookies and place on the prepared baking sheet. If using with ribbons, make a small hole near the top of each cookie with a wooden skewer – though remember that the hole will shrink in baking.

Bake the cookies in the preheated oven until golden-brown. With a palette knife transfer them to a wire rack to cool.

To make the icing: mix the sieved icing sugar with just sufficient hot water to make a soft pouring consistency and spread over each cookie. Alternatively, add less water to the icing sugar and produce a thicker mixture for piping around the edge of each cookie. When the icing is set, slip loops of ribbon through the holes on the cookies.

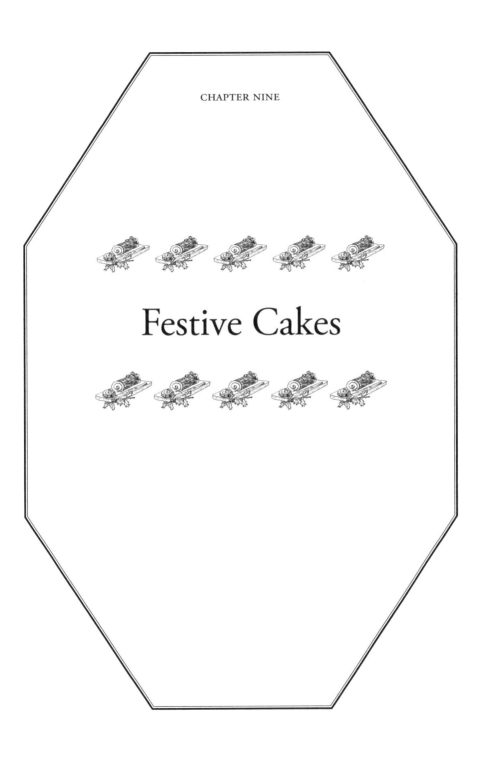

Festive Cakes

THE CONTENTS OF THIS CHAPTER

'It's fruitcake weather! Fetch our buggy. Help me find my hat.'...
Tomorrow the kind of work I like best begins: buying. Cherries and
citron, ginger and vanilla and canned Hawaiian pineapple, rinds and
raisins and walnuts and whiskey and oh, so much flour, butter, so
many eggs, spices, flavorings: why we'll need a pony to pull the buggy
home...

Truman Capote, *A Christmas Memory*, 1956

Man is born to celebrate was my mother's maxim. No event was too
trivial or commonplace to warrant a special cake: learning to swim
or ride a bike, the first melons or French beans from the garden,
the arrival of friends, were all marked by a display of her baking talents.
Astonishing birthday cakes were launched at our parties; decades before they
became standard fare on supermarket shelves, my brothers and I enjoyed
trains with trucks, cars with passengers, forts with soldiers, magic forests and
princess castles, gleaming with icing and glowing with lit candles.

Festive cakes are a great British custom, marking the seasons and celebrations
in our lives. A tiered wedding cake, for example, has long been imbued with
such importance that during the Second World War, when food was rationed
and ingredients were scarce, a cardboard model often decorated the table.
In *How We Lived Then*, Norman Longmate writes, 'One could borrow from
many bakers a splendid cardboard cover, looking like the most expensive type
of traditional iced cake.' Yet, such is our longing for celebratory cakes, that
inedible replica sometimes concealed a sad little sponge cake made with dried
eggs in place of the traditional fruit-rich wedding version.

When setting out to create a celebration cake for a birthday, particularly
for children, I usually start by baking some sponge cakes that can be cut or
carved into the desired shape. When my grandsons were three and five years

old they were each given a bicycle at a joint birthday party. I baked two chocolate sponge cakes in round tins and another in a swiss roll tin. Cutting the rectangular cake to make the frame, handlebars and saddle I assembled a bicycle cake, covered in chocolate frosting and decorated with Smarties. I piped a name on each wheel, and one was decorated with three candles, the other with five, so that each child could blow out his own.

Of course, baking a cake in a specially shaped tin – such as a large letter or number – simplifies the operation. Unless you make a great many of this kind, it may be sensible to rent or borrow rather than buy the cake tin from a kitchenware shop.

If you enjoy baking, festive cakes are fun to make though they normally take longer to prepare. This chapter includes a selection of my favourites, from the English Simnel Cake of Mothering Sunday, to the French Bûche de Noël, or a Rose Petal Angel Cake, and the choux-pastry Gâteau Paris-Brest, whose circular shape commemorates the inauguration of the famous cycle race.

There's an inevitable air of anticipation about a festive cake. Even if just rumoured or, indeed, known to exist, unveiling the confection should be an exciting theatrical moment which only enhances the cake's allure. Celebratory events are usually well-planned, yet some still sneak in unheralded. So a shrewd home baker needs a few tricks up their sleeve in order to respond to surprises. I keep spare candles and a packet of sparklers in a kitchen drawer. An angel cake or discs of baked puff pastry, stored in the freezer, can be sandwiched with thick cream and fresh fruit in a trice. Or a box of tiny meringues can be transformed into a towering Instant Celebration Cake shining with chocolate sauce. Bravo!

SIMNEL CAKE

Traditionally associated with Simnel Sunday, the mid-Lent date in the Christian calendar. Simnel derives from the Latin for fine flour – the kind used by pastry cooks. In Victorian times, it was customary for girls in service to return home on Mothering Sunday bearing a Simnel cake. Today this lovely cake with its characteristic layer of marzipan is usually reserved for Easter itself.

Oven: 150 °C/300 °F/gas mark 2 ♦ Baking time: 2¾ – 3 hours
Equipment: 18 cm/7 in. cake tin – buttered and lined
Makes: 8–10-portion cake

175 g/6 oz butter ♦ 175 g/6 oz pale muscovado sugar ♦ 3 eggs
finely grated zest of 1 lemon or orange ♦ 230 g/8 oz plain flour
1 tsp baking powder ♦ 1 tsp mixed spice
230 g/8 oz sultanas ♦ 175 g/6 oz currants ♦ 60 g/2 oz seedless raisins
60 g/2 oz glacé cherries, quartered ♦ 60 g/2 oz chopped candied peel
2 tbs milk ♦ 450 g/1 lb marzipan (recipe on p. 291)

decoration:
1 tbs of apple jelly or sieved apricot jam ♦ 1 tsp of beaten egg
60 g/2 oz icing sugar, sieved ♦ 2 tsp warm water
about 12 sugar flowers or fresh edible flowers

Cream the butter with the sugar until light and fluffy. Beat in the eggs, one at a time, with the grated lemon or orange zest. Sieve the flour, baking powder and spices on to a plate and add to the mixture a little at a time, alternately with the dried and candied fruit. Mix in the milk.

Spoon half the cake mixture into the prepared cake tin. Divide the marzipan and roll out one half to make a circle the same size as the cake tin. Gently place the marzipan on top of the mixture, and cover with the remaining mixture and smooth level.

Bake in the preheated oven until the cake is cooked and a wooden skewer comes out clean from the centre. Cool in the tin for 45 minutes then turn out on to a wire rack.

The decoration: when the cake is cold, roll out the rest of the marzipan to make a 18 cm / 7 in. circle. Brush the top of the cake with the jelly or jam and carefully place the marzipan on top. Roll lightly with a rolling pin. Press the prongs of a fork around the edge to make an attractive border. Brush the marzipan with the beaten egg and place under a high grill for a few minutes to give an attractive toasted golden crust. The cake is very pleasing left like this. But if you wish to prettify it further, mix the icing sugar with the water until smooth, and pour into the centre of the marzipan, leaving the border un-iced. Arrange the flowers around the edge of the icing, and tie a ribbon around the side of the cake.

EASTER NEST CAKE

An alternative Easter cake, specially for children and the young at heart. Prepare the cake to the recipe you prefer – I usually make a marble cake with the Easter colours of chocolate, yellow and vanilla (see p. 94), but a simple sponge cake (p. 76) works just as well – and cover it with chocolate butter icing.

Decoration for a 18–20 cm / 7–8 in. round cake

chocolate butter icing:
1 tbs cocoa powder ♦ 3 tbs hot water ♦ 230 g / 8 oz icing sugar
90 g / 3 oz butter, softened ♦ 2 tbs single cream or milk

nest decoration:
120 g / 4 oz plain or milk dessert chocolate
60 g / 2 oz Shredded Wheat, large size ♦ 60 g / 2 oz Bran Flakes
10–12 miniature sugar-coated eggs ♦ 10–12 miniature foil-wrapped eggs
1 or more fluffy artificial chicks

To make the icing, measure the cocoa into a bowl and blend in the hot water until smooth. Sift the icing sugar into the bowl and add the butter and cream or milk. Gently mix the ingredients together to make a soft, smooth spreading icing. Use a palette knife to coat the tops and sides of the cake, then leave the cake in a warm, dry place to firm slightly.

To make the nest, break the chocolate into pieces and melt in a bowl in a microwave oven or over simmering water. Remove from the heat and stir gently until smooth. Add both kinds of cereal, crumbled, and toss them together until coated with the chocolate. Spoon half the mixture into the centre of the cake and spread out to cover at least two-thirds of the surface. Spoon the rest of the mixture around the edge, building it up slightly to resemble a shallow bird's nest. Leave in dry place to set, then arrange the miniature eggs in the nest and place the chicks on top.

GÂTEAU MADELEINE

A handsome celebration cake: three layers of crisp meringue sandwiched with chocolate cream and decorated with chocolate shavings or caraque. The meringue layers can be made well ahead and the completed cake can be stored in the freezer overnight. Allow the cake to half defrost before serving – this makes it easier to cut.

Oven: 100 °C / 200 °F / gas mark ¼ ♦ Baking time: 2 hours plus overnight to cool
Equipment: 3 baking sheets – lined
Makes: 12–18-portion cake

meringue:
4 egg whites ♦ 230 g / 8 oz caster sugar

chocolate cream:
230 g / 8 oz plain dessert chocolate ♦ 4 tbs water
600 ml / 20 fl oz double cream

chocolate caraque:
60 g / 2 oz plain dessert chocolate

Use a pencil and a plate to draw three 20 cm / 8 in. diameter circles on the paper covering the baking sheets, and put a smear of butter under each corner to hold the paper in place.

In a large mixing bowl, whisk the egg whites until really stiff. Fold in half the sugar and whisk again before folding in the remaining sugar. Spread or pipe the mixture over the baking paper keeping just inside the drawn circles. Make the meringue as level as possible with a spatula or the back of a spoon.

Bake in the preheated oven for 50–60 minutes then exchange the positions of the baking sheets in the oven. Bake for another hour. Then turn off the oven and leave the meringue to cool overnight. Next day, peel the paper from the meringues and store each layer in a sealed plastic box until ready to assemble the gâteau.

To make the chocolate cream: break the chocolate into pieces in a small bowl and melt in a microwave oven or over simmering water. Stir gently until smooth and allow to cool slightly. Whisk the cream until it thickens but still looks glossy. Carefully pour the melted chocolate into the cream and fold together until well combined.

Place one meringue layer on a flat board or serving platter, spread with chocolate cream and cover with another layer. Repeat with the third layer then spread cream over the top and sides of the cake.

To prepare the chocolate caraque: break the remaining chocolate into pieces on to a plate and melt over hot water or in a microwave oven. Scrape the melted chocolate on to a marble slab or cold work surface and leave to set. With a long-bladed sharp knife, scrape thin curling layers from the set chocolate. I find the best way to do this is to hold the blade nearly upright to the surface and using a sawing movement drag the blade across the chocolate to form a scroll. Gently lift the scroll and place on top of the cake. Repeat until you have covered the top of the cake and used up all the chocolate. Then place the gâteau in a refrigerator for 2–3 hours before serving, or store in the freezer overnight.

PASSION-FRUIT CLOUD CAKE

Three layers of soft meringue sandwiched with citrus cream and fresh passion-fruit. If you prefer, though it calls for some dexterity, the meringue can be left in one piece and rolled around the cream filling – as for a Swiss roll – to make a meringue roulade.

Oven: 200°C/400°F/gas mark 6 ♦ *Baking time: 30 minutes*
Equipment: 32 x 24 cm/13 x 9 in. Swiss roll tin – lined
Makes: 10-portion cake

6 egg whites ♦ 350 g/12 oz caster sugar
60 g/2 oz pecan nuts, roughly chopped ♦ 2 tbs demerara sugar

citrus cream:
400 ml/14 fl oz double cream
1 tangerine or ½ orange, finely grated zest and juice
4–5 ripe passion-fruit

Whisk the egg white until stiff – ideally in a mixer or using an electric beater. Gradually whisk in half of the sugar, then fold in the remaining sugar using a balloon whisk. Spoon the meringue into the prepared cake tin and spread level. Sprinkle the chopped pecan nuts and demerara sugar over the top.

Bake in the middle of the preheated oven until the top of the meringue is golden brown and a wooden skewer comes out clean from the centre.

Remove from the oven and cool the meringue in the tin for 5 minutes, then turn it out on to a sheet of baking paper on the work surface. Carefully peel off the lining and allow the cake to cool. Then use a long sharp knife to cut across the cake in the shorter direction to make three oblong pieces.

To prepare the citrus cream: whisk the cream until fairly stiff though still glossy. Gently mix in the grated zest and strained juice of the tangerine. Cut the passion-fruit in half and scrape the flesh and seeds into a bowl or saucer.

Use a fish slice or wide spatula to transfer one piece of cake, smooth side uppermost, to a flat serving dish. Spread half the cream on top and spoon over half the passion-fruit. Use the fish slice to transfer the second cake layer on top but place it nut side uppermost. Spread over the remaining cream and passion-fruit. Then carefully cover with the third layer, nut side uppermost, to complete the cake.

Chill the cake in a refrigerator for 2–3 hours before serving until the cream is set and the cake is easier to cut into slices.

MARZIPAN AND MACAROON CAKE

Strictly for almond lovers and popular with my French friends. Adapted from my English Almond Cake (p. 175) but enriched with a layer of marzipan and crisp almond meringue.

Oven: 180 °C/350 °F/gas mark 4 ♦ Baking time: 30–35 minutes
Equipment: 20 cm/8 in. spring-clip tin – buttered and base-lined
Makes: 8-portion cake

120 g/4 oz butter ♦ 90 g/3 oz vanilla-flavoured caster sugar
1 egg ♦ 1 egg yolk ♦ 1 tbs milk
1–2 drops bitter almond essence (optional)
60 g/2 oz self-raising flour ♦ 60 g/2 oz ground almonds
225 g/8 oz prepared marzipan (p. 291) ♦ 1 egg white
30 g/1 oz caster sugar ♦ 30 g/1 oz flaked almonds

Cream the butter with the caster sugar until light and fluffy. Beat in the egg, egg yolk and milk with the almond essence. Fold in the sieved flour and the ground almonds. Spoon into the prepared cake tin and smooth level.

Roll out the marzipan to fit the cake tin and place gently on top of the mixture. Measure 1 tbs caster sugar and 1 tbs of flaked almonds on to a saucer and reserve. Whisk the egg white until stiff and whisk in the rest of the caster sugar. Fold in the rest of the flaked almonds and spread the meringue over the marzipan. Sprinkle the sugar and almonds from the saucer on top of the cake.

Bake in the preheated oven until the cake is cooked and just beginning to shrink from the tin. Cool in the tin for 10 minutes then release the clip on the cake tin and remove the side, slide the cake on its paper on to a wire rack to cool.

PRALINE CREAM GÂTEAU

Inspired by the virtuosity of French pâtisserie, I devised this gâteau a long time ago. Though it takes some time to prepare, the flavour makes it worthwhile. The praline mixture can be prepared days ahead and stored until needed.

Oven: 190°C/375°F/gas mark 5 ♦ *Baking time: 25 minutes*
Equipment: buttered sheet of baking paper; 28 x 18 cm/11 x 7 in. shallow tin –
buttered and lined; sugar thermometer (optional)
Makes: 8–10-portion cake

praline:
120 g / 4 oz blanched almonds ♦ 120 g / 4 oz caster sugar
2 tbs cold water

sponge cake:
120 g / 4 oz butter ♦ 120 g / 4 oz caster sugar
2 eggs ♦ 100 g / 3½ oz self-raising flour
30 g / 1 oz ground almonds

French butter cream:
120 g / 4 oz caster sugar ♦ 1 tbs water ♦ 2 egg yolks
120 g / 4 oz unsalted butter ♦ 60 g / 2 oz praline powder
30 g / 1 oz flaked almonds, toasted

glacé icing:
2 tsp instant coffee ♦ 2 tsp hot water ♦ 75 g / 2½ oz icing sugar

To prepare the praline: toast the almonds on a heat-proof plate, under a grill or in a hot oven, until golden-brown, turning them now and again. In a small pan, dissolve the sugar in the water over low heat. Raise the heat and watch the syrup until it caramelizes and turns golden brown. Remove from the heat, add the almonds and tip the mixture on to the buttered paper to set. When cold, remove the praline from the paper and place in a heavy duty plastic bag – or wrap in several layers of greaseproof paper – and crush with a rolling pin until a fine powder results. Store the praline powder in an air-tight container until needed.

To make the cake: cream the butter with the sugar until pale and fluffy. Gradually beat in the eggs. Fold in the sieved flour and the ground almonds. Spread the mixture evenly in the prepared cake tin. Bake in the preheated oven until the cake is golden brown and is just starting to shrink from the tin. Cool in the tin for 2 minutes, then turn out on to a wire rack. When cold, cut the cake lengthways, so that you have two pieces the same length as the cake tin but half the width.

To make the butter cream: dissolve the caster sugar in the water in a small pan over low heat. Raise the heat and bring the syrup to 110°C / 220°F, the point when it forms a short fine thread when pulled between finger and thumb – cool a little in a teaspoon first, before you make the test. Remove from the heat and slowly pour the syrup on to the egg yolks in a mixing bowl, whisking all the time with an electric hand-held beater. As the mixture cools, gradually beat in the butter, adding it in small pieces. Now beat in the praline powder in two or three additions. Use half the cream to sandwich the two pieces of cake, placing one on top of the other.

To make the glacé icing: mix the the coffee with the water in a cup or small bowl and blend in the sieved icing sugar to make a smooth pouring consistency. Pour the icing over the top of the cake, spreading it carefully with a knife. Spread the rest of the praline cream over the sides of the cake. Decorate the cake by arranging a line of overlapping flaked almonds around the top and the base. Leave the cake in a cold place for 5–6 hours before serving.

FRESH STRAWBERRY GÂTEAU or LE FRAISIER

A few years ago this attractive gâteau began to appear in the windows of Parisian pâtisseries. This is my version. Two layers of Genoese sponge cake are sandwiched with a liqueur-laced cream studded with halved strawberries and glazed with a strawberry purée.

Oven: 180°C/350°F/gas mark 4 ♦ Baking time: 20–25 minutes
Equipment: two 23 cm/9 in. sponge sandwich tins – buttered and base-lined,
dusted with caster sugar; 22 cm/8½ in. spring-clip tin
Makes: 10–12-portion cake

Genoese sponge cake:
4 eggs ♦ 120 g/4 oz caster sugar ♦ 60 g/2 oz cornflour
60 g/2 oz plain flour ♦ 45 g/1½ oz butter, melted

cream filling:
150 ml/5 fl oz double cream ♦ 2 tbs Grand Marnier or orange-based liqueur
6 leaves gelatine ♦ 2 tbs orange juice ♦ 2 egg yolks
60 g/2 oz caster sugar ♦ 1 egg white ♦ 1 tsp caster sugar
230 g/8 oz firm, ripe strawberries

glaze:
120 g/4 oz strawberries, quartered ♦ 2–3 tsp caster sugar
1 leaf gelatine

Use an electric beater or mixer to whisk the eggs with the caster sugar until light and foamy and the whisk leaves a trail over the surface. Sift together the cornflour and plain flour and replace in a sieve. Dust a thin layer of the flour over the surface of the egg mixture and gently fold in, using a balloon whisk. Repeat until all the flour is incorporated. Slowly dribble the melted butter into the mixture, gently folding it in. Divide the mixture between the two prepared cake tins and smooth level.

Bake in the preheated oven until the cakes are springy in the centre and are just starting to shrink from the tin. Cool the cakes in the tins for 2 minutes then turn out on to a wire rack.

Whisk the cream with the liqueur until stiff but glossy. Soften the gelatine in the orange juice in a small pan, then stir over low heat until dissolved. Whisk the egg yolks with 60 g / 2 oz sugar until foamy, trickle the gelatine into the mixture, whisking all the time. In a separate bowl, whisk the egg white until stiff, add the teaspoon of sugar and whisk again. Fold both egg mixtures into the thick cream until well combined.

To assemble the gâteau; place the sponge cakes on a level surface and with a small serrated knife trim a narrow strip from the edge of each cake to ensure they fit neatly inside the the spring-clip tin. Place one of the trimmed cakes in the base of the tin and cover with a thin layer of cream. Arrange halved strawberries around the edge of the cake with their cut sides facing the curved side of the tin. Spoon half the remaining cream on top. Slice the strawberries whch remain after constructing the perimeter and arrange them evenly on this layer of cream. Cover them with the rest of the cream and smooth level. Now carefully place the other sponge cake on top. Place a circle of baking paper on top of the cake and a cake or tart tin of the correct size on top of that. Then you can arrange three 120 g / 4 oz weights in this empty tin to gently compress the gâteau without damaging it in any way. Place the whole cake contraption in a refrigerator for at least 4 hours until the cream is set.

To make the glaze: warm the quartered strawberries with the sugar in a small pan over moderate heat for 3–4 minutes to draw out their juice. Press the mixture through a fine sieve back into the pan and add the gelatine. Stir over low heat until dissolved. Allow the glaze to cool slightly and when starting to set, remove the weights, tin and paper from the top of the gâteau and spoon it over the cake. Chill until the glaze is set. If you wish, the gâteau can be stored in the refrigerator for 24 hours.

To serve: wrap a hot cloth around the cake tin, carefully undo the clip and remove the side. Transfer the gâteau to a flat serving plate and use a very sharp knife to cut into portions.

GÂTEAU PARIS-BREST

A French pastry-chef created this gâteau to celebrate the famous cycle race from Paris to Brest that was launched in 1891. Rings of choux pastry – which, of course, inflate in the oven – represent bicycle wheels, sandwiched with a rich praline cream, though a quicker, easier coffee-flavoured cream is an alternative. The gâteau has remained popular with pâtisseries, particularly during the season of the annual Tour de France.

Oven: 220°C/425°F/gas mark 7 ♦ Baking time: 30 minutes
Equipment: baking sheet – lined;
piping-bag fitted with plain 1 cm/½ in. nozzle
Makes: 8–12-portion cake

choux pastry:
100 g/3½ oz plain flour ♦ 250 ml/9 fl oz boiling water
90 g/3 oz butter ♦ 3 eggs
1 tbs caster sugar ♦ 15 g/½ oz flaked almonds, lightly toasted

praline cream:
300 ml/10 fl oz whipping cream
120 g/4 oz prepared praline powder (p. 292)

coffee cream:
300 ml/10 fl oz whipping cream ♦ 3–4 tbs strong black coffee
2–3 tsp caster sugar or to taste ♦ 1 tsp icing sugar

Mark a circle of 18 cm/7 in. diameter on the baking paper lining the baking sheet.

Sift the flour on to a sheet of greaseproof paper and place near the cooker. Measure the water into a heavy-based pan and add the butter in small pieces. Stir until the butter has melted and bring the liquid to the boil. Remove the pan from the heat and add all the flour. Beat with a wooden spoon over moderate heat for a few minutes until the paste is smooth and forms a ball. Remove from the heat.

Lightly whisk the eggs in a cup or jug, then add them gradually to the pastry mixture, beating in each addition until combined. Now beat the mixture for 1 minute until smooth and glossy. Place the piping-bag in a bowl or jug to keep it upright and spoon in the choux paste. Pipe a ring of paste on the baking paper just inside the 18 cm / 7 in. circle; pipe another ring just inside the first. Pipe a third ring of paste on top over the join.

Bake in the preheated oven until the pastry has puffed up and is golden-brown. Remove the pastry from the oven and, using a cloth to protect your hand, cut through the cake with a long-bladed sharp knife to divide it equally (as if the Earth through the Equator). Use a teaspoon to remove most of the uncooked mixture and replace the pastry halves, cut side uppermost, in the oven for 5 minutes to complete baking. Carefully transfer the pastry to a wire rack to cool.

In a small pan, dissolve the sugar in a tablespoonful of water and bring to the boil. Remove from the heat and brush over the crust of the top half of the pastry. Sprinkle over the toasted flaked almonds.

To make the praline cream: whisk the cream until thick but still glossy, then fold in the praline powder. Place the bottom half of the pastry on a flat serving plate and spoon in the cream, heaping it up well. Cover with the top layer and dust lightly with the sieved icing sugar. Chill until ready to serve, ideally within 2 hours so that the choux pastry shell is still crisp.

To make the coffee cream: instead of filling the cake with a praline mixture, replace the praline powder with black coffee and fold in caster sugar for sweetness. Assemble the cake as above.

HOT LIMONCELLO CAKE WITH COOL LEMON CREAM

The contrast of hot cake with cool cream makes an enjoyable pudding or tea-time treat.

Oven: 180°C/350°F/gas mark 4 ♦ Baking time: 25–30 minutes
Equipment: 20 cm/8 in. square tin – buttered and base-lined
Makes: 10–12-portion cake

1 large lemon, wax-free ♦ 120 g/4 oz butter
120 g/4 oz golden caster sugar ♦ 2 eggs
120 g/4 oz self-raising flour
60 g/2 oz ground almonds ♦ 2 tbs caster sugar

lemon cream:
300 ml/10 fl oz double cream ♦ 2–3 tsp caster sugar
2–3 tsp lemon juice

25 ml/1 fl oz or ½ miniature bottle of limoncello

Halve the lemon and cut a thin slice from each half and set them aside. Squeeze the juice from the lemon into a cup and and finely grate the zest into a mixing bowl. Add the butter and sugar to the mixing bowl and beat the mixture until pale and creamy. Beat in the eggs, one at a time, then fold in the flour and ground almonds with 1–2 tablespoons of the strained lemon juice.

Spoon the mixture into the prepared tin and smooth level. Bake in the preheated oven until golden brown and a wooden skewer comes out clean from the centre. Remove the cake from the oven and leave in the tin. Reserve 2–3 teaspoons of lemon juice for the cream and stir the extra caster sugar into the remaining lemon juice in the cup. Spoon the mixture over the hot cake.

Beat the cream until thick but glossy. Sweeten to taste with the caster sugar and stir in the lemon juice.

Both cake and cream can now wait until ready to serve. Rewarm the cake, still in its tin, in a hot oven or turn it on to a plate and warm it in a microwave. Place the cake on a flat serving plate and pour the limoncello over the top. Pile the cream on top of the cake and decorate with the halved slices of lemon. Serve straight away.

HAZELNUT AND MUSCOVADO MERINGUE CAKE

Discs of hazelnut and caramel meringue sandwiched with whipped cream or coffee ice make a simple dessert or a rich cake for tea-time. The meringue layers can be stored in the freezer until needed, then assembled in a trice.

Oven: 150°C/300°F/gas mark 2 ♦ Baking time: 2 hours
Equipment: 2 baking sheets – lined
Makes: 8–10-portion cake

meringue:
120 g/4 oz toasted hazelnuts ♦ 2 tbs cornflour ♦ 4 egg whites
230 g/8 oz light muscovado sugar, sieved

filling:
300 ml/10 fl oz double cream, or 500 ml/1 pint coffee ice-cream
1 tbs icing sugar

Place a sheet of baking paper on each baking sheet. Use a pencil to mark a circle of 23 cm/9 in. diameter on each sheet. Finely chop the hazelnuts with the cornflour in a processor. Whisk the egg whites until stiff, then gradually add the sieved sugar, whisking all the time. Fold in the ground hazelnuts and cornflour.

Divide the mixture between the baking sheets, spreading it level and inside the pencilled circles. Bake in the preheated oven for 1 hour. Turn off the oven and leave the meringue for another hour. Remove from the oven and allow to cool. Gently slide a palette knife under each meringue layer to free it from the paper. If you wish to store the meringues until needed, place them, sandwiched with kitchen paper, in a lidded plastic box or a sealed plastic bag in a freezer.

When ready to serve, carefully transfer one layer of meringue to a flat serving dish. Whisk the cream until thick and spoon over this layer or, if you prefer the ice-cream variant, place spoonfuls of ice-cream on top. Cover this with the second disc of meringue and dust with sieved icing sugar. Serve an ice-cream filled cake straight away, or a cream-filled version within an hour.

SWISS ROLL WITH SPICED PRUNES AND PORT WINE FILLING

In *A Room of One's Own*, Virginia Woolf concedes that 'there are people whose charity embraces even the prune.' I'm fairly charitable about prunes, particularly in the spiced filling known as *lekvar* which I've combined with crushed amaretti biscuits and a layer of wine cream to give a distinctive and attractive flavour to this cake. *Lekvar* is an Eastern European word for a fruit butter and could apply to any fruit. The Slovaks, however, seem to be particularly fond of prune or plum *lekvar*.

Oven: 200°C/400°F/gas mark 6 ♦ *Baking time: 12–15 minutes*
Equipment; 30 x 20 cm/12 x 8 in. Swiss roll tin
– buttered and base-lined; tea cloth
Makes: 12-portion cake

3 eggs ♦ 90 g/3 oz caster sugar ♦ 90 g/3 oz plain flour
1 tbs caster sugar

filling:
265 g/9 oz pitted ready-to-eat prunes ♦ 2–3 tbs dark muscovado sugar
½ tsp ground cinnamon ♦ 6 tbs water
¼ tsp vanilla essence
60 g/2 oz amaretti biscuits, crushed

port wine cream:
300 ml/10 fl oz double cream ♦ 1 tbs caster sugar
2 tbs tawny port ♦ 1 tsp icing sugar

Whisk the eggs with the sugar until light and foamy using a mixer or hand-held electric beater and the whisk leaves a trail across the surface of the mixture. If you are doing this by hand, using a balloon whisk or mechanical egg beater, place the bowl over simmering water to shorten the time needed.

Sift a layer of flour over the surface of the mixture and gently fold in with a balloon whisk. Repeat until all the flour has been incorporated. Pour the mixture into the prepared tin and spread evenly.

Bake in the preheated oven until golden brown. Cool in the tin for 2 minutes then turn out on to a clean teacloth lightly dusted with the tablespoon of caster sugar. Peel off the baking paper and roll up the cake, keeping the cloth in the place where the filling will go. Place on a wire rack to cool.

To prepare the prune filling: simmer the prunes with the sugar, cinnamon and water in a covered pan over moderate heat for 20–30 minutes until soft. Cool slightly then purée the prune mixture with the vanilla essence in a food processor. Check the taste and add sugar or a dash of lemon juice to balance the flavours. Set the mixture aside until cold.

Whisk the cream with the sugar and port until stiff but glossy.

To assemble the cake: unroll the cake and spread the prune filling over it in an even layer. Scatter the crushed amaretti on top then cover with the port wine cream. Carefully re-roll the cake and place on a serving dish. Dust lightly with sieved icing sugar and set aside for 2–3 hours in a cold place before serving.

ROSE PETAL CAKE WITH ROSÉ CHAMPAGNE CREAM

A delicate shell-pink Angel Cake scented with rose-water and decorated with candied rose petals is ideal for a floral tea party served with nasturtium flower sandwiches and lavender biscuits. Serve the cake with thick cream enriched with pink champagne – perfect for a pink angel.

Oven: 160°C/325°F/gas mark 3 ◆ Baking time: 40–45 minutes
Equipment: 25 cm/10 in. non-stick ring tin, or 23 cm/9 in. spring-clip tin
– buttered and dusted with caster sugar
Makes: 16-portion cake

2–3 handfuls of fresh, unsprayed pink and red rose petals
1 egg white ◆ 30 g/1 oz caster sugar

sponge cake:
90 g/3 oz plain flour ◆ 15 g/½ oz cornflour ◆ 175 g/6 oz caster sugar
6 egg whites ◆ 1 tsp cream of tartar
1–2 drops cochineal or pink food colour ◆ 1–2 tsp rose-water

glacé icing:
175 g/6 oz icing sugar ◆ 5–6 tsp hot water ◆ rose-water to taste
1 drop cochineal or pink food colour

pink champagne cream:
300 ml/10 fl oz double cream
90 ml/3 fl oz pink champagne or similar
30 g/1 oz caster sugar ◆ 1 drop cochineal

Prepare the candied rose petals first: select about 20 of the firmest pink petals. Brush both sides of a petal with lightly whisked egg white then dust with caster sugar and place on baking paper on a cooling rack. Repeat with the other 19 petals. Set aside to dry.

Place the remaining petals and remaining caster sugar in a food processor and chop briefly until you have a fairly fine pink mixture for decorating the cake.

Sieve the flour with the cornflour and half the sugar, then tip back into the sieve. In a large bowl whisk the egg whites with the cream of tartar until stiff and fluffy but still a little moist – that is, the meringue slides across the bowl when it is tilted. Sprinkle the rest of the sugar over the meringue and whisk in. Add the rose-water and drop of cochineal and whisk in, aiming for a beautiful pale pink – the colour won't change much during baking. Sieve a layer of the flour/sugar blend over the top of the mixture and fold in with a balloon whisk. Repeat until all the blend has been incorporated. Pour the cake mixture into the cake tin and smooth level.

Bake in the preheated oven until a thin wooden skewer comes out clean from the centre of the cake. Cool in the tin for 2 minutes, run the blade of a small knife round the rim of the cake and then turn it out on to a wire rack. Leave the cake upside down.

To make the icing: sieve the icing sugar into a bowl and mix with sufficient hot water to make a smooth, spreading consistency. Flavour with rose-water and just one drop of cochineal to produce a shell-pink colour. Spoon and spread the icing over the top of the cake allowing it to run down the sides. Scatter the chopped rose petal mixture over the cake before the icing sets and decorate the top and around the base with the candied rose petals. Set aside until ready to serve.

To prepare the champagne cream: whisk the cream until thick but still glossy. Fold in the champagne and sugar to taste. If you wish to strengthen the colour add a droplet of cochineal. Spoon into a pretty bowl and decorate with a few rose petals. Chill until ready to serve with the cake.

GOLD VANILLA CAKE and SILVER ALMOND CAKE

Gold Cakes and Silver Cakes have appeared in cookery books for a century. They are produced by separating the eggs – the yolks go into the vanilla-scented gold cake and the almond-flavoured silver cake contains the whites. Both cakes are excellent weekend fare, with their marzipan filling and icing encrustation. If celebrating a wedding anniversary, either cake is suitable when decorated with gold- or silver-coated dragees and a gold or white ribbon tied round the cake ending with a bow.

Oven: 180°C/350°F/gas mark 4 ♦ *Baking time: 30–40 minutes*
Equipment: 20 cm/8 in. spring-clip tin – buttered and base-lined
Makes: 10–12-portion cake

Gold Vanilla Cake:
175 g / 6 oz butter ♦ 175 g / 6 oz caster sugar ♦ 6 egg yolks
¼ tsp vanilla essence ♦ 175 g / 6 oz self-raising flour
1 tsp baking powder ♦ 7 tbs milk

filling:
230 g / 8 oz marzipan ♦ 3 tbs apple jelly or sieved apricot jam

vanilla frosting:
45 g / 1½ oz butter ♦ 2 tbs water ♦ 120 g / 4 oz icing sugar
¼ tsp vanilla essence or seeds ♦ yellow food colouring

Cream the butter with the sugar until light and fluffy. Beat in the vanilla essence and mix in the flour sifted with the baking powder alternately with the milk. Spoon the mixture into the prepared tin and smooth level.

Bake in the preheated oven until springy in the centre and just starting to shrink from the tin. Cool in the tin for 2 minutes then open the clip and remove the side of the tin. Leave the cake to cool for 10 minutes then transfer to a wire rack.

Use a long serrated knife to cut the cake into two layers. Roll out the marzipan to fit the cake. Brush jam over the marzipan and place – jam side down – on the lower half of the cake. Brush the rest of the jam over the marzipan and cover with the other cake layer, gently pressing it into place.

Trim off any surplus marzipan and wrap the cake in a plastic bag and leave overnight.

To make the frosting: melt the butter with the water in a small pan and bring to the boil. Remove from the heat, cool for 1 minute, then pour on to the sifted icing sugar. Beat until smooth. Flavour to taste with the vanilla, add one small drop of food colouring if you wish, then pour over the top of the cake. Leave in a cool place until set, then decorate as you wish.

Silver Almond Cake:
6 egg whites ♦ 175 g / 6 oz caster sugar ♦ 175 g / 6 oz butter
few drops almond essence ♦ 120 g / 4 oz self-raising flour
120 g / 4 oz ground almonds

filling:
230 g / 8 oz marzipan ♦ 3 tbs apple jelly or sieved apricot jam

glacé icing:
120 g / 4 oz icing sugar ♦ 2 tsp hot water ♦ 1 drop almond essence

Whisk the egg whites until stiff, sprinkle one third of the caster sugar over the top and whisk again until really stiff.

Use the same beater to cream the butter with the rest of the sugar until light and fluffy. Mix in the almond essence. Use a tablespoon to fold in one quarter of the egg whites and then gently fold in one quarter of the flour and ground almonds. Repeat until all the ingredients have been incorporated. Spoon the mixture into the cake tin and smooth level.

Bake in the preheated oven until the cake is springy in the centre and just starting to shrink from the tin. Cool in the tin for 2 minutes then undo the clip and remove the side of the tin. Leave the cake to cool for 10 minutes then transfer to a wire rack.

At this point, repeat the splitting of the cake and the layering with marzipan and jam as in the previous recipe for Gold Vanilla Cake.

To make the glacé icing: sift the icing sugar into a small bowl. Mix in the hot water and almond essence and beat until smooth. Pour over the top of the cake then set aside until dry. Decorate the cake as you wish.

WILMA'S BIRTHDAY FLOWER HAT

A suitable cake for a dedicated gardener. The sponge can be whatever type you prefer: I chose a fat-free Royal Sponge which resembles an Angel Cake (p. 86). This pretty cake is decorated with edible flowers, a pistachio marzipan brim (or use 450 g / 1 lb bought pale green almond marzipan if you prefer) and a Happy Birthday ribbon. It is named after my mother, for whom I devised it.

Oven: 160 °C / 325 °F / gas mark 3 ♦ Baking time: 45 minutes
Equipment: 23 cm / 9 in. spring-clip tin
– lined with 100 x 38 cm / 39 x 13½ in. sheet baking paper
Makes: 16-portion cake

230 g / 8 oz granulated sugar ♦ 100 ml / 3½ fl oz water
4 eggs, separated ♦ 90 g / 3 oz plain flour ♦ 30 g / 1 oz cornflour
½ tsp cream of tartar ♦ ½ tsp vanilla essence
1 tsp orange flower water

pistachio marzipan:
300 g / 10 oz shelled pistachio nuts ♦ 150 g / 5 oz caster sugar
100 g / 3½ oz icing sugar ♦ 1 egg white ♦ 1–2 tbs brandy or sherry
½ tsp cornflour

glacé icing:
265 g / 9 oz icing sugar ♦ 2–3 tbs hot water
few drops rose-water ♦ drop of pink food colour (optional)

decoration:
30 cm / 12 in. diameter silver cake board
50 cm / 18 in. pink or green, 5 cm / 2 in. wide Happy Birthday ribbon
2–3 handfuls of pink edible flowers: pinks, rose petals, geraniums

Prepare the cake tin first: cut 23 cm / 9 in. from one end of the baking paper and cut a circle the same size as the cake tin. Fold the rest of the paper lengthways into 4 layers and line the side of the cake tin, fixing the ends together with a large paper clip. Place the paper circle in the base of the tin.

Measure the sugar and water into a heavy-based pan and place over low heat, stirring until dissolved. Remove from the heat. Use an electric beater to whisk the egg whites until stiff. Bring the sugar syrup to the boil and allow to reach 110°C / 225°F or short-thread stage. Remove the syrup from the heat and cool for 2 minutes while the egg whites are whisked again until they now form peaks. Gradually add the hot sugar syrup in a thin stream to the egg whites, whisking all the time. Whisk in the vanilla essence and orange flower water, then whisk in the egg yolks one at a time.

Use a balloon whisk to gradually fold in the dry ingredients. Tip the flours and the cream of tartar into a sieve and sift a layer over the mixture, fold in carefully, then repeat until all the flour mixture has been incorporated. Pour the mixture into the prepared cake tin and smooth level.

Bake in the preheated oven until golden and a wooden skewer comes out clean from the centre. Leave the cake to cool in the tin for 5 minutes then open the clip and lift off the side of the tin, carefully removing the paper around the side of the cake. Leave the cake to cool on the base of the tin.

To make the pistachio marzipan: the papery skins of the nuts need to be removed. Tip the pistachios into a saucepan and cover with cold water. Bring to the boil, pour off the hot water and replace with cold water. Peel away the brown skins and place the kernels on kitchen paper to dry.

Chop the nuts finely in a food processor with the caster sugar. Mix in the icing sugar, add the egg white and brandy and process until the mixture forms a soft dough.

Sprinkle some cornflour on a cake board and roll out the marzipan to a circle about 30 cm / 12 in. wide. Crimp the edge like a pie-crust with your fingertips and mark a 23 cm / 9 in. circle in the centre.

To make the glacé icing: mix the sieved icing sugar with the hot water, adding it gradually to make a pouring consistency. Add a little rose-water to flavour it and just one drop of pink food colour to produce a pale shade. Spoon some of the icing over the circle marked on the marzipan and place the cake on top. Pour the rest of the icing over the cake, letting it run down the sides a little. When set, tie a band of ribbon around the side of the cake, make a bow with the rest and pin to the join in the ribbon with a cocktail stick. Just before serving arrange the flowers prettily on the marzipan brim of the hat – one side can be curved upwards if you wish – with a few more on top of the hat. Add candles if you want.

CHOCOLATE LETTER OR NUMBER CAKE

This is a simple and effective celebration cake made in the shape of the initial letter of a name or the significant number to mark a birthday or anniversary. I bake the chocolate sponge cake in a large roasting tray and use a small serrated knife to cut out the shape. The cake cuttings can be used in other recipes such as the Chocolate Dreams on p. 198 or in a baked pudding.

Oven: 180°C/350°F/gas mark 4 ♦ *Baking time: 50–60 minutes*
Equipment: 28 x 18 cm/11 x 7 in. roasting pan – lined
Makes: single layer party cake of 12–20 portions

230 g/8 oz butter, softened ♦ 230 g/8 oz caster sugar
4 eggs ♦ ½ tsp vanilla essence
230 g/8 oz self-raising flour ♦ 1 tsp baking powder
60 g/2 oz cocoa powder

frosting:
200 g/7 oz plain dessert chocolate ♦ 60 g/2 oz butter
3–4 tbs black coffee or double cream
60 g/2 oz icing sugar
chocolate buttons, or gold or silver dragees
birthday candles in holders

Measure all the ingredients in a mixing bowl and beat together until the mixture is smooth. Spoon the mixture into the prepared cake tin and spread level.

Bake in the preheated oven until the cake is starting to shrink from the tin. Turn the cake out on to a cloth-covered board to cool. Draw and cut out a template of the letter or number that you wish to make and place on top of the cake. Use a small serrated knife to carefully cut out the shape, reserving the cuttings for use in another recipe. Transfer the cake to a foil-covered serving board.

To make the chocolate frosting: melt the chocolate with the butter in a bowl in a microwave oven or over simmering water. Stir gently and add sufficient coffee or cream to give a spreadable consistency. Cool slightly then spoon over the top of the cake. Mix the sifted icing sugar into the remaining frosting until smooth and spread over the sides of the cake. Arrange a line of chocolate buttons or gold or silver dragees around the edge of the cake and decorate with candles in holders. Leave the cake in a cold place for 2 hours for the icing to set.

ROUNDABOUT CAKE

I've been making roundabout cakes for decades – they have a lasting appeal as a birthday cake. Unless it's intended as a surprise, children enjoy helping to assemble this party centrepiece. For a May-time birthday, I opt for a Maypole Cake – simply omit the paper plate and attach streamers to the top of the maypole stretching down to the chocolate animals around the edge.

One 20 cm / 8 in. diameter cake,
for example the Quick-mix Victoria Sponge p. 77

chocolate icing:
100 g / 3½ oz plain dessert chocolate ♦ 30 g / 1 oz butter
60 g / 2 oz icing sugar

decoration:
20 cm / 8 in. diameter pretty paper plate
cardboard tube from roll of kitchen paper
decorative wrapping paper for covering tube
6–8 striped drinking straws
100 g / 3½ oz dolly mixture or Smarties
small animals in chocolate or biscuit shapes

To make the icing, break the chocolate into pieces and melt in a bowl in a microwave oven or over simmering water. Cool slightly then mix in the butter and sieved icing sugar until smooth. Spread the icing over the top and sides of the cake and transfer it to a flat serving plate or board.

Make a straight cut in the paper plate from the edge to the centre, then overlap the cut edges slightly to represent the roof of the roundabout. Use Sellotape to fix in place. Cover the tube with decorative paper and fix one end to the underside of the paper plate with tape. Push the other end of the tube into the centre of the cake. Support the edge of the plate by pressing drinking straws, cut to length, into the cake. Decorate the sides by pressing dolly mixture sweets or Smarties into the icing. Arrange the chocolate animals around the edge of the cake to represent the roundabout rides. Finally, write the child's name on a small paper flag and attach it to the top of the roundabout with a cocktail stick. Set aside in a cool place for 2 hours until the icing is set.

MOCHA MERINGUE TOWER

A simple last-minute celebration cake quickly assembled from store cupboard stand-bys. Two dozen small coffee meringues are piled high – ideally on a cake stand – with whipped cream. Pour chocolate sauce over the top and serve straight away.

300 ml / 10 fl oz double cream
4 tbs creamy milk ♦ vanilla sugar
24 small coffee-flavoured meringues (p. 196)

sauce:
120 g / 4 oz plain dessert chocolate ♦ 2 tbs strong black coffee
optional decorations: cake sparklers or coloured-flame candles

Whisk the cream with the milk and the sugar until thick but still glossy. Arrange nine meringues in a single layer on a serving dish and spoon over some cream. Now add another layer of meringues and cream, repeat until you have constructed a pyramid. If you wish, the cake can be stored in the freezer for a day. Allow to defrost for 1–2 hours before serving.

When ready to serve, make the sauce by melting the broken chocolate with the coffee in a microwave oven or in a heat-proof bowl over simmering water. Remove from the heat and stir gently; then spoon over the meringue tower. Add cake decorations, if desired, such as short-stemmed sparklers or candles with coloured flames, light them and serve the cake straight away.

GUY FAWKES BONFIRE CAKE

Bonfire parties need a festive cake. A pudding basin or a metal ice-cream bombe mould gives the right bonfire shape for covering with frosting and chocolate sticks. Since devising this cake for my own children, I've added a hidden surprise for their children – the centre of the cake is filled with coloured sweets to represent fireworks. Children are usually keen to make a marzipan 'Guy' to decorate the top of the cake.

Oven: 180 °C / 350 °F / gas mark 4 ♦ *Baking time: 1¼ hours*
Equipment: 1 litre / 2 pint oven-proof glass pudding basin or metal mould
– well buttered and dusted with caster sugar
Makes: 8–10-portion cake

175 g / 6 oz butter ♦ 175 g / 6 oz caster sugar ♦ 3 eggs
230 g / 8 oz self-raising flour ♦ 2 tbs milk

frosting:
1–2 packets dolly mixture, tiny jellies or Smarties ♦ 1 tbs cocoa
2 tbs hot water ♦ 60 g / 2 oz butter ♦ 150 g / 5 oz icing sugar
30 chocolate sticks

for the edible 'Guy':
230 g / 8 oz marzipan ♦ food colourings (optional)

Cream the butter and sugar until light and fluffy. Gradually beat in the eggs. Fold in the flour alternately with the milk. Spoon the mixture into the prepared basin or mould and smooth level.

Bake in the preheated oven until a wooden skewer comes out clean from the centre. Cool in the bowl for 5 minutes then turn out on to a wire rack – with a glass bowl you can see whether the cake is coming free as you unmould it.

To make the frosting, blend the cocoa with the hot water. Mix in the butter, gradually stir in the sieved icing sugar then beat until smooth.

Place the cake upside down on a serving board. Use a narrow serrated knife to cut a long narrow hole downwards from the top of the cake – but not all the way through – and discard the cake crumbs. Fill the hole with the small sweets. Spread frosting over the top and sides of the cake and arrange the chocolate sticks on end around the base and up the sides to resemble a bonfire. Leave for 1–2 hours for the icing to set.

To make the marzipan 'Guy': cut the marzipan into three roughly equal pieces. Shape the pieces to represent the body, limbs, and head. Use a cocktail stick to fix them together. Paint with the food colours if available. When ready to serve place the figure on top of the cake.

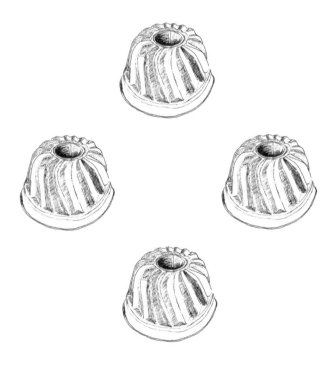

FESTIVE RING

An attractive American cake based on a plain sponge cake but decorated prettily for Christmas. A good cake to donate to a fund-raising event.

Oven: 190°C/375°F/gas mark ♦ Baking time: 45 minutes
Equipment: 18–20 cm/7–8 in. ring tin, capacity 1.2 litres/2 pints
– well buttered
Makes: 16-portion cake

175 g / 6 oz butter ♦ 175 g / 6 oz caster sugar
3 eggs ♦ ½ tsp vanilla essence
175 g / 6 oz self-raising flour

icing:
175 g / 6 oz icing sugar ♦ 3 tsp hot water
4 glacé cherries, rinsed, dried and halved
1–2 strips of candied angelica
8 pecan or walnut halves

Cream the butter with the sugar until light and fluffy. Gradually beat in the eggs and the vanilla essence. Fold in the sieved flour very gently. Spoon the mixture into the prepared tin and smooth level. Bake in the preheated oven until a wooden skewer comes out clean from the centre of the cake. Cool the cake in the tin for 4 minutes then turn out on to a wire rack.

To make the icing: blend the sieved icing sugar with the water until it is of pouring consistency. With the cake upside down on the wire rack, spoon the icing over the top so that it is well covered and the icing trails down the side to resemble a snow-capped mountain. Decorate with the halved cherries placed evenly around the cake. Place a halved pecan in the gaps between the cherries. Cut the angelica into small diamond shapes to represent leaves and place one or two on each side of the cherries. Leave the cake in a cold place for 1 hour until the icing is dry.

PANFORTE

The traditional Italian Christmas cake now identified with Siena. Richly spiced, crammed with candied fruit and nuts yet wheat flour-free, this is a delectable festive cake that's also simple to prepare.

Oven: 150 °C/300 °F/gas mark 2 ♦ Baking time: 30 minutes
Equipment: 20 cm/8 in. spring-clip tin
– buttered and base-lined with baking paper and rice paper
Makes: 10–12-portion cake

120 g/4 oz light soft brown sugar ♦ 150 g/5 oz clear honey
120 g/4 oz ground almonds
120 g/4 oz almonds, blanched and slivered
120 g/4 oz hazelnuts, toasted and halved
265 g/9 oz mixed candied peel, chopped
2 tsp ground cinnamon ♦ 1 tsp ground mace
1 tbs icing sugar

Weigh the sugar. Spread it out across the scale pan to make a bed for measuring the honey on top. Immediately tip sugar and honey into a pan and heat gently, stirring, until the sugar has dissolved. Remove from the heat but keep the mixture warm.

Measure all the other ingredients – except the icing sugar – into a bowl and mix well. Pour on the honey mixture and stir until it forms one mass. Transfer into the prepared cake tin and smooth as level as possible using the back of a spoon.

Bake in the preheated oven until the cake is golden brown. Cool slightly then run the blade of a knife around the cake to free it from the side of the tin. Open the clasp and lift off the curved edge. Leave the cake until cold, then slide it on its rice paper base on to a wooden board. Dust the top with the sifted icing sugar and set aside for at least 24 hours. Serve cut into narrow wedges. Alternatively, wrap the cake in cellophane and store in a cold place for up to one month before serving.

GLACÉ FRUIT AND NUT CELEBRATION CAKE

The gleaming candied fruit and nuts that decorate the top give this cake an immediate appeal. My own preference is this natural style rather than the traditional marzipan and icing. The fruit cake itself could be the Christmas Cake recipe given below or the Dundee Cake on p. 102. A cake decorated with glacé fruits in this way makes a fine present or a prize at a fund-raiser.

This quantity covers the top of a 20 cm/8 in. square cake

4 tbs apple jelly or sieved apricot jam
175–200 g / 6–7 oz mixed glacé fruits – cherries, apricots, pineapple, greengages, etc
30 g / 1 oz pecan or walnut halves
30 g / 1 oz whole almonds, blanched and toasted
a few brazil or macadamia nuts

Gently heat the jelly or sieved jam in a small pan until liquid. Brush some of this over the top of the cake. Leave the cherries whole but halve or cut the rest of the glacé fruit into neat pieces. Arrange the fruit and nuts on top of the cake in a random fashion or in diagonal rows across the cake, making sure that all of the surface is covered. Now spoon the remaining jelly over the fruit and nuts to give a shiny glaze. Tie a cake band around the sides of the cake. I usually make a cake band from white tissue paper: fold it into three layers and make 1 cm / ½ in. cuts close together along the top and bottom edges to make a fringe. Secure the overlapping ends with sticky tape and tie white or gold ribbon around the cake finishing in a bow. This cake will keep well in a cold dry place for at least one month.

BÛCHE DE NOËL

The famous chocolate Christmas cake from France, made to resemble a Yule log. If need be, the cake can be stored in the freezer for up to a month. This is ideal as a seasonal present, when an alternative to the fresh cream filling may be called for. So I also give the recipe for a coffee butter-cream filling which has the advantage that the cake can then travel in a cool-box without the need for refrigeration.

Oven: 200°C/400°F/gas mark 6 ♦ *Baking time: 12–15 minutes*
Equipment: 32 x 23 cm/13 x 9 in. Swiss roll tin
– buttered and base-lined; tea cloth
Makes: 8–10-portion cake

60 g/2 oz self-raising flour ♦ 30 g/1 oz cocoa
pinch ground cinnamon ♦ 100 g/3½ oz dark muscovado sugar
3 eggs ♦ 1 tbs caster sugar

coffee cream filling:
300 ml/10 fl oz double cream ♦ 4 tbs strong black coffee
4 tsp caster sugar

coffee butter-cream filling:
100 g/3½ oz butter ♦ 100 g/3½ oz caster sugar
50 ml/2 fl oz hot strong black coffee

chocolate frosting:
200 g/7 oz plain dessert chocolate ♦ 60 g/2 oz butter
100 ml/3½ fl oz double cream ♦ 1 tbs rum or brandy (optional)
1 tsp icing sugar

Sift the flour with the cocoa and ground cinnamon on to a sheet of paper and set aside. Sift the sugar into a bowl – set over simmering water if mixing by hand – and add the eggs. Whisk the mixture until light and foamy and the whisk leaves a trail across the surface of the mixture. Sift some of the flour mixture on to the eggs and fold in gently with a balloon whisk, repeat until all the flour has been incorporated. Pour the mixture evenly into the prepared cake tin.

Bake in the preheated oven until risen and springy to the touch. While the cake is cooking, spread a clean tea cloth on a pastry board or work surface and sprinkle with the tablespoon of caster sugar. Remove the cake from the oven, leave for one minute then loosen the sides of the cake from the tin with the blade of a small knife and turn the cake out on to the cloth. Gently peel off the baking paper and use a sharp knife to trim off any crisp edges. Fold one end of the cloth over the short side and carefully roll up, taking the cloth too – so that the cloth temporarily replaces the filling – to make a log shape. Place the cloth-covered cake on a wire rack to cool.

To make the fresh coffee cream: whisk the cream until thick but still glossy, gradually adding the coffee and sugar. Carefully unroll the cake, leaving it on the cloth. Spread the coffee cream evenly over the cake and re-roll without the cloth. Transfer the cake to a flat serving plate or cake board.

To make the coffee butter-cream: cream the butter with the sugar, using an electric beater, until light and fluffy. Gradually beat in the coffee, a spoonful at a time, until the mixture is smooth and the grains of sugar have dissolved. Unroll the cake and spread the cream evenly over the surface before re-rolling. Transfer the cake to a flat serving plate or cake board.

To make the chocolate frosting: break the chocolate into pieces in a heat-proof bowl, add the butter and cream, and place over simmering water, or in a hot oven or a microwave, until the chocolate is melted. Remove from the heat and add the rum or brandy. Gently stir until smooth, then cool slightly. Spread this evenly over the cake, covering the curved surface and the ends. As the chocolate sets, drag the prongs of a fork over it all to resemble the bark – with knots – of a tree. Leave until set, then decorate with a ribbon bow. Just before serving, place the icing sugar in a fine sieve and tap the edge while moving it across the cake to provide a festive dusting of snow.

In the Ardèche region of France, they fill the cake with sweetened chestnut purée in place of the coffee cream.

TRADITIONAL CHRISTMAS CAKE

A dark, rich, fruit cake that is suitable for Christmas or other celebrations such as a birthday, anniversary or wedding. If stored for about a month, the flavour intensifies. Trickling brandy or sherry into the cake now and again does no harm. A useful tip when making a cake with so many ingredients is to begin by measuring each one on to a plate or saucer, or a sheet of kitchen paper, to help you check them against the recipe. Then, before you spoon the mixture into the cake tin, check every plate is empty! For a Christmas or anniversary cake I prefer a 20 cm / 8 in. square cake tin since it is easy to cut economically – up to fifty portions – and I find it less demanding to decorate. The marzipan can be added to the cake about a week before, and the icing and decoration are applied about 4 days before the cake is cut.

Oven: 150 °C / 300 °F / gas mark 2 for 1½ hours,
140 °C / 275 °F / gas mark 1 for 2–2½ hours
Baking time: 3½–4 hours
Equipment: 20 cm / 8 in. square or 23 cm / 9 in. round tin – buttered and lined
Makes: 20 cm / 8 in. cake serving 30–50 portions

230 g / 8 oz butter ♦ 230 g / 8 oz dark muscovado sugar
3 tbs black treacle or molasses ♦ 4 eggs
300 g / 10 oz plain flour ♦ ¼ tsp bicarbonate of soda
½ tsp salt
1 tsp mixed spice ♦ ½ tsp ground cinnamon
½ tsp grated nutmeg or ground allspice
230 g / 8 oz seedless raisins
60 g / 2 oz seeded or muscatel raisins, chopped (optional)
230 g / 8 oz sultanas ♦ 230 g / 8 oz currants
120 g / 4 oz glacé cherries, quartered ♦ 120 g / 4 oz candied peel, chopped
60 g / 2 oz blanched almonds, slivered or chopped
2 tbs sherry, stout or milk

Cream the butter and sieved sugar until pale and fluffy. Gradually beat in the treacle and eggs, adding a little flour towards the end. Sieve the remaining flour with the bicarbonate of soda, salt and spices on to the egg mixture and stir a few times. Add the fruit and nuts to the bowl with the liquid. Stir well with a wooden spoon until all the ingredients are combined. Spoon the mixture into the prepared tin and smooth level.

Bake just below the centre of the preheated oven for 1½ hours, then lower the heat and bake for a further 2–2½ hours. Allow the cake to cool in the tin before turning out and peeling off the paper. Wrap the cake in clean greaseproof paper and store in a lidded plastic box. After a week or so, unwrap the cake and pierce holes with a wooden skewer and pour brandy, rum or sherry into the cake. Then wrap the cake again and store in the lidded container in a cold place.

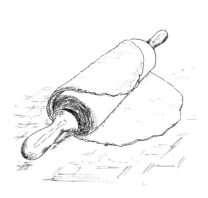

MARZIPAN

This recipe makes approximately 700 g / 1 lb 8 oz marzipan or almond paste, sufficient to cover the top and sides of a 20–23 cm / 8–9 in. cake. Divide the ingredients by three to make 230 g / 8 oz marzipan.

175 g / 6 oz icing sugar ♦ 175 g / 6 oz caster sugar
350 g / 12 oz ground almonds ♦ 1 egg or 2 egg whites
2 tsp lemon juice ♦ 1 tbs brandy
few drops of almond essence (optional)

Note that if you wish to replace the raw egg in this recipe, simply double the quantity of lemon juice and brandy.

Sift the icing sugar into a bowl and stir in the caster sugar and ground almonds. In a cup, mix the egg with the lemon juice, brandy and almond essence, then pour on to the dry ingredients. Stir together until the mixture forms a smooth, firm dough. The marzipan can be wrapped in greaseproof paper and kept in a plastic bag in the refrigerator for 4 weeks.

To marzipan the Christmas cake: brush the top of the cake with sieved apricot jam or apple jelly. Sift a small amount of icing sugar on to a pastry board or work surface and roll out half the marzipan to fit the top of the cake. Lower the cake, upside-down, on to the marzipan and cut round it with a sharp knife to remove the surplus. Place the cake the right way up and knead together the trimmings with the rest of the marzipan and divide in two. Roll out each piece to make a long narrow strip to fit two sides of the cake, if you are making a square cake, or half the circumference if you are making a round one. Brush jam or jelly on to the sides of the cake and roll the cake on to the marzipan strips, cutting off the surplus and making sure that the joins are not at the corners (if you are doing the square sort) and are well made. Stand the cake the right way up and roll it all over with the rolling pin to give a smooth surface. Wrap the cake loosely in a clean tea cloth and set aside for 2–3 days to dry before icing.

ROYAL ICING

If you use an electric beater to make the icing, so much the better; otherwise wait until you feel energetic and use a good-sized bowl and a wooden spoon. It will take 5–10 minutes of steady mixing but you will be pleased with the result. Royal icing can be so hard that it's difficult to eat unless an emulsifier is added in the form of glycerine or honey. So my recipe includes this. But if you prefer a rock-like icing, leave out the glycerine.

This quantity of royal icing covers the top and sides of a 20–23 cm / 8–9 in. cake

900 g / 2 lb icing sugar ♦ 4 egg whites
2 tsp lemon juice ♦ 2 tsp glycerine

Sift the icing sugar into a bowl, then tip it on to a plate or a sheet of paper. In a mixing bowl, whisk the egg whites until frothy. Gradually add half the icing sugar in spoonfuls, beating it in well each time. Now beat well for 5–10 minutes until the icing grows in bulk and becomes quite fluffy. Stir in the lemon juice and glycerine and gradually add the other half of the icing sugar, beating all the time until the icing stands up in peaks and has lost its shininess. Cover the bowl with a damp cloth if you are not using the icing within half an hour.

To ice the cake: use a palette knife or spatula to spread the icing generously over the marzipan on the top and sides of the cake until there is an even thickness. Now use the end of a smaller knife to swirl the icing, to give a roughened snow effect, making sure that you have not lost the shape of the cake. Cut a piece of wide, red satin ribbon almost as long as the diagonal or diameter of the cake and cut a V-shape from each end to neaten it. Gently place the ribbon on the wet icing and use a ruler to press it into place. Use more ribbon to make a looped bow and pin it about one-third of the way from the end of the flat ribbon, Add a sprig of holly, or whatever is suitable, and place the cake in a dry, cool place for 3 days to dry out.

CHAPTER TEN

Decorating Cakes

THE CONTENTS OF THIS CHAPTER

Leaving a cake plain, just the way it emerges from the oven with its appetizing golden crust, is often the nicest way of serving it. A light dusting of caster or icing sugar may be all that's called for; or clear honey brushed over the surface and set aside until dry. For a shallow chocolate cake with a level top, a delicate layer of sieved cocoa powder can provide the finishing touch. If the top of the baked cake is not level, then adopt the French method of simply turning it over. The flat side of the cake that has been in contact with the baking tin provides an easily decorated surface.

The simplest way to produce an even layer of icing sugar or powdered cocoa is to spoon a little into a fine-mesh sieve. Hold the sieve above the cake, and as you move it across the surface tap the side with a teaspoon to release a fine drift of the powder.

For a more stylized effect, place a stencil on top of the cake, then dust with sieved icing sugar or cocoa powder. Remove the stencil to reveal the decorative design. Plain strips of paper evenly spaced across the top of the cake before adding sieved icing sugar produce a striped effect on top of the cake when they are removed, or if the strips overlap diagonally a pleasing diamond pattern results. Children enjoy making their own stencil – start with a piece of paper the same size as the cake and fold in half. Then repeat two or three times to produce a dart shape, before cutting small pieces from the folded edges. Unfold the stencil, place on top of the cake, dust with sugar and carefully remove – to a small child the decoration that results seems like magic.

Should you want a name or greeting on top of a cake and wielding an icing nozzle does not appeal, letter and number stencils can work surprisingly well.

Paper stencils can be as simple as a paper circle cut in half with a wavy line: place the stencil on the cake and remove one half, dust the cake with sieved icing sugar and cover with its stencil, remove the other half and dust with sieved cocoa or brush the surface with clear honey and sprinkle with chopped nuts. Remove both stencils, and hey presto! a two-tone cake decoration.

Another easy technique is to trail glacé icing or melted chocolate over the top of a cake by drizzling a spoonful of a fairly liquid mixture quite quickly back and forth across the cake, starting at one side and working across the surface to leave a fine tracery of parallel lines.

Even the least practised cook can spoon thick cream over the top of a cake then sprinkle with toasted flaked almonds, grated chocolate or fine shreds of citrus peel.

Although usually reserved for special cakes such as Simnel and Battenberg, a thin layer of marzipan is an attractive and delicious decoration, made with either ground almonds, hazelnuts or pistachio nuts, left in their natural state or subtly tinted with a food colouring. Remember to first brush the surface of the cake with sieved apricot jam before covering with the marzipan. Then, you should use a rolling pin to gently press it into place. If the fancy takes you, small marzipan decorations – moulded by hand or cut to shape – can be applied to this foundation, using a thin layer of beaten egg white as an adhesive. Alternatively, a lightly toasted finish is attractive: brush the marzipan with beaten egg yolk and place under a hot grill until just changing colour, remove immediately and set aside to cool.

Large shallow cakes full of fresh fruit might be decorated with a layer of toasted meringue just before serving. Whisk two egg whites until stiff, then gradually fold in 2–3 tablespoons of golden caster sugar. Pile spoonfuls of the meringue over the cake and place in a moderate oven or under a hot grill – though not so close that it scorches – until set and golden brown. Serve the cake within 30 minutes.

Occasionally, the appearance of an iced or frosted cake does not come up to expectations. In that case, a rapid disguise is called for before the icing sets: sprinkle over some chopped nuts – toasted or tinted with a drop of food colouring, crumbled meringues or amaretti biscuits, or grated chocolate. If time is short, resort to chocolate vermicelli. Children love decorating cakes with small sweets – dolly mixture, chocolate buttons, hundreds and thousands, Smarties and Barbie sprinkles. A charming summer decoration is easily made by scattering small edible flowers or their petals over the top of a cake.

If you are a dab hand with a piping-bag, then decorating a cake can be very quick. But take care not to overdo it – leave parts of the iced cake plain so that the contrast is pleasing.

When you need to cut a cake into layers before filling and decorating, use a very sharp or a finely-serrated knife with a long blade in a gentle sawing action across the cake to cut it into even layers. When cutting a slab of cake into pieces for decorating, use a smaller knife and, if necessary, check the cutting lines with a ruler. It's worth bearing in mind that it is easier to spread icing or cream over the smooth baked surface of a cake rather than across a cut surface, whose uneven crumb will also absorb the filling.

Readers who specialize in decorated cakes or who bake for a cake stall may wish to give their work an additional distinctive flourish with home-made motifs such as marzipan letters and chocolate leaves. Since this kind of cake decoration is enjoyable but time-consuming to prepare, it is sensible to make a supply well ahead whenever possible.

CHOCOLATE LEAVES

The mature leathery leaves from a rose bush are best, due to their strong vein pattern. Choose clean dry leaves from an spray-free plant, hold each leaf by the stem, and brush the underside with melted chocolate. Place the leaves, chocolate side up, on a sheet of baking paper – leave some leaves flat and curve others over a wooden spoon. Chill the leaves until the chocolate is set, then gently peel off the green leaf to reveal the chocolate version. Store the these on crumpled kitchen paper in a lidded plastic box placed in the fridge.

CHOCOLATE SHAPES

Pour melted chocolate to a depth of 5 mm / ¼ in. into a Swiss roll tin lined with baking paper, then chill until set hard. Turn the sheet of chocolate on to a flat surface and use a ruler and knife to cut out small squares and triangles. Use small, sharp petit-four pastry cutters to cut out numerals, letters and other shapes. Store the shapes between layers of baking paper in a lidded plastic box in the fridge.

PIPED CHOCOLATE MOTIFS

Spoon some melted chocolate into a piping-bag fitted with a small plain writing nozzle. Pipe the chocolate on to a sheet of baking paper into pretty motifs such as figures of eight, music clefs, and other twirly shapes. Chill the chocolate until set hard, then gently lift the motifs from the paper and store between layers of baking paper in a lidded plastic box in the fridge.

CHOCOLATE SHAVINGS

Slightly warm a bar of chocolate, then shave along the longer edge with a sharp vegetable knife or a potato peeler to produce long decorative curls. These are best used straight away since they are fragile. To produce longer, cigar-shaped chocolate curls known as chocolate caraque, turn to the recipe for Gâteau Madeleine on pages 244–5.

GRATED CHOCOLATE

Chill a bar of chocolate, then draw the edge of the bar downwards against one side of a box grater to produce small shavings that can be stored in a lidded plastic box.

MARZIPAN LETTERS AND NUMERALS

Use natural-coloured marzipan or marzipan tinted with food dyes. On a pastry board dusted with a little cornflour, roll out the marzipan until 5 mm / ¼ in. thick. Use small, sharp petit-four cutters to make miniature letters and numerals. Store the shapes in a lidded plastic box.

MINIATURE MERINGUES

Prepare a meringue mixture (recipe on p. 196) and divide between three small bowls. Use only a drop or two of food colour to subtly tint each bowl – pale shades of pink, green and yellow look pretty. Spoon the meringue into a piping-bag fitted with a 1 cm / ½ in. star nozzle and pipe small rosettes on to lined baking sheets. Bake in an oven preheated to 100°C / 200°F / gas mark ¼ for 1½ hours then leave in the oven overnight. Transfer the meringues to a lidded plastic box and store in a dry place.

There are, of course, many kinds of of icings, frostings and cream available to cake-makers. This list supplements and develops some of those that appear in the baking chapters. I hope it will help you to create your own individual cakes, by marrying together a cake from earlier in the book with a cream, frosting or filling from the recipes below. Bear in mind, though, that the finished cake will be more successful and memorable if you enhance the flavour of the cake with a decoration that results in a happy balance of taste and texture.

WHIPPED DAIRY CREAM

Possibly the quickest and easiest filling for a cake that is to be served straight away or within a few hours – provided the cake is stored in a refrigerator to preserve the cream from spoiling. Whipped double cream can be spooned, spread or piped over a cake; the chilled cream is whisked by hand with a balloon whisk, a rotary egg beater or a hand-held electric beater until thick but still glossy. Take care not to whisk the cream too long or it may separate. While plain cream may take your fancy, you can also flavour it. For example:

Vanilla cream: mix in a few drops of vanilla essence and sweeten to taste.
Raspberry cream: mix in 1–2 tbs puréed raspberries and sweeten to taste.
Passion-fruit cream: mix in the flesh and juice of one or two ripe passion-fruit and sweeten to taste.
Coffee cream: mix in 1–2 tbs strong black coffee and sweeten to taste.

ENGLISH BUTTER CREAM

A velvet smooth cream made by blending butter with caster sugar, then gradually beating in a warm liquid which dissolves the sugar crystals. This cream can be spooned, spread or piped and can be stored at room temperature for 2–3 hours before serving.

Vanilla butter cream: Heat 3 tbs milk with the seeds scraped from a finger of vanilla pod for 4 minutes, set aside but keep warm. Blend 100 g / 3½ oz unsalted butter with 100 g / 3½ oz caster sugar until pale and light, gradually beat in the vanilla milk a tsp at a time. Taste the cream, and if need be add a few drops of home-made vanilla essence (recipe on p. 292). Chopped nuts such as toasted hazelnuts or almonds can be mixed into this butter cream before using, if desired.

Coffee butter cream: replace half the vanilla milk with hot strong black coffee.

Orange butter cream: mix 1–2 tbs strained orange juice and ½ teaspoon finely grated orange zest into the vanilla butter cream.

Lemon butter cream: mix 1–2 tbs strained lemon juice and ½ teaspoon finely grated lemon zest into the vanilla butter cream.

Chocolate butter cream: blend 60 g / 2 oz melted plain chocolate into the vanilla butter cream.

FRENCH BUTTER CREAM or CRÈME AU BEURRE

A rich silky-smooth cream made with egg yolks, butter and hot sugar syrup – an electric hand-held beater saves effort and although a sugar thermometer is not essential, it is helpful.

120 g / 4 oz caster or granulated sugar ♦ 100 ml / 3½ fl oz water
5 egg yolks ♦ 230 g / 8 oz butter

Dissolve the sugar in the water, stir over low heat then bring the syrup to the boil and cook until the syrup reaches 110°C/220°F on a sugar thermometer. Alternatively, remove the pan from the heat and drop a blob of syrup on to a saucer. Place the tip of a teaspoon in the syrup and lift slowly: if the syrup forms a fine thread that breaks after an inch or so, this should be the correct temperature. Whisk the egg yolks in a mixing bowl and continue whisking while you add the syrup in a thin stream. Place the bowl in cold water and continue whisking until the mixture is cool. Whisk in the butter in small pieces until incorporated. Set the cream aside until ready to use.

Vanilla butter cream: mix in a few drops of vanilla essence (recipe p. 292).

Coffee butter cream: mix in 1–2 tbs strong black coffee.

Praline butter cream: mix in 1–2 tbs praline powder (recipe p. 292).

CHOCOLATE BUTTER CREAM

120 g / 4 oz caster or granulated sugar ♦ 3 tbs water
2 egg yolks ♦ 120 g / 4 oz plain chocolate ♦ 120 g / 4 oz butter

Measure the sugar and water into a small pan and stir over low heat until the sugar has dissolved. Raise the heat and bring the mixture to 110°C/220°F (the short-thread stage) then remove from the heat. Use a hand-held beater to whisk together the egg yolks, continue beating while adding the hot syrup in a slender trickle until the mixture is pale and thick. Cool the mixture by standing the bowl in cold water.

Meanwhile break the chocolate into pieces and melt with the butter in a bowl using a microwave oven, or by placing the bowl over a pan of simmering water. Gradually stir spoonfuls of chocolate into the egg foam and then set aside until cool.

GLACÉ ICING

This is the simplest icing to make, just icing sugar blended with hot water to produce a spreadable icing which dries to a glossy surface. Add the water gradually – it's easy to overdo it – just remember that the more water you add the runnier the icing. For icing the top of a cake, the mixture should be thin enough to pour but thick enough to cover without running down the sides. To make glacé icing thick enough for piping a name or a message, add rather less water.

120 g / 4 oz icing sugar ♦ 2–3 tsp hot water

Sieve the icing sugar into a small bowl and gradually mix in the water. Flavour or colour the icing with a drop or two of essence.

Coffee glacé icing: in the recipe above, add 2 tsp of hot, black coffee and about 1 tsp hot water.

BUTTER ICING

A blend of butter and icing sugar that is easy to make and is highly popular in North America. Variations of this vanilla version can be made in the same way as for English butter cream above.

60 g / 2 oz butter ♦ 120 g / 4 oz icing sugar ♦ ¼ tsp vanilla essence

Cream the butter in a bowl until soft, gradually mix in the sieved icing sugar until you have a smooth spreadable mixture. Flavour to taste with a drop or two of the vanilla essence.

LEMON FROSTING

90 g / 3 oz butter ♦ 1 small lemon ♦ 230 g / 8 oz icing sugar, sifted

In a small glass or stainless steel pan, melt the butter with 3 tbs of the strained lemon juice. Bring to the boil, allow to bubble for 30 seconds, then remove from the heat and cool for 1 minute. Stir in the icing sugar and beat until smooth. Stand the pan in cold water for one minute to cool the frosting, then mix and use while still spreadable.

CHOCOLATE FROSTING

90 g / 3 oz icing sugar ♦ 30 g / 1 oz cocoa powder
60 g / 2 oz pale muscovado sugar ♦ 60 g / 2 oz butter ♦ 2 tbs water

Sift the icing sugar and cocoa into a bowl. Measure the muscovado sugar, butter and water into a small pan and stir over low heat until dissolved, then bring to the boil. Remove from the heat, cool for half a minute then pour on to the sugar / cocoa mixture and beat until smooth. Pour the frosting over the cake, allowing it to trickle down the sides. Leave the cake in a cool place for 2 hours to set.

FUDGE FROSTING

60 g / 2 oz butter ♦ 120 g / 4 oz light muscovado sugar
1 tbs single cream

Melt the butter in a pan over moderate heat, stir in the sugar and cream until dissolved. Bring the mixture to the boil and simmer for 2 minutes. Remove from the heat and cool the pan by standing it in cold water for 2–3 minutes. Beat the filling until it is thick but still spreadable.

CREAM CHEESE FROSTING

45 g / 1½ oz cream cheese ♦ 175 g / 6 oz icing sugar
1–2 drops vanilla essence or ¼ tsp finely grated lemon zest

Beat the cream cheese in a small bowl until smooth and gradually blend in the sifted icing sugar, adding more or less according to how stiff you want the frosting. Add vanilla essence or lemon zest to taste and use the frosting straight away.

VANILLA YOGHURT FROSTING

175 g / 6 oz icing sugar ♦ 2–3 tbs thick plain natural yoghurt
1–2 drops vanilla essence

Sift the icing sugar into a bowl and gradually blend in the yoghurt, a little at the time until the frosting is as spreadable as you wish. Mix in vanilla essence to taste. Spread the frosting over the cake while still soft.

SEVEN-MINUTE FROSTING

2 egg whites ♦ 350 g / 12 oz caster sugar ♦ ¼ tsp cream of tartar
4 tbs hot water ♦ ¼ tsp vanilla essence

Whisk the egg whites with the sugar, cream of tartar and hot water in a large mixing bowl set over a pan of simmering water. This usually takes about seven minutes, hence the icing's name. The frosting is ready when the meringue is thick enough to stand up in peaks. Remove the bowl from the heat, stand it on a folded cloth and continue whisking until the mixture is cool. Whisk in the vanilla essence and use while the frosting is still spreadable.

CHOCOLATE GANACHE

This rich mixture is a smooth blend of melted chocolate and thick cream which – depending on how much cream is added – produces a mixture either soft enough to pour or spread on to a cake, or firm enough to pipe into decorative shapes.

Piping ganache:
265 g / 9 oz plain dark chocolate ♦ 120 ml / 4 fl oz double cream

Pouring ganache:
265 g / 9 oz plain dark chocolate ♦ 150 ml / 5 fl oz double cream

Break the chocolate into pieces into a heat-proof bowl. Add the cream and heat until the chocolate melts, either in a microwave oven or over simmering water. Gently stir until smooth. As the mixture cools, it thickens and is suitable for pouring. To thicken further, use an electric beater to whisk the mixture for 3–5 minutes or until the ganache is paler and lighter. Take care not to beat too long or the ganache can separate. Use straight away for filling and decorating a cake before the mixture sets.

MARZIPAN or ALMOND PASTE

An easy-to-prepare traditional recipe with an excellent flavour. These quantities make 450 g / 1 lb.

230 g / 8 oz ground almonds ♦ 120 g / 4 oz caster sugar
120 g / 4 oz icing sugar, sieved ♦ 1 egg or 2 egg whites
1 tbs brandy or lemon juice
1–2 drops almond essence (optional)

Measure all the ingredients into a bowl and mix together until well combined. Shape the marzipan into a ball and use straight away, or wrap in plastic and chill until needed.

VANILLA ESSENCE

Home-made vanilla essence has a pure flavour and is simple to prepare.

Use scissors or a sharp knife to cut open a plump, moist vanilla pod lengthways. Snip the pod into short pieces and feed these into a small screw-top bottle or jar. Fill the bottle with eau-de-vie, dry sherry or brandy, seal the bottle and shake gently. Store in a warm place, giving the bottle a shake each day, for 2–3 weeks before use. Top up the bottle with more alcohol as necessary, and replace the vanilla pod when all its flavour has been extracted.

PRALINE

Toasted almonds encased in caramel are known as praline, and it is a classic ingredient in French pâtisserie. When crushed to a powder it is one of the most attractive flavours for adding to creams and fillings.

Place 120 g / 4 oz blanched split or halved almonds under a hot grill and toast to a golden brown, taking care not to let the nuts burn or the taste will be bitter. Spread the toasted almonds on a baking tray lined with baking paper. In a small pan, dissolve 120 g / 4 oz caster or granulated sugar in 4 tbs of water while stirring over low heat. Then increase the heat and cook until the syrup turns to a golden caramel, taking care that it does not darken too much. Immediately pour the syrup over the nuts and set aside until set. When the praline is cold, remove from the paper and break into pieces into a processor, then grind to a fine powder. Tip the praline powder into a screw-top jar and seal tightly until ready to use.

Index

biscuit de Savoie, 73
biscuits (see also cookies)
  almond tuiles, 220
  Anzacs, 224
  butterscotch, 221
  chocolate Paddington Bears, 234
  cinnamon stars, 235
  coffee maryses, 223
  digestive, 217
  Easter, 218
  gingerbread people, 229
  hazelnut macaroons, 222
  parliament cakes or parlies, 228
  shortbread, 215
  wholemeal shortbread, 216
blackberries
  autumn fruit and nut upside-down cake, 126
  plum and blackberry crumble cake, 124
blueberries
  blueberry cornmeal muffins, 64
  fig and nectarine galette with raspberry coulis, 117
  quatre-quarts aux framboises et aux abricots, 119
blueberry cornmeal muffins, 64
boiled fruit cake, 109
bonfire cake, 268–9
brandy snaps, 232–3
brazil nuts
  celery, chive and brazil nut teabread, 60
brioche-style sponge cake with sherry sabayon sauce, 83
brownies, Canadian, 154
bûche de Noël, 273–4
butter, 15
butter cream, 286
  chocolate butter cream, 286, 287
  coffee butter cream, 85, 171, 222, 286, 287
  French butter cream, 248–9, 286
  lemon butter cream, 286
  orange butter cream, 286
  praline butter cream, 287
  vanilla butter cream, 286–7
butter icing, 188, 288

butter tarts, 189
butterfly cakes, 194
butterscotch biscuits, 221
cakes, butterfly, 194
cakes, japonais, 188
cakes, queen, 187
Canadian brownies, 154
Canadian crullers, 66
candied fruit
  angelica and almond cake, 170
  children's chocolate cake, 150
  chocolate cracker cake, 141
  Devonshire saffron loaf, 62
  florentines, 190
  glacé fruit and nut celebration cake, 272
  Gudrun's Norwegian chocolate raisin cake, 147
  orange raisin lunch-box cake, 112
  orange, polenta and almond cake, 177
  panforte, 271
  pineapple fruit cake, 107
  pumpkin, rice and maple syrup cake, 168
  ring fruit cake, 106
  truly ginger cake, 160
  wine cupboard fruit cake, 113
caraque, chocolate, 244–5
caraway seed loaf, 165
cardamom
  apricot, pine nut and cardamom loaf, 166
carrot cake, frosted, 161
celery, chive and brazil nut teabread, 60
champagne cream, rosé, 258–9
cheese
  apéro cake, 63
  savoury scone ring, 53
chequer-boards, 230–1
cherries
  cherry compote, 146–7
  cherry shortbread biscuits, 215
  fresh cherry cake, 116
  quatre-quarts aux framboises et aux abricots, 119
  quick-mix glacé cherry and almond cake, 105
cherry compote, 146–7

INDEX